THE *CAROLE*
A STUDY OF A MEDIEVAL DANCE

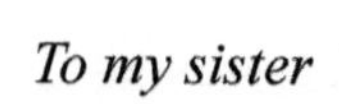

To my sister

The *Carole*

A Study of a Medieval Dance

ROBERT MULLALLY

LONDON AND NEW YORK

First published 2011 by Ashgate Publishing

Published 2016 by Routledge
2 Park Square, Milton Park, Abingdon, Oxfordshire OX14 4RN
711 Third Avenue, New York, NY 10017, USA

First issued in paperback 2016

Routledge is an imprint of the Taylor & Francis Group, an informa business

British Library Cataloguing in Publication Data
Mullally, Robert.
The carole: a study of a medieval dance.
1. Dance – England – History – To 1500. 2. Dance – France – History – To 1500. 3. Dance music – 500–1400.
I. Title
793.3'1942'0902-dc22

Library of Congress Cataloging-in-Publication Data
Mullally, Robert.
The carole : a study of a medieval dance / Robert Mullally.
p. cm.
Includes bibliographical references and index.
ISBN 978-1-4094-1248-9 (hardcover : alk. paper) 1. Carole (Dance) 2. Carole (Dance)–Social aspects. 3. Choreography. I. Title.
GV1796.C17M85 2010
793.3–dc22

2010046652

ISBN 13: 978-1-138-25201-1 (pbk)
ISBN 13: 978-1-4094-1248-9 (hbk)

Contents

List of Plates

The Plates are located between pages 80–81.

List of Music Examples

Acknowledgements

The writing of an extensive work inevitably involves the help and co-operation of others. This is particularly true of a work such as this, which, because of its interdisciplinary nature, crosses many boundaries. It is therefore an agreeable task to record here my indebtedness to the individuals and institutions that made the completion of my project possible. In particular I should like to thank my sister, Evelyn, for her support and encouragement throughout the years that I have been engaged in writing this work.

I should also like to take this opportunity to acknowledge the advice and suggestions of those who have helped to make my contribution to the study of medieval dance more accurate and informative than it otherwise might have been. First, I wish to express my gratitude to Karen Pratt, of the Department of French, King's College London, for her keen observations and comments. Readers will be aware that my investigation entailed the examination of texts in several languages, and I would want to record here the advice and suggestions of Carlotta Dionisotti of the Department of Classics at King's who read some of my translations from Latin. Likewise I would like to thank Janet Cowen of the Department of English who read a draft of my last chapter and gave me some pointers. The palaeography of medieval music is a field of research where resources do not abound. I was particularly grateful, therefore, to be able to enlist the help of several distinguished scholars: Daniel Leech-Wilkinson of the Department of Music at King's who read an early draft of Chapter 8, and made some interesting comments and also Mark Everist of the Department of Music at the University of Southampton who read a later draft of the same chapter, and returned it to me with the expected magisterial observations. My thanks are also due to Nicolas Bell, Curator, Music Collections at the British Library, who checked my transcriptions of a number of medieval dance tunes. In connection with this chapter too, I would like to thank Daphne J. Harvey, who performed the indispensable function of répétitrice at a session when I tested the practicalities of performing the *carole* with a number of her fellow music students at King's rounded up for the occasion, and whose help I acknowledge here. In the almost wholly uncharted waters of the iconography of the medieval dance, I am especially grateful to Susie Nash of the Courtauld Institute of Art (University of London), for her copious suggestions on possible sources of information. This is also the place to acknowledge the assistance of those people, too many to mention by name, who answered my diverse queries.

It goes without saying that a large proportion of one's time is spent in libraries. I would wish it to be known that the help and expertise in many fields of their members of staff has not gone unrecognized. Most notably I should like to thank Jim Sutton and Stuart Bond of Information Services and Systems at King's for their clarity, expertise and patience in dealing with my multifarious computer problems. Here, too, I want to mention in particular the librarians and assistants of the following libraries: the Bodleian Library, The British Library, the University of London Library, the Conway Library of the Courtauld Institute of Art, the library of Lincoln's Inn, the Taylorian Institute, the Département des Manuscrits (Division Occidentale) of the Bibliothèque Nationale de France.

For the inclusion of photographic reproductions in this work I wish to acknowledge permission granted to me by the following institutions and organizations: the Bodleian Library, University of Oxford (Plates 3, 4 and 6); The British Library, London (Plates 5 and 7); the Bibliothèque Nationale de France, Paris (Plates 1 and 2); the Servizio Musei Comunali di Firenze and ATS Italia Editrice srl, Rome (Plate 8); the Comune di Siena and Edizioni Lombardi, Siena (Plate 9).

An undertaking such as this inevitably necessitates visits to libraries away from home with the consequent additional expenses. In my case such trips were facilitated by a number of small grants. I would like, therefore, to thank those funding bodies who made them: the University of London Central Research Fund for a grant for a short stay in Paris while I studied manuscripts at the Bibliothèque Nationale; the Humanities Research Committee of King's College, London for a grant for the same purpose at the Bodleian Library, Oxford. Finally I would also like to thank the School of Advanced Studies of the University of London for bursaries to attend one-day seminars on aspects of palaeography.

List of Abbreviations

Battaglia	*Grande dizionario della lingua italiana.* Ed. Salvatore Battaglia *et al.* 21 vols. Turin, 1961–2002
FEW	*Französisches etymologisches Wörterbuch.* Ed. Walther von Wartburg. Bonn, 1928–
Godefroy	*Dictionnaire de l'ancienne langue française et de tous ses dialectes du IX*[e] *siècle au XV*[e] *siècle.* Ed. Frédéric Godefroy. 10 vols. Paris, 1880–1902
Huguet	*Dictionnaire de la langue française du seizième siècle.* Ed. Edmond Huguet. 7 vols. Paris, 1925–67
Index	*The Index of Middle English Verse.* Ed. Carleton Brown and Rossell Hope Robbins. New York, 1943
LBL	London, The British Library
MED	*Middle English Dictionary.* Ed. Hans Kurath, Sherman Kuhn *et al.* 14 vols. Ann Arbor, MI, 1956–99
MGG 2	*Die Musik in Geschichte und Gegenwart.* 2nd ed. Ed. Ludwig Finscher. 9 vols. Kassel, 1994–98
New Grove 1	*The New Grove Dictionary of Music and Musicians.* Ed. Stanley Sadie. 20 vols. London, 1980
New Grove 2	*The New Grove Dictionary of Music and Musicians.* 2nd ed. Ed. Stanley Sadie and John Tyrrell. 29 vols. London, 2001

OBL	Oxford, The Bodleian Library
OED	*The Oxford English Dictionary*. 2nd ed. Ed. J. A. Simpson and E. S. C. Weiner. 20 vols. Oxford, 1989
PBN	Paris, la Bibliothèque Nationale de France
Sahlin	Margit Sahlin. *Etude sur la carole médiévale: l'origine du mot et ses rapports avec l'église*. Uppsala, 1940
Tobler-Lommatzsch	*Altfranzösisches Wörterbuch*. Ed. Adolf Tobler and Erhard Lommatzsch. 11 vols. Berlin, 1925–2002

Introduction

In the vast corpus of medieval French literature, we frequently encounter the dance term *carole*. One explanation of its frequent occurrence is that dancing provides a device for social interaction in literary works. Another, no doubt, is the popularity in France of dancing itself. The *carole*, in particular, was performed by all classes of society – kings and nobles, shepherds and servant girls. It is described as taking place both indoor and outdoors. Its central position in the life of the people is underlined by references not only in what we might call fictional texts, but also in historical (or quasi-historical) writings, in moral treatises and even in a work on astronomy. Yet in spite of this centrality, we do not know precisely what kind of dance the *carole* was. That is not to say that commentators have ignored the dance. Indeed the contrary is true, and a considerable literature has accumulated over the centuries. But in spite of the attention devoted to the subject, we have no definitive answer about any aspect of the dance – about its choreography, its music, its iconography or even about the etymology of the word itself.

Much of the scholarly interest, from the sixteenth to the eighteenth centuries, concentrated on the etymology, and although by that time the dance had passed into oblivion, the term was revived as an archaism in the sixteenth century and, perhaps for this reason, attracted the attention of early lexicographers. This philological aspect continued to engage academic interest into the twentieth century. The topic, nevertheless, has remained one of great controversy with half a dozen competing theories about the origin of the very word *carole*. Both the phonological and the semantic aspects have been examined in detail. With regard to the latter, a critical issue in the argument is whether the word could be derived from a Latin term for dance or from one entirely unconnected with it.

While the etymology has been the focal point of academic endeavour, and therefore cannot be neglected in any study that aims to cover the subject of the dance comprehensively, the purpose of the present one is focussed on the dance itself. My intention is to discover those characteristics of the dance already mentioned that have hitherto remained unidentified. This is self-evidently a prerequisite to any other discussion. Thus any hint of a sociological or literary critical approach has been avoided, and consequently no references will be found to works that tend to adopt such approaches. The emphasis is very much on details relevant to the history, choreography and performance of the dance as revealed in the primary sources. This methodology involves attempting to isolate the term *carole* from other dance terms not only in French, but also in other languages.

This procedure is all the more necessary as the considerable accumulation of writing on the dance has not been done by dance historians, but rather by lexicographers, literary historians, and to a cetain extent by musicolgists. This circumstance has produced, not surprisingly, a variety of views on the nature of the dance. Unfortunately dance historians have been too often content to follow their literary predecessors.

The trouble with the endeavours of previous commentators, both literary and musical, is that they failed either to examine the primary sources carefully, or to relate their statements to any dance or dance type. Thus, not only have their conclusions about the *carole* varied with one another, but the lack of specific information also raises questions about what constitutes a dance lyric or a dance tune.

Iconography can play an influential role in the understanding of a subject, especially of one such as a dance. Here we are, of course, not dealing with art history, but simply with the fact of representation, and what it might tell us about the subject in question. Yet at the same time one must be aware that what is being depicted may depend on artistic licence or the artist's competence in reproducing the aspect of the work in which we are interested.

A more precise idea of the dance can only be gained from a comprehensive study of the different primary sources – literary (in the broadest sense), musical and iconographical. As no treatise or manual exists to instruct us on how the dance was performed, we must glean the requisite information from a variety of texts and iconographical items. We then have to decide whether or not the details thus obtained provide us with a coherent view of the dance. Sometimes the particulars that we seek are only to be found in one or two texts or even a single manuscript. The literary and the iconographical sources have to be compared for similarities or differences. And if there are differences, which source do we trust? Yet in spite of all the difficulties it is possible by a diligent search to find all the required information.

Chapter 1
The History of the Term *Carole* since c. 1400

The term, *carole*, as a reference to a dance still performed disappears from French writing about 1400. The characteristics of the dance while it was still in vogue will be the subject of the following chapters. Meanwhile we may note that a new dance, the *basse danse*, is first cited about 1416, and it is this dance that was to dominate the social scene throughout the rest of the fifteenth century and the first half of the sixteenth.[1] Hence the designation *basse danse* or the simple term *danse* is generally employed by fifteenth-century authors for the principal social dance of that period. But although the word *carole* no longer referred to a contemporary choreographic form, it survived as an archaism.

One circumstance that ensured its continued use was the enduring popularity of the *Roman de la Rose*, of which there are numerous fifteenth-century manuscripts. This celebrated poem, composed in the thirteenth century, includes a lengthy description of allegorical figures dancing a *carole*. In these later manuscripts, as in the earlier ones, the term *carole* is still actually used although the word *danse* is very occasionally substituted in some manuscripts.

Citations are also found, if infrequently, in works composed in the fifteenth century. For instance, in the biography of Jacques Lalaing we read:

> Puis quand ce vint après souper et que les tables furent levées, danses et carolles encommencèrent par la grande salle du chasteau de Lalaing; trompettes et ménestrels commencèrent à jouer de leur mestier. Là y avoit qui jouoient de plusieurs instrumens mélodieux; chacun d'iceux s'y acquittoit au mieux qu'il pouvoit. Après toutes danses et esbattemens faits, l'heure vint que tous s'en allèrent coucher … .[2]

---

[1] For the citation see Alain Chartier, 'Le Livre des Quatre Dames' (ll. 2399–402) in *The Poetical Works of Alain Chartier*, ed. J. C. Laidlaw (London, 1974). Other dates proposed as the earliest for the appearance in print of the term *basse danse* do not, in fact, refer to dancing.

[2] 'Le Livre des faits du bon chevalier messire Jacques de Lalaing' in Georges Chastellain, *Oeuvres de Georges Chastellain*, ed. Baron Joseph Kervyn de Lettenhove (Brussels, 1866), VIII, 8. This biography is now considered to be mainly by Jean Le Fevre (1395/96–1468).

> (Then when the moment arrived after supper, and the tables were removed, dances and *caroles* began in the great hall of the château of Lalaing; trumpeters and minstrels began to ply their trade. There were some there who played several melodious instruments, and each of them acquitted himself in the best manner possible. After all the dances and entertainments had finished, the time came when everyone went to bed … .)

At first sight the reference here to 'danses et carolles' might seem to indicate an actual performance of *caroles* and other dances, but in fact it simply repeats a stock phrase found, for example, earlier in Froissart and later in Moreau, and is probably no more than a general reference to dancing.[3] Still, it shows how the word *carole* had, to a certain extent, become embedded in the language.

At least for one author, however, the word had a particular significance. The chronicler, Jean Wavrin, describes the reception that Murad II, the Sultan of Turkey, gave in 1442 for Wlad of Wallachia whose territory Murad hoped to seize:

> Et audehors dudit pavillon estoit assis a terre sur coussins et tapis de drap dor le dit seigneur de la Valaquie a la dextre dudit Turcq et a sa senestre estoit assis son bellarbay, qui vault autant a dire comme seigneur des seigneurs, et tous les autres nobles furent assis comme en une grant carolle partant de la main dextre et senestre en tele maniere que le Grant Turcq les povoit tous veoir mengier.[4]

> (And outside the said tent the said Lord of Wallachia was seated on cushions and a carpet of cloth of gold with the said Turk on his right and his *bellarbay*, which can be translated approximately as lord of lords, seated on his left, and all the other nobles were seated in a great *carole* to the left and to the right so that the Great Turk could see them all eating.)

Here obviously there is no question of dancing, as *carole* is used in a simile, and clearly means that those present were placed in a circle.

Yet a choreographic sense for the word *carole* seems likely in the following extract from a poem composed sometime in the late fifteenth century, although one should note that the word is used to form a rhyme, and may therefore represent nothing more than a useful archaism:

---

[3] Jean Froissart, *Chroniques de J. Froissart*, ed. Siméon Luce *et al.* (Paris, 1869–1975), I, 76, XIII, 161, XIV, 133 (referring to various events that took place in the fourteenth century); Sébastien Moreau, *La Prinse et délivrance du roy* [etc.], ed. L. Cimber and F. Danjou, *Archives curieuses de l'histoire de France depuis Louis XI jusqu'à Louis XVIII*, 1re série (Paris, 1835), II, 323 (referring to an event that took place in 1526) .

[4] Jean de Wavrin, *Recueil des croniques et anchiennes istories de la Grant Bretaigne, a present nomme Engleterre*, ed. Sir William Hardy and Edward L. C. P. Hardy (London, 1891), VI/1, 6–7. Redactions of this text date from 1445 and 1469 and were continued until 1471.

Fille, quant serez en karolle,
Dansez gentiment par mesure,
Car, quant fille se desmesure,
Tel la voit qui la tient pour folle.[5]

(Girls, when your are in a *carole*, dance modestly and with decorum, for, when a girl behaves without decorum, there will be some who think her wanton.)

It is definitely as an archaism that the word is used by sixteenth-century authors.[6] Late in that century the term is defined by Maurice de la Porte thus: 'douce, mesuree, trepignante, amoureuse. C'est un vieil mot françois lequel signifie danse, auquel tu auras recours pour t'aider des epithetes qui lui sont attribués' (gentle, measured, lively, tender. It is an old French word, which means *dance*, to which you will have recourse to help you with the [foregoing] epithets that are attributed to it).[7] The poet, Joachim du Bellay, employs *carollant* for *dansant* in his translation of two books of the *Aeneid* in order to avoid words in common usage and to achieve a more elevated style:

C'est pourquoy ne voulant tousjours contraindre l'escriture au commun usage de parler, je ne crains d'usurper quelquefois en mes vers certains mots, et locutions dont ailleurs je ne voudroy user, et ne pourroy sans affectation, et mauvaise grace. Pour ceste mesme raison, j'ay usé de gallees, pour galleres, endementiers, pour en ce pendant: isnel, pour leger: carrolant, pour dansant, et autres dont antiquité (suyvant l'exemple de mon aucteur Virgile) me semble donner quelque majesté au vers, principalement en un long poëme, pourveu toutefois que l'usage n'en soit immoderé.[8]

(That is why, not always wishing to restrict my style to the usage of common speech, I have not been reluctant to import sometimes certain words and locutions into my verses that otherwise I would not, and could not, use without affectation or disagreeable effect. For this same reason I have used *gallees* for *galleres*, *endementiers* for *en ce pendant*, *isnel* for *leger*, *carrolant* for *dansant*, and other words whose antiquity (following my author Virgil) seem to me to impart some majesty to the verse especially in a long poem, provided that the use of such words is not excessive.)

---

5 'Le Doctrinal des filles à marier' in *Recueil de poésies françoises des XVe et XVIe siècles – morales, facétieuses, historiques*, ed. Anatole de Montaiglon (Paris, 1855), II, 19.

6 See Huguet, 'Carole', for an extensive list of sixteenth-century citations.

7 Maurice de la Porte, *Les Epithetes de M de la Porte, Parisien* (Paris, 1571), fol. 47^{v}, 'Carole'.

8 Virgil, *Deux Livres de l'Eneide de Virgile, a scavoir le quatrieme et sixieme traduicts en vers francois par J. du Bellay, Angevin* (Paris, 1560), fols 3^{v}-4^{r}.

The word *carole*, then, had generally fallen out of use. It was to be employed only for specific purposes, and then only occasionally.

Yet in spite of its rarity in actual usage, *carole* as a choreographic term was starting to appear about this time as a headword in the emerging field of lexicography. The senses that dictionaries of the time attributed to it will be examined later. Suffice it to say here that at least from Nicot's publication of 1573 onwards the word is frequently included in dictionaries published in France, whether these are French–Latin publications, where obviously the French term is explained in Latin, or French–French dictionaries.[9] Many of the French–Latin dictionaries attempt an explanation of the etymology. Indeed a preoccupation with this aspect continued to be a subject of interest well into the twentieth century. Nevertheless, the lexicographers were also concerned with the choreographic sense of the term, although their definitions are limited to stating or implying that it is an obsolete word for *danse*.

In the second half of the eighteenth century the etymology was re-examined, and the original meaning of the word was re-assessed. This re-evaluation was due to Jean-Baptitse de la Curne de Sainte-Palaye, a scholar widely read in Old French, and therefore much in advance of his time, who completed a historical dictionary of the French language in 1762, although it was not published until more than a century later.[10] Indeed his dictionary, when eventually published, proved a valuable starting point for Godefroy's dictionary of Old French (1880–1902). This publication, in turn, counted among the growing number of lexicographical works published from the late nineteenth century onwards in which *carole* is included among the entries. As might be expected, definitions in more general dictionaries were followed by more specialized compilations of dance terms of which Aeppli's study (1925) is particularly significant.[11] The closing decades of the twentieth century saw the publication of dictionaries specifically devoted to dance, such as the *Tanz Lexikon* and the *International Encyclopedia of Dance*, both of which cite the *carole*.[12]

The lexicographical activity that took place in the late nineteenth century was matched by works devoted to the increasing interest in the social life of the Middle Ages. Exploration of aspects of everyday life included a consideration of medieval

[9] *Le Grand Dictionaire françois-latin augumenté*, ed. Jean Nicot *et al.* (Paris 1573), 'Carolle'. I have not seen an earlier edition.

[10] *Dictionnaire historique de l'ancien langage françois ou glossaire de la langue françoise depuis son origine jusqu'au siècle de Louis XIV*, compiled by Jean-Baptiste La Curne de Sainte-Palaye, ed. L. Favre and M. Pajot (Paris, 1875–82).

[11] Fritz Aeppli, 'Die wichtigsten Ausdrücke für das Tanzen in den romanischen Sprachen', *Beihefte zur Zeitschrift für romanische Philologie*, 75 (1925), 33–36; see also 90–95.

[12] Otto Schneider, *Tanz Lexikon* (Frankfurt-am-Main, 1985), 'Carole'; Ingrid Brainard, 'Medieval Dance', *International Encyclopedia of Dance: A Project of Dance Perspectives Foundation*, ed. Selma Jeanne Cohen *et al.* (New York, 1998).

pastimes, including dance. An early specialist entry into this field was Albert Czerwinski's *Geschichte der Tanzkunst* (1862), which, however, does not mention the *carole*.[13] But the term *carole*, and how it might be differentiated from *danse*, was about to become the focus of attention, having its origins in Liliencron's study (1848) of the poems of Neidhart von Reuental in which he contrasted the terms *reie* and *tanz*.[14]

Yet another area of the subject was also being opened up. Once the *carole* was a little better known, it became evident that the dance was always accompanied by singing. Being counted among the earliest extant specimens of French lyrics these dance pieces were of the greatest historical importance. Not surprisingly, therefore, they featured prominently in the first major study of the genre, Jeanroy's *Les Origines de la poésie lyrique en France au Moyen-Age*, first published in 1889.[15] This investigation was the subject of a comprehensive review by Gaston Paris, which addressed at greater length the etymology and choreography of the *carole*.[16] These two works were in turn cited as authorities on the *carole* in a more general survey of dance in the thirteenth century verse by Joseph Bédier in his article, 'Les Plus Anciennes Danses françaises'.[17] This essay, together with the two studies already mentioned, has also, in a way, continued to influence the thinking about the nature of medieval dance in general, and about the *carole* in particular. A further addition to works of this kind was Verrier's three-volume publication, *Le Vers français*.[18] Verrier had much to say on every aspect of the *carole*, including its choreography, and in an article written at the same time as his history, 'La Plus Vieille Citation de carole', he sets out at some length his discovery of what he believed was the earliest occurrence of the term.[19] This piece, too, entered the select canon of authors commenting on the dance. Further histories of French

---

13 Albert Czerwinski, *Geschichte der Tanzkunst bei den cultiven Völkern* [etc.] (Leipzig, 1862).

14 R. von Liliencron, 'Über Neidharts höfische Dorfpoesie', *Zeitschrift für deutsches Alterthum*, 6 (1848), 79–83.

15 Alfred Jeanroy, *Les Origines de la poésie lyrique en France au Moyen-Age* (Paris, 1889). Later editions were published in 1904 and 1925 (the edition used in this study). See especially pp. 102–13 and 387–431.

16 Gaston Paris, rev. of *Les Origines de la poésie lyrique en France au Moyen-Age* by Alfred Jeanroy, *Mélanges de littérature française du Moyen Age*, ed. Mario Roques (Paris, 1912), see especially pp. 588–609. This review had previously appeared in the *Journal des Savants* (novembre 1891; mars, juillet 1892).

17 Joseph Bédier, 'Les Plus Anciennes Danses françaises', *Revue des Deux Mondes*, 31 (jan.–fév. 1906), 398–424.

18 Paul Verrier, *Le Vers français: formes primitives, développement, diffusion* (Paris, 1931–32). On the *carole*, see especially I, 23–55.

19 Paul Verrier, 'La Plus Vieille Citation de carole', *Romania*, 58 (1932), 380–421 and 61 (1935), 95–97.

poetry with references to the *carole* have since appeared since Verrier's, but these have added nothing new to our knowledge of the dance or, indeed its lyrics.

If literary studies, such as those by Jeanroy, Gaston Paris, Bédier and Verrier, formed the basis of much of the later comment on the nature of the *carole*, a radically different view of the dance was put forward in Margit Sahlin's monograph, *Etude sur la carole médiévale*. This work was originally submitted as a doctoral thesis to the University of Uppsala, and was published in 1940. It is the only major study of the *carole* to date. Sahlin differed from her predecessors, both as regards the etymology of the word itself and also as regards the general form of the choreography. Her work was the subject of a dozen reviews during the 1940s. While acknowledging the originality of her contribution, her critics, nevertheless, generally rejected her arguments. In spite of this, her study has continued to be widely cited. Sahlin's *Etude* is fairly wide-ranging in its examination of the *carole* both from a linguistic and literary perspective. Yet her investigation does not discuss in any detail, for example, the choreography or its accompanying lyrics and music or its iconography.

The linguistic and the literary historians were not the only scholars to concern themselves with dance in general and with the *carole* in particular. A dance must perforce be accompanied by music, and consequently musicologists have become engaged in this topic. Activity in this field seems to have begun with Pierre Aubry and his article 'La Danse au Moyen Age' in which the *carole* is specifically mentioned.[20] Most of these purely musicological studies are, in fact, concerned with medieval instrumental music and few with the dance. Notable exceptions are the two histories of medieval music by Théodore Gérold, in which he tries to relate known dances of the period to extant music.[21] Stevens and Page, in their respective books published in the 1980s, have also given some attention to the *carole*.[22] As for standard music reference works, the *Handwörterbuch der musikalischen Terminologie* has no entry for 'Carole' as it is not a musical term.[23] 'Carole' or 'Carola', however, does appear as a head word in numerous other music dictionaries notably those in English, German, French and Italian. It figures

[20] Pierre Aubry, 'La Danse au Moyen Age' *La Revue Musicale*, [originally *La Revue d'Histoire et de Critique Musicales*], 9 (1909), 109–15.

[21] Théodore Gérold, *La Musique au Moyen Age* (Paris, 1932), pp. 299–301 and *Histoire de la musique des origines à la fin du XIVe siècle* (Paris, 1936), pp. 304–05.

[22] John Stevens, *Words and Music in the Middle Ages: Song, Narrative, Dance and Drama, 1050–1350* (Cambridge, 1986), pp. 159–98; Christopher Page, *Voices and Instruments of the Middle Ages: Instrumental Practice and Songs in France 1100–1300* (London, 1987), 77–84; also *The Owl and the Nightingale: Musical Life and Ideas in France, 1100–1300* (London, 1989), pp. 110–33.

[23] *Handwörterbuch der musikalischen Terminologie*, ed. Heinrich Eggebrecht (Stuttgart, 1972–94).

in both editions of *The New Grove Dictionary of Music and Musicians*.[24] In the second edition of the standard German dictionary on the subject, *Die Musik in Geschichte und Gegenwart*, the *carole* is treated in the general context of dance and dance music.[25] Inevitably most of these contributions rely on the earlier literary studies mentioned above, or do little to relate the music to dancing.

Music that has been edited and discussed but somewhat overlooked in connexion with the *carole* can now be shown to be related to that dance. A seminal publication here was Friedrich Gennrich's *Rondeaux, Virelais und Balladen*.[26] Although he was qualified as a linguist and a musicologist to undertake such an editorial task, his emendations of the lyric texts in particular have been questioned. A more recent and valuable contribution to the musical aspect of the subject has been Maria Vedder Fowler's unpublished dissertation, 'Musical Interpolations in Thirteenth- and Fourteenth-Century French Narratives'.[27] Neither of these publications, however, relates the tunes to dance.

Possibly because they feel less directly connected with dance, art historians and iconographers have been less forthcoming. Nevertheless John Fleming's study on the *Roman de la Rose* deals briefly with the illustration of the *carole* within the context of the work as a whole.[28] The only monograph on the subject of medieval representations of the *carole* (or *Reige* to use his exact term) has been provided by Walter Salmen in his article 'Ikonographie des Reigens im Mittelalter'.[29] But his interpretation of the term and its depiction, it must be said, is far too generalized.

Thus in the centuries since its demise as a social dance, the *carole* has never been entirely absent from public consciousness. Indeed, interest in its various aspects has increased from the late nineteenth century, although it must be said that almost nothing of relevance has appeared in print in the opening decade of the twenty-first century. Yet in spite of multifarious endeavours, we have no precise information about the *carole* or how it was performed, although it was the most popular dance in francophile regions in the late Middle Ages. There is even no agreement about what kind of dance the *carole* was.

---

[24] See John Stevens, 'Carole', *New Grove 1*; but for a different view, see Robert Mullally 'Carole', *New Grove 2*.

[25] Sibylle Dahms, 'Tanz. 1. Mittelalter', *MGG 2*.

[26] Of the three volumes of *Rondeaux, Virelais und Balladen*, ed. Friedrich Gennrich, those particularly relevant to the present study are the first two published in Gesellschaft für romanische Literatur, namely 43 (1921) and 47 (1927).

[27] Maria Vedder Fowler, 'Musical Interpolations in Thirteenth- and Fourteenth-Century French Narratives', PhD. Diss. Yale University, 1979.

[28] John V. Fleming, *The* Roman de la Rose: *A Study in Allegory and Iconography* (Princeton, NJ, 1969), p. 84.

[29] Walter Salmen, 'Ikonographie des Reigens im Mittelalter', *Acta Musicologica*, 52 (1980), 14–26.

Chapter 2
The Etymology of the Word *Carole*

The word *carole* is obviously French. French is a Romance language, and is therefore derived from Latin. The origin of a large number of French words clearly illustrates this: for example the word *mur* (a wall) obviously derives from the Latin *murus*. In other cases the derivation is not so easily discernible but, following the laws of phonology, such a derivation can be made; thus *trouver* (to find) presupposes a hypothetical Latin form **tropare*. As for the word *carole* neither of the above procedures has provided an agreed solution. Consequently, the search for an answer has given rise to much argument and speculation going back as far as the thirteenth century.

Some of the suggested origins have been frivolous, and have been rightly dismissed by Sahlin, such as, for example, that *carole* derives from the Latin *carrus* (a cart) or *Carolus* (Charles).[1] An ingenious but nonetheless erroneous theory was put forward by Lacroix-Novaro, namely that the word comes from **charagula*, a diminutive of *charagus*.[2] According to this theory, an oriental cult of magic reached the West in the fourth century AD. This cult involved the construction of a circular palisade within which a dance was performed led by a magician called a *charagus* from which the name of the dance itself, *charagula*, was derived, and this word subsequently developed into *carole*. This explanation, intriguing as it is, remains, purely speculative.

We are left, then, with six theories that can be, in some manner at least, supported by phonological laws or from some historical perspective. These six naturally involve the two aspects of etymology: semantics and phonology. Let us examine these theories.

Middle Breton, *coroll* (Modern Breton, *koroll*)

In the years between 1135 and 1138, Geoffrey of Monmouth composed his famous *Historia Regum Brittanie* (The History of the Kings of Britain).[3] In it he described Stonehenge as the *chorea gigantum* (the Giants' Dance). Subsequently Wace made a verse translation into Anglo-Norman of this work, which he called *Le Roman de*

---

[1] Sahlin, pp. 72–3.

[2] Yves Lacroix-Novaro, 'La Carole: ses origines', *Revue de Musicologie*, 19 (1935), 1–26, for what follows in my text.

[3] Geoffrey of Monmouth, *The* Historia Regum Britannie *of Geoffrey of Monmouth*, ed. Neil Wright and Julia C. Crick (Cambridge, 1985–91), I, 90.

Brut, and which he completed in 1155. The reference to Stonehenge is rendered in the following lines:

> E Merlin les pieres dreça,
> En lur ordre les raloa;
> Bretun les suelent en bretanz
> Apeler carole as gaianz,
> Stanhenges unt nun en engleis,
> Pieres pendues en franceis.[4]

> (And Merlin set up the stones, returning them to their original order. The Bretons in the Breton language usually call them the Giants' Carole. They are known as Stonehenge in English or Hanging Stones in French.)

The statement 'Bretun les suelent en bretanz' apparently suggested to some scholars that the word *carole* was derived from Breton, or at least had some influence on its etymology.[5] Others contested this view maintaining categorically that the word was French.[6] Indeed no evidence was advanced as to how this derivation from Breton took place. Conclusive proof that this theory is faulty is provided by the fact the Breton *coroll* cannot be traced back further than the second half of the fifteenth century, whereas *carole* in French has been attested centuries earlier.[7]

Latin, *chorus* or **chorulus*

It might seem obvious that in French, being a Romance language, an etymon might be found in a Latin word for *dance*. Not surprisingly, therefore, in an anonymous commentary in a thirteenth-century manuscript of the *Dictionarius* of

---

[4] Wace, *Le Roman de Brut de Wace*, ed. Ivor Arnold (Paris, 1938–40), ll.8173–8. The date of composition is given in ll.14864–7.

[5] Notably Friedrich Diez, *Etymologisches Wörterbuch der romanischen Sprachen* (1853; 5th ed. Bonn, 1887), 'Carole'; Urban T. Holmes, 'Old French Carole', *Language*, 4 (1928), 28–30; Max Förster, 'Can Old French *caroler* be of Celtic Origin?', *Language*, 4 (1928), 200–01; *A Dictionary of Old Breton: Dictionnaire du vieux breton,* ed. Léon Fleuriot (1964; rpt Toronto, 1985), '(Cor)'.

[6] C. Nigra, ' Notes étymologiques et lexicales', *Romania*, 31 (1902), 519, n. 2; Förster, *ibid.*; *FEW*, 'Choraula'; Leo Jordan, 'Der Reigentanz Carole und seine Lieder', *Zeitschrift für romanische Philologie*, 51 (1931), 335; *Romanisches etymologisches Wörterbuch*, ed. W. Meyer-Lübke, Sammlung romanischer Elementar-und Handbücher, 3rd Series, No 3 (1911–20, 3rd ed., Heidelberg 1935), '*Choreola'; Sahlin, p. 73.

[7] See *Geriadur istorel ar brezhoneg* [etc]: *Dictionnaire historique du Breton*, ed. Roparz Hemon, (2nd ed. Quimper, 1979–), 'Koroll', where the earliest attestation given is a Breton–French–Latin manuscript vocabulary of 1464.

Johannes de Garlandia, the text of which was written between 1218 and 1229, we find the following explanation: 'choream, Gallice *charole*, ab hoc nomine chorus' (*Chorea*, in French *carole*. *Chorus* comes from this noun [i.e. from *chorea*]).[8] This commentary on Johannes de Garlandia, then, provides us with the earliest suggested etymology. The word *chorus* itself, however, cannot be the etymon, since it does not account for the ending *–ole* in French, and thus even if it were to be the ultimate source, must necessarily have passed through a diminutive form, *chorolus*. A few commentators have followed this line of thought, but in general this theory has gained little acceptance.[9] Indeed the derivation seems highly suspect since *chorulus* would produce the form *chorle*.

Latin, chorea or **choreola* (or *choriola*)

If *chorus* could not provide an indisputable origin for the French *carole* then possibly another Latin word for dance, *chorea*, might supply the answer.[10] Some early lexicographers believed the word might be derived from the root form itself.[11] But even before them, as early as 1573, another lexicographer, Nicot, realized that, as with *chorus*, the French word could only be derived from a diminutive: 'carolle: chorea, chorus saltatio, videtur dici quasi choreola' (*carole*, *chorea* or *chorus*, a dance.[12] It seems to be derived from *choreola*). Some much more recent etymologists have also been attracted to this solution.[13] Others are unconvinced

---

[8] 'The *Dictionarius* of John de Garlande' in *A Library of National Antiquities*, I, *A Volume of Vocabularies*, ed. Thomas Wright (n. p., 1857), 'Chorea'.

[9] Diez, 1st ed. (Bonn, 1853), 2nd ed. (Bonn, 1861–62) and 5th ed., 'Carole'; Rudolf Haberl, 'Neue Beiträge zur romanischen Linguistik', *Zeitschrift für romanische Philologie*, 36 (1912), 309–10; *Dictionnaire étymologique de la langue française*, ed. Albert Dauzat (Paris, 1938), 'Carole'; *Trésor de la langue française: dictionnaire de la langue du XIXe et du XXe siècle (1789–1960)*, ed. Paul Imbs (Paris, 1971–94), 'Carole'; *Dictionnaire du moyen français: la Renaissance*, ed. Algirdas Julien Greimas and Teresa Mary Kane (Paris, 1992),'Carole'.

[10] Hans Spanke, rev. of Sahlin, *Literaturblatt für germanische und romanische Philologie*, 64 (1943), 107, believes that the root word might have had some influence on the etymological development of the form.

[11] For example, *Trésor de recherches et antiquitez gauloises et françoises, reduites en ordre alphabétique*, ed. P. Borel (Paris, 1655), 'Carole'; *Nouveau Dictionnaire françois*, ed. Pierre Richelet (Amsterdam, 1732), 'Carolle'.

[12] *Le Grand Dictionnaire françois–latin augumenté*, ed. Jean Nicot *et al.* (Paris, 1573), 'Carolle' and following him, *Thrésor de la langue francoise, tant ancienne que moderne*, ed Aimar Ranconnet (rev. Jean Nicot) (1621; facsimile, Paris, 1960), 'Carolle'.

[13] Föster, p. 201, Meyer-Lübke, '*Choreola'; J. Jud, rev. of Sahlin, *Vox Romanica*, 5 (1940), 302–4.

by this derivation on various grounds.[14] As Diez and Lerch note, the phonology here is defective as the theory fails to account for the loss of the palatal /j/ in the transition from *choreola* to *carole.*[15]

Latin, *corolla*

As *carole* cannot be proved to derive from either of the Latin words for *dance*, an alternative line of investigation suggests that it comes from a different Latin word. Some scholars, believing that the *carole* was a circular dance, proposed *corolla* (a garland) a diminutive of *corona* (crown) as the etymon. This derivation was put forward by La Curne de Saint-Palaye in 1762.[16] He was widely read in Old French literature, and had considered the different meanings of the French dance term carefully. A small but firmly convinced group of commentators have followed him.[17] Yet objections on semantic grounds had already been raised as the transition from 'garland' to 'dance' was far from clear.[18] The etymology was also rejected on phonological grounds.[19] Gaston Paris, for example, pointed out that *corolla* would produce *coroule* in French.[20]

Greek, *Kyrie eleison*

At this juncture none of the suggested Latin etymologies has proved satisfactory. Sahlin, the only person to date to publish a monograph on the *carole*, adopted a

---

14 W. Foerster, 'II Etymologisches', *Zeitschrift für romanische Philologie*, 6 (1882), 109–10; Holmes, p. 202, in reply to Förster; Leo Jordan, 'Der Reigentanz Carole', 335; FEW, 'Choraula'; Sahlin, pp. 74–5; Eugen Lerch, rev. of Sahlin, *Cultura Neolatina*, 1 (1941), 236–7.

15 Diez (2nd ed.), 'Carole'; Lerch, *ibid.*

16 *Dictionnaire historique de l'ancien langage françois ou glossaire de la langue françoise depuis son origine jusqu'au siècle de Louis XIV*, compiled by Jean-Baptiste de la Curne de Sainte-Palaye, ed. L Favre and M. Pajot (Niort, 1875–82), 'Carole'.

17 W. Foerster, p. 110; G. Gröber, 'Vulgärlateinische Substrate romanischer Wörter', *Archiv für lateinische Lexikographie und Grammatik*, 1 (1884), 'Corolla'; *Lateinisch–romanisches Wörterbuch (Etymologisches Wörterbuch der romanischen Hauptsprachen),* ed. Gustav Körting (1890; 3rd ed. Paderborn, 1907), No 2525; see also No 2145; Curt Sachs, *Eine Weltgeschichte des Tanzes* (Berlin, 1933), p. 183 and *World History of the Dance*, trans. Bessie Schönberg (London, 1938), p. 271.

18 Diez, 5th ed., 'Carole', Halberl, p. 309; Leo Jordan, 'Wortgeschtliches' in *Festschrift zum XII. allgemeinen deutschen Neuphilologentagen in München*, Pfingsten, 1906, ed. E. Stollreither (Erlangen, 1906), p. 61; Sahlin pp. 73–4; Spanke, 107 *et al.*

19 FEW, 'Choraula'; Meyer-Lübke, '*Choreola'; Sahlin, p. 74–5; Lerch, p. 236.

20 Gaston Paris, rev. of W. Foerster, 'Carole', *Romania*, 11 (1882), 444–5.

totally different approach.[21] Her concept of the dance will be examined in the next chapter, but suffice it to say here that, rather than being a circular dance, as others had suggested, she argued that it was, in fact, a processional dance for couples. In their progress, she maintained, the participants exclaimed the refrain 'Kyrie eleison' (Lord, have mercy) and it was from this Greek phrase that the French term was derived: KYRIELEISON > *kyrielle* > *karielle* > *kariole* > *karole*.[22] Lerch agreed with Sahlin on the etymon but differed from her on the origin and development of the term.[23] He explained 'Kyrie eleison' as a popular expression of joy in north-eastern France as the cart (*cariole*) bringing the last of the harvest arrived. *Kyrie eleison* then passed through the intermediary stages of *cariole* and *kerole*. Lerch was alone in his acceptance of Sahlin's etymology; most scholars were generally united in rejecting it. Some expressed a general feeing of scepticism; others advanced more detailed criticisms.[24]

First there were the objections on semantic grounds. There was simply no evidence that the *carole* was a processional couple dance.[25] Likewise no proof existed that *Kyrie eleison* was a song, and for Sahlin's theory to be acceptable this phrase would have had to have been first a song and then a dance derived from that song, but *carole*, as Sahlin herself admitted, was always a dance and never a song.[26]

Sahlin's phonology also posed numerous difficulties. Spitzer queried a host of her etymological deductions.[27] Jud noted that the change from countertonic /i/ to /a/ in KYRIELEISON > *carole* was not explained satisfactorily.[28] Jud and Falk were perplexed by the change of the suffix *–elle* to *–ole* (*kyrielle* > *kariole*).[29] Both Falk and Suchier cast doubt on the change of the tonic /e/ to /ɔ/ (as in the preceding example).[30] Furthermore Falk pointed out that /j/ in hiatus (KYRIELEISON) was always retained, and that in any case words containing such forms are modern.[31] More generally he observed that Sahlin herself had admitted that her etymology 'ne suit pas strictement le "lois phonétiques"' (does not strictly follow the 'rules

---

21 Sahlin, pp. 82–94.

22 Sahlin, p. 91.

23 Lerch, pp. 237–42, for what follows in my text.

24 Mario Roques, rev. of Sahlin, *Romania*, 67 (1942–43), 419–20; Paul Zumthor, rev. of Sahlin, *Zeitschrift für romanische Philologie*, 64, 1944), 182–4; Henri Guiter, rev. of Sahlin, *Revue des Langues Romanes*, 69 (1945), 345–6.

25 Paul Falk, rev. of Sahlin, *Studia Neophilologica*, 13 (1940–41), 136–8; Hans Rheinfelder, rev. of Sahlin, *Volkstum und Kultur der Romanen*, 15 (1942–43), 186–8.

26 Walther Suchier, rev. of Sahlin, *Deutsche Literaturzeitung*, 62 (1941), col. 1215; Spanke, 107.

27 Leo Spitzer, rev. of Sahlin, *Modern Language Notes*, 56 (1941), 222–5.

28 Jud, p. 303.

29 Jud, *ibid*,; Falk, p. 135.

30 Falk, p. 135; Suchier, col. 1215.

31 Falk, *ibid*.

of phonetics'), which is a decisive reason for disregarding her argument.[32] It must be added, however, that her etymology has been widely noted in various studies.

Greek, χοραυλης

We are left with the one remaining theory, which appears to have been first enunciated by Diefenbach in 1857.[33] According to this etymology the Old French *carole* is ultimately derived from the Greek noun *χοραυλης* (one who accompanies a chorus on the aulos).[34] From this etymon came the Latin form *choraula* and thence *carole*. This etymology found favour in varying degrees with scholars with some taking the derivation from the Latin form rather than from the Greek.[35] Yet here again objections have been as wide ranging as with the other theories.

Lerch observed that it was not obvious how a learned word became a term for a folk dance, or how the Latin masculine noun *choraula* became the Old French feminine noun, *carole*.[36] The more general argument, however, was that the etymology left unexplained how a word for a person in Greek and Latin became a word for a thing – a dance – in French.[37] The phonological development was also judged to be unsatisfactory. In particular it was felt that argument for the development of / ko-/ to /ka-/ (cho*raula* to ca*role*) could not be sustained.[38]

From the foregoing survey it might seem that none of the proposed theories provides an acceptable explanation of the origin of the term *carole*. Yet this last has a better claim, and the objections raised against it can be satisfactorily answered.

First, the *carole* cannot be called a folk dance for, as will become evident in later chapters, it was a social dance performed by people of every class. The semantic and grammatical changes involved in the transition from χοραυλης to *choraula* and thence to *carole* are no hindrance to the acceptance of the etymology

---

32 Sahlin, p. 90, Falk, *ibid.*

33 *Glossarium Latino–Germanicum Mediae et Infimae Aetatis*, ed. Laurentius Diefenbach (Frankfurt-am Main, 1857), 'Cho-'.

34 I have taken the definition from *A Greek–English Lexicon*, ed. Henry George Liddell and Robert Scott rev. Sir Henry Stuart Jones *et al.* (1843; 9th ed., Oxford, 1940), for which see under 'χοραυλεω'; I have, however, substituted *aulos*, which was a reed instrument, for the incorrect *flute*. A verbal form, *χοραυλειν*, is found in Strabo's *Geography* (written between 20 and 7 BC), XVII.1.11, but it cannot be the etymon of the French noun.

35 Diez, 5th ed. 'Carole'; Nigra, pp. 519–20; *Untergegangene und veraltete Worte des französischen im heutigen Englisch*, ed. Hugo Brüll (Halle, 1913), 'Charole'; Körting, '*Choraulo, -are'; Jordan, 'Wortgeschichtliches', pp. 61–3 and also 'Der Reigentanz', pp. 336–7; FEW, 'Choraula' *et al.*

36 Lerch, p. 237. Lerch overstates the case when he says that *choraula* is a learned word.

37 Sahlin, pp. 76–7; Lerch, p. 237.

38 Lerch, p. 236.

either. Arguments on the grounds of change in gender can be rejected immediately. One might note in passing that Probus gives *choraula* as actually being of common gender: *hic et haec choraula*.[39] As for changes as words passed from Latin to French, one need only cite such examples as *flos* (Accusative Case, *florem*), which is masculine in Latin, but gives the feminine French, *fleur*, and *dens* (Accusative Case, *dentem*), which is also masculine in Latin, but its derivative, *dent*, is both masculine and feminine in Old French and feminine in Modern French.[40] As for shifts in meaning, Falk views these as evolutionary: 'joueurs de flûte', 'coryphée', 'jongleur', 'chanteur', 'danseur' (flute player, leader of the dance, entertainer, singer, dancer).[41] Here one might be tempted to concede to Lerch that the sense remains that of a person not of a musical instrument or a dance.[42] Yet even such radical shifts are possible (in this case from an instrumentalist in Greek to a dance in French). Thus, for instance, Classical Latin *cohortem*, which can mean 'a space surrounded by farm-buildings, farmyard' becomes *cour* (court) in French, signifying not only the place but also the people in it.[43] More relevant to our present purpose, since it indicates the change in meaning from people to an inanimate object, is the Classical Latin *collegium*, which refers to people, for example 'a guild, club, society, fraternity', and is the etymon of the French *collège*, 'college'.[44] It is therefore possible to accept a change in meaning from an instrumentalist to a dance.

The phonology, too, is demonstrably regular. The earliest citation of the noun, χοραυλης, occurs in an epigram of Lucillius who lived in the reign of Nero (54–68 A.D.)[45] There are examples, too, of memorial inscriptions in Greek.[46] Transliterated into the Roman alphabet as *choraules*, it is recorded in this form in the works of Petronius, Pliny the Elder, Martial and Juvenal.[47] A native Latin form, *choraula*, which shows the normal replacement of the Greek ending -ης by the Latin *–a* (c.f. ΝΑΥΤΗΣ > *nauta*), is also used by Petronius and Martial as well as by Suetonius

39 *Probi, Donati, Servii Qui Feruntur de Arte Grammatica Libri*, ed. Heinrich Keil, Grammatici Latini (Hildesheim, 1961), IV, 85.

40 For the examples cited here and for others, see Alfred Ewert, *The French Language* (1933; rpt London, 1969), pp. 136–42.

41 Falk, pp. 138–9.

42 Lerch, p. 237.

43 *Oxford Latin Dictionary* (Oxford, 1968–82), 'Cohors'.

44 *Oxford Latin Dictionary*, 'Collegium'.

45 *Epigrammatum Anthologia Palatina*, ed. Friedrich Dübner (Paris, 1872), II, 286.

46 See *Paulys Real-Encyclopädie von classischen Alterumwissenschaft*, ed. August Friedrich von Pauly, rev. Georg Wissowa *et al.* (Stuttgart. 1893–1978), 'Choraules'.

47 Petronius, *Satyricon*, 53; Pliny, *Pline l'Ancien, histoire naturelle*, ed. and trans. E. de Saint Denis (Paris, 1972), XXXVII, 3.6; Martial, *Epigrams*, V, 56, 9, IX, 77, 6, XI, 75, 3; Juvenal, *Satires*, VI, 77.

and many later writers.[48] Although the Greek and Latin forms appear more or less contemporaneously, the Latin form obviously derives from the Greek. The form *coraula* or *coraules* with the loss of the strong initial aspiration, is found in glosses (in manuscripts dating from the seventh to the tenth centuries).[49] Similarly the form *coraulem* is to be found in a manuscript reading of the tenth century of the works of Pliny the Elder.[50] It also occurs in manuscript readings dating from the ninth to the eleventh centuries of the works of Apuleius and Servius.[51]

Of particular interest are manuscripts of two works by Venantius Fortunatus (530–609 AD). The first work is a poem addressed to a Bishop Felix.[52] In 11 of 13 manuscripts, dating from the ninth to the eleventh centuries, we find the form *coraula*.[53] In the two remaining manuscripts, the first dating from the eighth or ninth centuries and the second dating from the tenth century, however, the word appears as *coralla*. Here we see the normal development of the stressed diphthong /au /, represented by the graph *au*, to an open back monophthong /ɔ/, represented here by the graph *a* or *o* (c.f. CAUSAM > *cose*, Modern French, *chose*).

The other citation from Venantius Fortunatus that concerns us is a passage in his prose biography of St Radegund, the *Vita Sanctae Radegundae*.[54] In five of the six manuscripts cited by Krusch the reading *corolla* occurs; the remaining one has *carolla*. These examples illustrate a feature also found in other sources where a vacillation takes place between a graph *o* and a graph *a* in a countertonic syllable indicating a phonological shift from /o: / to /a/ or /ə/. Thus a ninth-century manuscript of the Tironian *notae* transcribes the symbol for *choreuontes* as *chareontes*; three other manuscripts of the ninth and tenth centuries have

---

48 For the development of Gk. -ης > Lat. –*a*, see C. H. Grandgent, *An Introduction to Vulgar Latin* (1934; rpt New York, 1962), p. 22; for examples of the Latin ending, see Petronius, 69; Martial, VI, 39, 19; Suetonius, *Lives of the Caesars*, Nero, 54 and Galba, 12. An extensive list of citations will be found in *Thesaurus Linguae Latinae* (Leipzig, 1900–), 'Choraules'.

49 *De Glossariorum Latinorum Origine et Fatis*, ed. Georg Goetz *et al.* (1888–1923; rpt Amsterdam, 1965), III, 84, 172, IV, 44, 325, V, 594, 596.

50 *Pline l'Ancien*, XXXVII, 3.6 (in the Codex Bambergensis, M.V.10).

51 Apuleius, 'Du Dieu de Socrate' in *Apulée: opuscules philosophiques*, ed. and trans. Jean Beaujeu (Paris, 1973), p. 33: Servius, *Servii Grammatici Qui Feruntur in Vergilii Carmina Commentarii*, ed. Georg Thilo and Hermann Hagen (Leipzig, 1927), III, 64 (and note on Virgil, *Eclogues*, 5.89).

52 Venantius Fortunatus, *Venance Fortunat: poèmes*, ed. and trans. Marc Reydellet (Paris, 1994), I, 94.

53 Venantius Fortunatus, *ibid.*

54 LBL, Additional, 11880 (s. ix^int^) was the manuscript consulted; the edition used was Venantius Fortunatus, *Venanti Honori Clementiani Fortunati Presbyteri Italici Opera Pedestria*, ed. Bruno Krusch, Monumenta Germaniae Historica, Auctorum Antiquissimorum Tomi IV Pars Posterior (Berlin, 1885), pp. 47–8.

careontes, one (also from the ninth century) has *careuntes*.[55] We also find an attestation in a tenth-century gloss in which the Latin equivalent of the Greek *χοραυλαι* is given as *charaulę*.[56] These changes represent the reduction of the back vowel to a central position. The fact that this countertonic vowel can have a more central position is exemplified by the development COLUCULAM > *quenouille* (c.f. *querole*, a variant spelling of *carole*). Thus the main objection to the transition of *κοραυλπς* or *choraula* to *carole* is overcome.

A filiation can therefore be drawn up, which is not based on theory or on hypothetical forms but on attested examples:

> ΧΟΡΑΥΛΗΣ > *choraules* > *choraula* > *coraula* > *coralla* / *corolla* / *carolla* > *carole*
> [khɔraulɛːs > khɔ'raula > kɔ'raula > kə'rɔlə > ka'rɔl or kə'rɔl].

A widespread belief exists that the French word has cognates in other European languages. Salmen, for example, implies the extensive dissemination of the *carole* by grouping together the terms *chorea, carole, carôlo, quirola, kirola, carola, chorella, corola, rey, querolle, ronde*.[57] Most of these, if they exist, are cognates derived from the French. *Chorea* is discussed in the next chapter, *querolle* is simply a variant spelling of *carole*, *rey* is a totally unrelated term, *ronde* is not a specific dance term. In Occitan *carola*, as a dance term, occurs only once as the equivalent of *baltz* in a discussion of rhymes in the *Donatz Proensals*.[58] This occurrence is unique. The term is unknown to dictionaries of the language so that even if any other attestations were to be found, they are likely to be borrowings from the French.[59] In spite of assertions to the contrary there are no citations of cognates in either Spanish or Portuguese.[60] In fact, no evidence exists for cognates in any European language with the exception of some examples of an Italian form, *carola*, and, of course, the English form, *carol*, both of which derive from the French. These two examples will be discussed in later chapters.

---

55 *Comentarii Notarum Tironianarum cum Prolegomenis Adnotationibus Criticis et Exegeticis* [etc.], ed. Guilelmus Schmitz (Leipzig, 1893), Tab[ula] 106, [No]17.

56 *De Glossariorum Latinorum Origine et Fatis*, III, 10.

57 Walter Salmen, 'Ikonographie des Reigens im Mittelalter', *Acta Musicologica*, 52 (1980), p. 15.

58 Uc Faidit, *The* Donatz Proensals *of Uc Faidit*, ed. J. H. Marshall (London, 1969), p. 189.

59 The Occitan dictionaries are *Lexique roman ou dictionnaire de la langue des troubadours* [etc.], ed. François Renouard, (Paris, 1838–44), and *Provenzalisches Supplement-Wörterbuch: Berichtigungen und Ergänzungen zu Raynouards Lexique roman*, ed. Emil Levy *et al.* (Leipzig, 1894–1924).

60 M. Bataillon, rev. of Sahlin, *Bulletin Hispanique*, 42 (1940), 328–31; Rafael Lapesa, rev. of Sahlin, *Revista de Filología Española*, 25 (1941), 122–4.

In the end the need did not exist for a number of conflicting theories about the etymology of the word *carole* or for a proliferation of supposed cognates. Diefenbach's etymology proves to be the correct one, and this etymology is amply supported by documentary evidence.

Chapter 3
The Earliest Citations of the Term *Carole* and the Relationship of *Carole* to *Chorus* and *Chorea*

Some of the earliest citations of the word *carole* appear as translations of Latin terms for dance: *chorus* and *chorea*. We saw in the last chapter that neither of these words can plausibly be accepted as the etymon of the French; a relationship, nevertheless, exists between them and *carole*. There also remains the problem of establishing a date (albeit an approximate one) for the first appearance of the word in French, and also of determining whether *chorus* or *chorea* in medieval texts can invariably be translated as *carole*.

The most significant statement to date about the earliest occurrence of the term *carole* was made by Verrier.[1] He claimed that the earliest citation was in the form *chorolla* found in an account of the legend of the dancers of Kölbigk. This is the tale of a supposed miracle that took place in Saxony in the second decade of the eleventh century. It relates how a group of men and women who, in spite of the protests of the priest, persisted in dancing around a churchyard while Mass was being celebrated on Christmas Eve, and were consequently condemned to continue their dance for a whole year. There are three versions of this narrative, one anonymus, one by Othbert,and one by Theoderic.[2] All three are in Latin. The version that concerns us here is Theoderic's, the earliest extant copy of which is contained in a manuscript transcribed by Ordericus Vitalis (fl. 1124–42). The word for 'dance' employed throughout this text, is, with two exceptions, *chorus*. The two exceptions appear in the following passage in which the now repentant Theoderic recounts the event:

> Mittimus geminas puellas, Mersuinden et Vuibecynam, que similes similem de ecclesia allactarent ad iniquitatis nostre choream, quam venabamur predam. Quid hoc aucupio facilius? Adducitur Ava ut avicula irretita, colligitque advenientes

---

1 Paul Verrier, 'La Plus Vieille Citation de carole', *Romania*, 58 (1932), 380–421, 622–3 and 61 (1935), 95–7.

2 The full text of all three versions will be found in Ernst Erich Metzner, *Zur frühesten Geschichte der europäischen Balladendictung: der Tanz in Kölbigk* [etc.], Frankfurter Beiträge zur Germanistik, No 14 (Frankfurt-am-Main, 1972), pp. 30–48. Metzner uses his own revisions of the three versions as edited by Karl-Heinz Borck, 'Der Tanz zu Kölbigk', *Beiträge zur Geschichte der deutschen Sprache und Literatur*, 76 (1954), 243–320.

> Bovo, tam etate prior quam stulticia. Conserimus manus et chorollam confusionis in atrio ordinamus.[3]
>
> (As if hunting prey, we sent the twin girls, Mersuinden and Vuibecyna, so that the like-minded might entice the like-minded from the church to take part in our iniquitous dance. What snare could be easier? Ava was led forth like a bird in a net, and Bovo, being the more advanced in age and stupidity, gathered together all those who had assembled. We joined hands, and began the dance of our confusion in the churchyard.)

Here *chorea* and *chorolla* are synonymous with *chorus* employed elsewhere in the text. *Chorolla* here is not a form of *carole*, as Verrier claimed, but a diminutive of *chorus*.[4] Neither is it, as we saw in the last chapter, an intermediary Latin form in the development of the etymology of *carole*.

A more likely candidate for a French word, 'affublé … en latin' (disguised in Latin), to use Verrier's phrase, is *caraula*, which appears in the autobiography of Guibert de Nogent. The composition of this work dates from between 1114 and 1117, although the text is preserved only in a sixteenth-century copy.[5] Guibert, in this early excursion into archaeological research, speculates on the antiquity of his monastery of Nogent-sous-Coucy, and deduces that the site is probably of pre-Christian origin because the tombs are arranged in a circular fashion unlike Christian burials:

> Quia enim non in morem nostrorum ordo disponitur sepulchrorum, sed circulatim in modum caraulae sepulchrum unius multa ambiunt, in quibus quaedam reperiuntur vasa, quorum causam nesciunt christiana tempora, non possumus aliud credere, nisi quod fuerunt gentilium, aut antiquissima christianorum, sed facta gentili more.[6]

---

[3] PBN, fonds lat. 6503 (between 1124 and 1142), fol. 61^r. The relevant passage, which is possibly an interpolation, is reproduced in facsimile in *Matériaux pour l'édition de Guillaume de Jumièges*, ed. Jules Lair with a preface and notes by Léopold Delisle (n.p., 1910), Appendix 3. The manuscript has *colligitque* and *stulticia* where Metzner (p. 43) has the readings *colligit* and *stultitia* respectively. Verrier ('La Plus Vieille Citation', pp. 381–2, *passim*), incorrectly states that the text was composed by Ordericus Vitalis, not merely copied by him (see Metzner, pp. 40–41).

[4] In Medieval Latin diminutive endings do not necessarily have the significance of a diminutive; c.f. *avicula* in the foregoing quotation; see *A Primer of Medieval Latin: An Anthology of Prose and Poetry*, ed. Charles H. Beeson (1953; rpt, Folkestone, 1973), p. 14.

[5] Guibert de Nogent, *Autobiographie*, ed. and trans. Edmond-René Labande, Les Classiques de l'Histoire de France au Moyen Age, No 34 (Paris, 1981), p. 210.

[6] *ibid.*

(The graves are not arranged according to our custom, but in a circle in the manner of a *carole*, with many graves encompassing a single one in the middle. Some urns have been found buried in them, the purpose of which is unknown to us Christians. I can find no other explanation but that either they are of pagan or very ancient Christian origin continued according to pagan custom.)

Sahlin seems to suggest that *caraula* might be one of a number of retranslations from the French.[7] Certainly Bourgin, in his edition of Guibert, writes of the author 'latinisant les mots de la langue vulgaire' (Latinizing words in the vernacular).[8] It is indeed possible that the Latin form is derived from the French, but the contrary is also possible. What we do not have, either in Theoderic's version of the legend of Kölbigk or in Guibert's autobiography, is a word that is indisputably French. No dating, therefore, can be based on either of these citations, and one must look elsewhere for the earliest citation of the term *carole*.

There exists a considerable number of manuscripts of biblical texts dating from the twelfth century in which the Latin word *chorus* is translated by the French word *carole*. Among such sources is *The Oxford Psalter*.

The Oxford Psalter, now in the Bodleian Library, is also known as *The Montebourg Psalter* from its earlier location. It is written in the Anglo-Norman dialect of Old French. Some have considered this manuscript to date from the second half or even from the end of the twelfth century, but others (including more recent studies) place it in the first half of the twelfth century.[9] The citation that concerns us is Psalm 149 verse 3, which in the Vulgate reads:

Laudent nomen eius in choro, in tympano et psalterio psallant ei.

(Let them praise his name in the dance, let them play to him on drum and harp.)

---

[7] Sahlin, p. 79.

[8] Guibert de Nogent, *Guibert de Nogent: histoire de sa vie* (1053–1124), ed. Georges Bourgin (Paris, 1907), p. xlix.

[9] See, *Répertoire des plus anciens textes en prose française depuis 842 jusqu'aux premières années du XIIIes siècle*, ed. Brian Woledge and H. D. Clive, Publications romanes et françaises, No 79 (Geneva, 1964), p. 99 (end of the 12th century); *Grundriss der romanischen Literaturen des Mittelalters*, ed. Jürgen Beyer and Franz Koppe (Heidelberg, 1968–70), VI/2, 63 (second half or end of the 12th century). For a more recent dating, see Dorothy A. Sneddon, 'The Anglo-Norman Psalters: I, A Note on the Relationship between the Oxford and Arundel Psalters', *Romania*, 99 (1978), p. 396. On information received from M. B. Parkes, she gives a dating of the first half of the 12th century. This dating is accepted by Ian Short, 'Patrons and Polyglots: French Literature in Twelfth-Century England', *Anglo-Norman Studies*, 14 (1991), who concludes that *The Oxford Psalter* is therefore 'the earliest recorded in the French language' (p. 233).

The Oxford Psalter does not give the Latin text, but its translation of this verse runs as follows:

> Lódent le num de lui en caróle; en týmpane é saltiér cántent a lúi.[10]
>
> (Let them praise his name in *caroles*; let them play to him on drum and harp.)

There are half a dozen other manuscripts related to *The Oxford Psalter* dating from the twelfth or the first half of the thirteenth century, but this manuscript is the earliest.[11]

Another Psalter with an Anglo-Norman translation dating from the middle of the twelfth century also provides us with two instances where *chorus* is translated as 'charole'. This is *The Cambridge Psalter*, again named after its present location.[12] It is alternatively know as *The Canterbury Psalter*, from the place where it was copied, or *The Eadwine Psalter*, from its traditional association with the scribe of that name.

Two other similar sources are worth mentioning. One is a translation in the Lorraine dialect (c. 1208) of a sermon by St Bernard of Clairvaux (before c. 1090–d. 1153) where the original Latin *chorus* is again translated as 'kerole'.[13] The other is an Anglo-Norman translation of I Samuel of which the earliest and best manuscript dates from the late twelfth century, where in the narrative of Saul and David we have 'charolantes'.[14]

---

[10] OBL, MS Douce 320 (s. xii[1]), fol. 73[v]. The significance of the diacritics in this and other Anglo-Norman texts remains unexplained; they are possibly stress marks to help the reader. The manuscript has been published under the title, *Libri Psalmorum Versio Antiqua Gallica e Cod. MS. in Bibl. Bodleiana Asservato una cum Versione Metrica aliisque Monumentis Pervetustis*, ed. Francisque Michel (Oxford, 1860) where the line quoted can be found on p. 230.

[11] These MSS are listed in Woledge and Clive, p. 98.

[12] Cambridge, Trinity College, MS R.17.1 (s. xii[med]). A facsimile of the manuscript has been published under the title *The Canterbury Psalter*, and is provided with an introduction by M. R. James (London, 1935). For an edition, see *Le Livre des psaumes: ancienne traduction française publiée pour la première fois d'après les manuscrits de Cambridge et de Paris*, ed. Francisque Michel (Paris, 1876), where the relevant psalms can be found on pp. 30 and 158.

[13] St Bernard of Clairvaux, *Sancti Bernardi Primi Abbatis Claravallensis Sermones de Tempore, de Sanctis, de Diversis, ad Tertiam Editionem Mabilloniam cum Codicibus Austriacis, Bohemicis, Styriacis Collatam* (Vienna, 1891), I, 197; St. Bernard of Clairvaux, *Li Sermon Saint Bernart: älteste französische Übersetzung der lateinischen Predigten Bernhards von Clairvaux* [etc.] , ed. Wendelin Foerster (Erlangen, 1885), p. 142.

[14] I Samuel, 18, 6–7. The manuscript has been edited as *Li Quatre Livre des reis: die Bücher Samuelis und der Könige in einer französischen Bearbeitung des 12. Jahrhunderts* [etc.], ed. Ernst Robert Curtius, Gesellschaft für romanische Literatur, 26 (Dresden, 1911), p. 36.

The preponderance of these Anglo-Norman translations has been ascribed to the long tradition of biblical glosses in England, which was carried over in the new official language after the Conquest.[15] But the dominance of this dialect of French in the culture of the period must also have played a part.

Chorus in these biblical translations clearly signifies *dance*, and is also employed in this sense in Theoderic's version of the legend of the dancers of Kölbigk as we have seen. But a shift in meaning to *choir* was already taking place. The relationship between the earlier and later meanings is recognized by Honoré of Autun (b. 1080/90–d. 1156):

> *Chorus* psallentium a chorea canentium exordium sumpsit, quam antiquitas idolis ibi constituit, ut videlicet decepti deos suos et voce laudarent, et toto corpore eis servirent.[16]
>
> (*Chorus* as it relates to choirs had its origin in the dancing of singers, which the ancients established for the worship of idols so that those infidels might praise their gods with their voices, and serve them with their whole bodies.)

It will have been noticed that the word used here for 'dance' is *chorea*, the Latin word used in the later Middle Ages, and which is frequently translated into French as *carole*. This brings us to a consideration of the relationship between these two terms.

The earliest citation of *chorea* relevant to our purpose is to be found in Geoffrey of Monmouth's *Historia Regum Britannie* mentioned in Chapter 2.[17] At one point he relates how Merlin advises that a circle of huge stones should be brought from Ireland, and set up as a memorial to those whom the war-monger ('bellator') Hengist had killed in battle: 'si perpetuo opere sepulturam uirorum decorare uolueris, mitte pro chorea gigantum que est in Killarao monte Hybernie' (if you wish to adorn the graves of these men with an everlasting monument, send for the Giants' Dance, which is on Killaraus, a mountain in Ireland).[18] The transportation of the stones, with the help of Merlin's magic, is duly accomplished, and they are re-erected in a circle according to the narrative, 'in montem Ambrii' (on the mount of Amesbury). The designation of Stonehenge as the 'chorea gigantum' is subsequently repeated several times in the text.[19]

---

[15] Short, p. 232.

[16] Honoré of Autun, *Honorii Augustodunensis Operum Pars Tertia Liturgica: Gemma Animae* [etc.], Patrologiae [Latinae] Cursus Completus, ed. J-P Migne, (Paris, 1854), CLXXII, 587.

[17] Geoffrey of Monmouth, *The* Historia Regum Britannie *of Geoffrey of Monmouth*, ed. Neil Wright and Julia C. Crick (Cambridge, 1985–91), I, 90. The 217 MSS of this text are listed in III, xv–xxii (Cambridge, 1989).

[18] Historia, I, 90.

[19] Historia, I, 93, 94, 100.

Geoffrey's *Historia* enjoyed enormous success. In particular, the magical origin of Stonehenge, the 'chorea gigantum', caught the imagination of several writers in Latin. The most important of these for our purpose was Gervase of Tilbury who gathered together, in the years between 1209 and 1214, a collection of interesting stories, which he called *Otia Imperialia*, for the delectation of the Holy Roman Emperor, Otto IV. The monument, he says, was erected at Amesbury at the instigation of Aurelius Ambrosius:

> … fecitque ad memoriam nobilium, qui pridem in proditione Saxonum per Vortigernum fuerant peremti, lapides olim in Childardo monte Yberniae collocatos, ad Ambresbiriam per Merlinum locari in modum choreae, sicut a gigantibus fuerant dispositi.[20]

> (… and as a memorial to the nobles who long since had perished through Vortigern's betrayal of the Saxons, he had the stones, which were formerly on Mount Killaraus in Ireland, gathered together, and arranged by Merlin in the form of a dance at Amesbury, just as they had been set up by the giants.)

Geoffrey's and Gervase's works were both translated into French. Notable among those of the *Historia* was Wace's version quoted in Chapter 2. An interpolation in this work underlines the origin of the monument and its circular form:

> Pert uncore el quadreduble cerne
> De la charole que fud as jaianz
> Des bis rochiers e merveillus e granz.[21]

> (It is still seen in the quadruple circle of the *carole* that the giants made of grey-brown slabs, both great and marvellous.)

---

[20] Gervase of Tilbury, *Gervasii Tilberiensis Otia Imperialia ad Ottonem IV Imperatorem*, Scriptores Rerum Brunsvicensium Illustrationi Inservientes, ed. Godfried Wilhelm Leibnitz (Hanover, 1707), I, 935. The manuscript tradition of this work is discussed in three articles by James R. Caldwell. In 'The Autograph Manuscript of Gervase of Tilbury (Vatican, Vat. Lat. 933)', *Scriptorium*, 11 (1957), 87–98, he examines this MS and 26 others, and provides (p. 87) the date given in my text. In the same article he concludes that the Vatican MS contains Gervase's holograph corrections. In 'Manuscripts of Gervase of Tilbury's *Otia Imperialia*', *Scriptorium*, 16 (1962), 28–45, he gives brief descriptions of 29 MSS including Wolfenbüttel MS Helms 481 (s. xiii or s. xiv) – the manuscript that Leibnitz used as the base manuscript for his edition, while in 'The Interrelationship of the Manuscripts of Gervase of Tilbury's *Otia Imperialia*', *Scriptorium*, 16 (1962), 246–74, he establishes stemmata for four groups of MSS, but notes evidence of contamination (p. 274).

[21] For this interpolation together with others, see Sylvie Lefevre, 'Le Fragment Bekker et les anciennes versions françaises de *l'Historia Regum Britanniae*', *Romania*, 109 (1988), 225–46. The lines quoted appear on p. 234 of her article.

There were two French translations of the *Otia Imperialia*. The first was made at the end of the thirteenth century by Jean d'Antioche, in which Merlin's magical achievement is recounted as follows:

> Et de ces pierres fist Merlin ung merveilleux edifice en la Grant Bretaigne a Mont Ambre pres de Salesbiere; et les fist par grant engin et par grant soutileté et est durable a tousjours mays et l'appelle l'on la Querole des Geans et illecq gist le dit Aurelius qui mourut par poyssons de venin.[22]
>
> (And with these stones Merlin made a wonderful construction in Great Britain at Mount Amesbury near Salisbury. He made it with great skill and ingenuity, and it will last for evermore. It is called the *Giants' Carole*, and the said Aurelius, who died from poisoning, lies buried there.)

Jean de Vignay made the other translation about 1330 in which, speaking of 'Aurelien filz Ambroise' (Aurelius, son of Ambrose), he says:

> … et fist mettre grans pierres que Merlin avoit pieça mis en la montaingne de Childart en Yllande en manere d'une karolle si conme les jaians les avoient ordenees … .[23]
>
> (… and he had the great stones, which Merlin had long since placed [sic] on Mount Killaraus in Ireland, placed in the manner of a *carole* just as the giants had arranged them … .)

It is not only in connexion with the origin of Stonehenge in the passages cited that *chorea* is rendered into French as *carole*. For example, in Ralph Bocking's life of St Richard of Chichester, dating from the end of the thirteenth century, the author speaks of the saintliness of Richard in his youth, 'unde coreas, tripudia et vana consimilium spectaculorum genera sic detestando fugiebat' (whence he fled *caroles* and *tresches* and other worthless performances of the kind, detesting them all).[24] Shortly afterwards Pierre d'Abernon of Fetcham made a verse translation in Anglo-Norman in which the foregoing quotation is rendered as follows:

---

[22] Gervase of Tilbury, 'Le Livre de grant delict', trans. Jean d'Antioche, nicknamed Harent d'Antioche, PBN, fonds fr. 9113 (s. xiii^{ex}), fol. 52^{r}. This passage has not been edited before.

[23] Gervase of Tilbury, 'Le Livre des oisivetez des emperieres', trans. Jean de Vignay, PBN, MS Rothschild 3085. IV.I. 5 (c. 1330), Ch. 59 (there is no foliation or pagination). This work also remains unedited.

[24] The Latin text quoted here is given in Pierre d'Abernon (also known as Pierre de Fetcham or Pierre de Peckham), *La Vie de Seint Richard, evesque de Cycestre*, ed. D. W. Russell, Anglo-Norman Text Society, No 51 (London, 1995), p. 119.

En despit
Aveit caroles e vein delit
Des tresches, e de tel folie
Ke veer, son voil, ne le voleit mie.[25]

(He held *caroles* in contempt and the vain pleasure of *tresches* to be such folly that he never wished to see them.)

To these citations one could add other examples of *chorea* being translated as *carole*, such as the commentary on Johannes de Garlandia's *Dictionarius* cited in Chapter 2 or Jean Lefevre's French translation made in the 1380s of the *Lamentationes Matheoli* composed c. 1298.[26]

The foregoing texts and translations might lead one to conclude that *chorea* in Latin could invariably be translated into French as *carole*. In fact this equivalence is implied by Sachs when he draws up a list of dance terms.[27] Falk is explicit and emphatic that the two terms are synonymous:

Quand les gens du moyen âge écrivaient en latin, ils employaient le mot *chorea* pour désigner la *carole*. C'est un fait avéré. Les quatre dictionnaires latin–français les plus anciens du XIIIe et du XIVe siècle, p.p. M. Roques, rendent tous *chorea* par *carole*.[28]

(When people in the Middle Ages wrote in Latin, they used the word *chorea* to signify the *carole*. This is an established fact. The four earliest Latin–French dictionaries, dating from the thirteenth and fourteenth centuries, as cited by Roques, all give the equivalent for *chorea* as *carole*.)

Other writers have also taken it for granted that the two terms are exact equivalents.

---

[25] *La Vie*, ll. 186–8. Russell, in his edition, prints *d'estresches*, and, in a note (p. 119), explains that 'this is a form of estrete, "street", (here he cites the *Anglo-Norman Dictionary*, 'Estrete'), adding that 'the translation stresses the public nature of these diversions by explicitly mentioning the street as the site of these amusements'. It is clear, however, following the *tripudia* of the Latin text that the reading should be 'des tresches', signifying a kind of dance. I have consequently emended the reading. I am indebted to my sister, Dr Evelyn Mullally, Queen's University Belfast, for drawing my attention to this edition and its anomaly.

[26] Jean le Fevre, *Les Lamentations de Matheolus et le Livre de Leesce de Jehan Le Fevre de Resson*, ed. Anton Gérard van Hamel (Paris, 1892–1905), ll. 3555–8; trans. ll. 2911–19.

[27] Curt Sachs, *Eine Weltgeschichte des Tanzes* (Berlin, 1933), p. 182 and *World History of the Dance*, trans. Bessie Schönberg (London, 1938), p. 269.

[28] Paul Falk, rev. of Sahlin, *Studia Neophilologica*, 13 (1940–41), 137, n. 1.

It may be true that the four dictionaries cited by Roques, who is quoted approvingly by Falk, give *carole* as the French equivalent of *chorea*, and indeed that is the case in the example cited earlier from Johannes de Garlandia. But *chorea* is not always defined as *carole*. If Johannes de Garlandia gives such a definition in one work, in another, the *Unum Omnium*, he glosses *corea* as 'thesche' (*recte, tresche*), which is a different dance.[29] Guillaume de Nangis makes the following remark about the festivities following the coronation of King Philip III of France in 1271:

> ... mandavit comes Attrebati omnes dominas et domicellas illius patriae, ut cum uxoribus burgensium urbis choreas ducentes, et laetitiae et exultationi intendentes, totam laetificarent civitatem.[30]

> (... the Comte d'Artois ordered all the ladies of that region (both young and old) to lead *choreas* with the citizens' wives, and, by devoting themselves to joy and exultation, bring happiness to the whole city.)

In what appears to be a contemporary translation, we read:

> Le conte d'Artois manda les dames et les demoiselles du pays pour faire tresches et quaroles avec fames aux bourgois, qui s'estudioient en toutes les manieres de danser et d'esplinger et se demenoient en toutes les manieres qu'elles pouoient qui deust plaire au roy.[31]

> (The Comte d'Artois ordered the ladies of that region (both young and old) to perform *tresches* and *caroles* with the citizens' wives, and they strove in every way to dance, and behave in a lively manner in every way that they could that might please the king).

What is evident from text and translation here is that the term *choreas* covers both 'tresches' and 'quaroles'. Thus *chorea* in the foregoing examples can apparently adumbrate two different dances.

Even when *chorea* is applied to a single dance it can mean different things. In the *Lamentationes Matheoli* the participants in the *chorea* do not dance in a circle, but perform a wide variety of movements and gestures in which they advance and retire, rise and lower themselves while bending backwards, chase one another, and

---

29 Johannes de Garlandia,'Les Gloses en langue vulgaire dans les MSS de *l'Unum Omnium* de Jean de Garlande', ed. Tony Hunt, *Revue de Linguistique Romane*, 43 (1979), 165.

30 Guillaume de Nangis, *Gesta Philippi Regis Franciae Filii Sanctae Memoriae Regis Ludovici*, ed. [P.] Daunou and [J.] Naudet, Recueil des historiens des Gaules et de la France (Paris, 1840), XX, 468.

31 Guillaume de Nangis, p. 469. I have added apostrophes to the edition.

are chased – actions that are by no means made clear in Le Fevre's translation.[32] A *chorea* can be led through streets and squares ('per vicos et plateas'), thereby implying a linear dance.[33] Etienne de Bourbon relates how certain youths were accustomed to enter a churchyard and even the church itself: 'et super equum ligneum ascendere, et larvati et parati choreas ducere' (and masked and dressed up, mount wooden horses, lead *choreas*).[34] This *chorea* is far removed from being a circular dance. Even more strikingly different is the well-known unhappy incident as recounted in a medieval Latin chronicle, aptly illustrating the diversity of the meaning of *chorea*: the 'Bal des Ardents' (the Dance of the Burning Men), which took place in 1393. It tells how King Charles VI of France and five young nobles disguised in hairy costumes and masks entered the royal hall:

> … et gestus deformiores huc illucque discurrendo ceperunt exercere, et tandem more lupino horrissonis vocibus ululantes. Nec absoni a voce deinde motus fuerunt; sed tripudiando choreas sarracenicas inceperunt, et, ut firmiter creditur instinctu dyabolico agitati.[35]
>
> (… and, running hither and thither, they began to make even more horrible gestures, and then to howl like wolves. Nor were their movements any different. They began to dance Saracen *choreas* acting, as people firmly believe, through the incitement of the Devil.)

The costumes caught fire and, although the king and one of the nobles escaped, the other four were burnt to death, hence the title of the event. In this entertainment the dancers did not form a circle either but ran hither and thither.

Thus although *chorea* is frequently translated as *carole*, it could also signify a variety of other kinds of dance. It will be noted that in the above description the dances are called 'choreas sarracenicas' indicating that *chorea* is being used here as a general term. In conclusion we may say that in Medieval Latin as in Classical Latin *chorea* is usually best translated simply as the general term 'dance'.

Carole, as considered so far, has been examined exclusively as a translation of the Latin *chorus* or *chorea*. It remains, however, to give some consideration to the earliest citation of the word in original French texts. Possibly the first occurrence is to be found in the *Roman de Troie* by Benoît de Sainte-Maure, a work composed

---

32 *Lamentationes*, ll. 3559–70. The equivalent passage is translated in ll. 2929–31, which, as van Hamel notes (p. 212), is very loose, and alters the original.

33 See the quotation from a sermon by Pierre de Bar-sur-Aube in Jean Barthélemy Hauréau, *Notices et extraits de quelques manuscrits latins de la Bibliothèque Nationale* (Paris, 1893), VI, 243–4.

34 Etienne de Bourbon, *Anecdotes historiques, légendes et apologues tirés du recueil inédit d'Etienne de Bourbon*, ed. Richard Albert Lecoy de la Marche (Paris, 1877), p. 168.

35 *Chronique du religieux de Saint Denys, contenant le règne de Charles VI, de 1380 à 1422*, ed. and Fr. trans. L. Bellaguet (Paris, 1840), II, 66.

about 1155–60, and of which the first complete manuscript citing the verb *caroller* dates from the end of the twelfth century.[36] But this poem depends heavily on Latin works, and may therefore simply be continuing the tradition of translation. For a totally original composition we should perhaps turn to the romances of Chrétien de Troyes. In *Erec et Enide* (composed at the earliest c. 1170) we are told 'puceles querolent et dancent' (girls carol and dance).[37] Somewhat later is *Le Chevalier de la Charette* (possibly composed c. 1177–81) in which there is reference to 'baules, et quaroles et dances'.[38] Finally we have the *Conte du Graal* (called *Perceval* by later scribes), which was probably begun in 1181, but was left unfinished at the poet's death c. 1190.[39] In this romance the queen's young ladies 'chantent et querolent et dancent' (they sing and carol and dance). Manuscripts of these three works, however, all date from the thirteenth century. It is possible, therefore, that the copies are not free from scribal intervention.[40]

The term *carole* appeared in the first half of the twelfth century and throughout the rest of that century is found mainly in biblical translations. A notable exception is Wace's translation of Geoffrey of Monmouth. In this translation, and in works derived from it in one way or another, the word *chorea* is translated as *carole* and is applied to Stonehenge. This implies that *chorea* and *carole* referred to circular dances. On the other hand *chorea* could indicate a diverse range of dances. Could this be equally true of *carole*?

---

[36] Benoît de Sainte-Maure, *Le Roman de Troie*, ed. Léopold Constans (Paris, 1904–12), 'E li pöete e li devin / Qui la furent i querolerent' (ll. 29160–61). The manuscripts with their datings are described VI, 1–57.

[37] Chrétien de Troyes, *Eric et Enide*, Les Romans de Chrétien de Troyes, I, ed. Mario Roques (Paris, 1952), 1, 1993.

[38] Chrétien de Troyes, *Le Chevalier de la Charrette*, Les Romans de Chrétien de Troyes, III, ed. Mario Roques (Paris, 1958), l, 1646.

[39] Chrétien de Troyes, *Le Conte du Graal (Perceval)*, Les Romans de Chrétien de Troyes, V, ed. Félix Lecoy (Paris, 1972–75), l, 8722.

[40] Apart from one manuscript of *Cligès*, which may possibly date from the end of the 12th century, all the manuscripts of Chrétien's romances are later, for which see Terry Nixon, 'Romance Collections and the Manuscripts of Chrétien de Troyes', in *Les Manuscrits de Chrétien de Troyes: The Manuscripts of Chrétien de Troyes*, ed. Keith Busby *et al.*, Etudes de la Langue et Littérature Françaises, No 72 (Amsterdam, 1993), p. 17.

Chapter 4

Theories about the Choreography

The main difficulty in arriving at a concept of the *carole* as a dance is that we have no specific and comprehensive account of it. No dance manuals or treatises exist from before the fifteenth century. We are obliged, therefore, to rely on various statements made in widely scattered literary sources, and to draw our own conclusions. Not surprisingly, when different commentators cite a plethora of references, and use them in different ways they obtain different results.

The broadest interpretation of the term is that it might adumbrate such a diversity of choreographies that it is impossible to define the term more precisely. This appears to be the view of Godefroy, who concludes the definition in his dictionary with the words 'divertissement dont la danse fait partie' (an entertainment of which dancing forms a part).[1] Brüll, in a linguistic monograph, is similarly all-inclusive: 'ronde, danse, réjouissance, cercle, réunion' (round, dance, rejoicing, gathering, meeting).[2] Not surprisingly therefore, we find that a dictionary of Middle French can explain the term as 'danse en rond, danse en général' (a round dance, dance in general).[3] This generalized concept finds its most interesting expression in Stevens's study of medieval music: 'the *carole* must surely have been not *a* single form but a potential form, a dance-*idea* waiting to be realized in various forms' (his italics).[4]

Other scholars, however, are more specific. A few are of the opinion that the term might include a theatrical kind of dance, that is to say one containing elements specific to an individual choreography, as well as designating a purely social kind of dance. This concept may have originated with Jeanroy for whom the *carole* might, on occasion, be a figure dance.[5] Bédier follows Jeanroy in believing that the dance might incorporate a dramatic episode, which he calls a *balerie*.[6] He also maintained that such dramatic scenes on their own could also be denominated *caroles*. While Stevens in a later work, as we saw above, considers

---

1 Godefroy, 'Carole'.

2 *Untergegangene und veraltete Worte des französischen im heutigen Englisch*, ed. Hugo Brüll (Halle, 1913),'Charole'.

3 *Dictionnaire du moyen français: la Renaissance*, ed. Algirdas Julien Greimas and Teresa Mary Kane (Paris, 1992), 'Carole'.

4 John Stevens, *Words and Music in the Middle Ages: Song, Narrative, Dance and Drama, 1050–1350* (Cambridge, 1986), p. 175.

5 Alfred Jeanroy, *Les Origines de la poésie lyrique en France au Moyen Age* (1889, 3rd ed., 1925), p. 394, n. 1.

6 Joseph Bédier, 'Les Plus Anciennes Danses françaises', *Revue des Deux Mondes*, 31 (jan–fév 1906), p. 401.

the nature of the dance to be indefinable, in an earlier article he stated that it could be 'circular or processional' but 'in its more elaborate forms the *carole* became a little dramatic scene'.[7] This view, he acknowledges, he derived from Bédier. But Bédier's *baleries* are not designated in their sources as *caroles*. Neither has any evidence been adduced to show that such dramatic involvement is an essential, or even a commonly occurring, feature in the *carole*.

The more generally held view is that the *carole* was exclusively a social dance; but even here ideas on what form the dance took vary. Some understand it to be a couple dance. Schneider defines it thus: 'mit diesem Namen bezeichneten die französischen Minnegesänger den bei den mittelalterlichen Tanzpaaren üblichen geschrittenen Vortanz' (French trouvères used this name to indicate the medieval foredance for couples, which was normally walked).[8] He adds that it contrasted with an ensuing hopped dance, the *espringle*. He does not, however, provide any textual authority for these statements. A more prominent exponent of the theory of the *carole* as a couple dance is, of course, Sahlin, who actually draws on medieval French sources to support her concept of the dance. While admitting that there is some evidence for a circular or chain formation, she concludes that 'ce que suggèrent cependant la plupart des textes, c'est plutôt l'idée d'un cortège de personnes marchant cérémonieusement deux à deux ou trois à trois' (what most texts suggest, however, is rather the idea of a procession of people walking ceremoniously two by two or three by three).[9] She points out that in some instances one person takes another by the hand, that in others the word *procession* is used, although she concedes that in still others it is rather a line of people – but not a circle – that is implied, such as suggested by the word *encontre*. Convincing as this assembly of evidence may seem at first sight, it is far from being conclusive.

One can certainly cite texts where the couples take hands. Yet this does not necessarily mean that they dance as couples. As Falk remarks there is nothing to preclude a couple from then joining other couples to form a circle.[10] Sahlin's other deductions are also open to question. She sometimes misinterprets the texts to which she refers. For example, there is no mention of dancing in the passages that she cites from Bartsch's anthology, or from *Guillaume de Dole* (ll, 2508–27) or from *Blancandin* (ll, 6147–54) or from the particular passage that she quotes from the *Tournoi de Chauvency* (ll, 4115–30).[11]

---

[7] John Stevens, 'Carole', *New Grove 1.*

[8] Otto Schneider, *Tanz Lexikon* (Frankfurt-am-Main, 1985), 'Carole. The foredance is the first of a pair of dances, but the concept does not appear to have evolved before the pair of the hove dance followed by the *carole* – a pairing that did not take place until the second half of the 14th century.

[9] Sahlin, p. 25.

[10] Paul Falk, rev. of Sahlin, *Studia Neophilologica*, 13 (1940–41), 137.

[11] Sahlin, pp. 27–30; *Romances et pastourelles françaises des XIIe et XIIIe siécles: altfranzösische Romanzen und Pastourellen*, ed. Karl Bartsch (Leipzig, 1870), II, 27, 93ff, quoted in Sahlin, p. 28.

As for the inclusion of *processions* in some texts, the word as found in some of Sahlin's citations does not refer to the *carole* itself, but rather to events taking place before or after it. In one case, however, the word actually relates to the dance. This occurs in a moral treatise, *Le Mireour de monde*: 'les processions au déable sont caroles' (*caroles* are processions to the Devil).[12] The anonymous author here is arguing that those who take part in this dance transgress the covenant that their godparents made to God on behalf of the person being baptized. In the course of this sacrament the godparents promise to renounce the Devil and all his works. The Latin for this last phrase is 'et pompis ejus', which literally means 'and all his processions'. The author of *Le Mireour* is translating the word literally, and not in the sense it which it is actually used – an example of the etymological fallacy.

Sahlin is almost alone in her belief that the *carole* was a couple dance. The overwhelming majority of commentators believe that it was a communal dance, and among them some are of the opinion that it was linear. They point to sources where words such as *contre* or *encontre* are used. Again they cite texts where, although it is not explicitly stated that the formation is linear, that interpretation seems to be implied, as for instance in lines from the *Roman des Sept Sages*:

> Li jougleour vont vielant
> Et les borjoises karolant;
> Grant joie font por le signor
> Tout revertira a doulour.[13]
>
> (The minstrels go playing the vielle, and the citizens go carolling; they evince great joy on account of their lord, but all will turn back to grief).

These passages will be discussed in the next chapter. One quotation often cited in support of a linear form for the dance is to be found in *La Manekine*: 'Tel carole ne fu veüe; / Pres d'un quart dure d'une lieue' (Such a *carole* was never seen, it extends out nearly a quarter of a league).[14] This apparent contradictory evidence will be discussed in Chapter 6.

Others who have concluded that it was a social dance consider that it was a linear dance, a circular dance, or both. Thus Jeanroy, in addition to thinking that it might be a figure dance, believed it could be a performed in a circle, and in this, as with his view that the dance could have a dramatic form, he was followed by

---

[12] *Le Mireour du monde: manuscrit du XIV* siècle découvert dans les archives de la Commune de la Sarra*, ed. Félix Chavannes, Mémoires et documents publiés par la Société d'Histoire de la Suisse Romande, No 4 (Lausanne, 1845), p. 163.

[13] *Le Roman des Sept Sages*, ed. Jean Misrahi (Paris, 1933), ll. 697–700.

[14] Philippe de Remi, *Le Roman de la la Manekine*, ed. and trans. Barbara Sargent-Baur with contributions by Alison Stones and Roger Middleton, Etudes de la langue et littérature françaises, No 159 (Amsterdam, 1999), ll. 2305–6.

Bédier, who added that it could also be a chain.[15] In his earlier history of medieval music, Gérold stated categorically that the *carole* was a round dance or chain dance: 'les caroles étaient comme l'on sait, des rondes ou des chaînes, composées soit de femmes seules, soit d'hommes et de femmes, les danseurs se tenant par la main' (*caroles* were, as is well known, rounds or chains, composed either of women alone or of men and women, with the dancers holding one another by the hand).[16] This notion of the dual form of the dance became widely accepted in the lexicography, and we find phrases such as 'en ronde ou en chaîne' (in a round or in a chain), 'Reigen- oder Kettentanz' (round or chain dance), 'in tondo o a catena' (in a round or chain), 'line and circle group dances'.[17]

A particular variation of this theory is that in its linear form it resembled the farandole. This view seems to have originated with a misinterpretation of a passage in a review of Jeanroy by Gaston Paris:

> Toutefois il semble que la chaîne non fermée et suivant un conducteur s'appelât proprement *tresque*. Aux Faeroe, il ne paraît pas que la chaîne soit close. Dans nos rondes de paysans de l'Ouest, si je ne me trompe, elle l'est toujours; mais l'ancienne *tresque* paraît subsister dans la *farandole* provençale.[18]
>
> (Nevertheless it seems that an open chain following a leader might properly be called a *tresque*. In the Faeroes, it does not appear that the chain was closed. In our [folk dance] rounds of the west [of France], if I am not mistaken, it still is; but the old *tresque* seems to be still extant in the Provençal farandole.)

---

15 Jeanroy, p. 394, n. 1; Bédier, pp. 398–401.

16 Théodore Gérold, *La Musique au Moyen Age* (Paris, 1932), p. 299.

17 *Encyclopédie de la musique*, ed. François Michel (Paris, 1958–61), 'Carole'; *Lexikon des Mittelalters*, ed. Liselotte Lutz *et al.* (Munich, 1979–), 'Carole'; *Dizionario enciclopedico universale della musica e dei musicisti*, ed. Alberto Basso (Turin, 1983–90), 'Carola'; John Stevens, 'Carole', *New Grove 1*; Ingrid Brainard, 'Medieval Dance', *International Encyclopedia of Dance: A Project of Dance Perspectives Foundation*, ed. Selma Jeanne Cohen *et al.* (New York, 1998). Christopher Page, *The Owl and the Nightingale: Musical Life and Ideas in France, 1100–1300* (London, 1989), p. 116, also defines the *carole* as a 'festive company dance performed in a line, ring or chain'. Similar variations are implied in Timothy J. McGee, 'Medieval Dances: Matching the Repertory with Grocheio's Descriptions', *The Journal of Musicology*, 7 (1989), p. 507. Peter Grosskreuz, 'Tanzquellen des Mittelalters und der Renaissance', *Gutenberg Jahrbuch*, 66 (1991) makes a different point by separating the *carole* (which he calls a 'mittelaltlicher Rundtanz') from what he calls a 'Schängelreigen' (Farandole), p. 324.

18 Gaston Paris, rev. of *Les Origines de la poésie lyrique en France au Moyen Age*, by Alfred Jeanroy, in Mélanges de littérature française du Moyen Age, ed. Mario Roques (1892; rpt Paris, 1912), 594, n. 4.

Thus it is the *tresque* (i.e. *tresche*) and not the *carole* that Paris associates with this southern French folk dance. Yet the belief that the *carole* is in some way to be associated with the farandole has found favour with many dance historians.

The farandole, as Paris states, is a folk dance of southern France. Some have claimed that its ancestry, and that of the *carole*, can be traced back to ancient Greece.[19] Yet the farandole seems to have been unknown in the Middle Ages; the term is not found in dictionaries of Old French or of Old Occitan (formerly called Old Provençal). Alford in her article on the farandole, does not mention the *carole*.[20] It is, in fact, first recorded in the French form *farandoule* in 1776 as being derived from the Occitan *farandoulo*, a word of uncertain origin.[21] There is no evidence, therefore, that the farandole resembled any kind of medieval dance.

Another firmly held view is that the *carole* was exclusively a circular dance, and for some it actually contrasted in this respect with a couple dance, a theory particularly upheld by German scholars. In 1848, Liliencron noted the juxtaposition of *tanz* and *reie* in the poems of Neidhart von Reuental, and inferred from this fact that the two types were opposed.[22] This opposition was then transferred to the French terms *danse* and *carole*, Alwin Schultz citing a phrase from Chrétien de Troyes 'puceles querolent et dancent' (*Eric et Enide*, l. 1993, girls carol and dance).[23] Bertoni, an Italian writing on the Germanic influence on the Italian language, offered another example often since quoted: 'li uns dance, l'autre querolle' (Herbert, *Dolopathos*, l. 2810, some dance, others carol).[24] Bertoni's interpretation differed from others holding a distinction between the two terms in that for him the *danse* was circular, but that in the *carole* one turned around oneself ('girando su se stessi'). Aeppli, in an examination of dance terms, declared emphatically in favour of the distinction between the circular and the couple dance citing a host of examples to prove his point.[25] Not surprisingly, therefore, Sachs pronounced dogmatically 'kein Zweifel, dass es sich hier um je zwei getrennte, ja gegensätzliche, sich ergänzende Begriffe handelt' (there is no doubt that we

---

19 For example Jean Baumel, *Les Danses populaires, les farandoles, les rondes, les jeux chorégraphiques et les ballets du Languedoc méditerranéan* (Paris, 1958), p. 66.

20 Violet Alford, 'The Farandole', *Journal of the English Folk Dance and Song Society*, 1 (1932), 18–33.

21 *Le Grand Robert de la langue française*, ed. Paul Robert, 2nd ed. rev. Alain Rey (Paris, 1985),'Farandole': Its earliest appearance in English is in *A Dictionary of Musical Terms*, ed. J. Stainer and W. A. Barrett (London, [1876]),'Farandola'.

22 R. von Liliencron, 'Über Neidharts höfische Dorfpoesie', *Zeitschrift für deutsches Alterthum*, 6 (1848), 79.

23 Alwin Schultz, *Das höfische Leben zur Zeit der Minnesinger* (1879; 2nd ed. Leipzig, 1889), I, 544.

24 Giulio Bertoni, *L'elemento germanico nella lingua italiana* (Genoa, 1914), pp. 245–6.

25 Fritz Aeppli, 'Die wichtigsten Ausdrücke für das Tanzen in den romanischen Sprachen', *Beihefte zur Zeitschrift für romanishcePhilologie*, 75 (1925), 33.

have here two separate, indeed opposed, concepts, which supplement each other).[26] The contrast between *carole* and *danse* and their supposed cognates in various European languages is an idea expanded by Salmen.[27] The theory has more recently been restated in an article in *MGG 2*.[28] Yet, in spite of such overwhelming and apparently incontrovertible support, this theory has been challenged.

Harding, in her study of medieval German dance terms, approvingly quotes Sahlin to the effect that the *carole* was a procession of couples: 'again in the case of the French material there is no evidence that a circling action is involved in the 13th and 14th centuries'.[29] She is equally adamant that there was no circular dance in Germany before about 1450.[30] Contrary to the deductions of the other scholars cited above, she states that the *reie* (or *reige*) was a 'lively processional dance'. At the same time she affirms that 'throughout the [medieval] period *tanz* is used as a general term for courtly merry-making ("dancing"), rather than as the name of a specific dance or type of dancing'.[31] Consequently she concludes that 'there is no evidence to suggest that *reie* and *tanz* were ever regarded as contrasting styles of dancing'.[32]

Harding's conclusions about medieval German dance would seem to demolish the theory of contrasting styles as far as German dance is concerned and, by implication, the French. Her acceptance of Sahlin's theory is, however, questionable, as will be seen in the next chapter. The possibility of some other difference between *carole* and *danse*, will also be discussed later.

Among those who have considered the *carole* to be a circular dance, some have interpreted the term in a very particular way – one that associates the medieval dance with the Renaissance *branle*. Godefroy gives 'branle' as his first definition of *carole*.[33] Gaston Paris believed that the *carole* was like a dance from the Faeroe Islands the choreography of which he describes in terms reminiscent of a sixteenth *branle*:

> ... hommes et femmes se prennent par les mains et forment une chaîne: le mouvement consiste simplement en ce que l'on fait en mesure trois pas *vers la*

---

[26] Curt Sachs, *Eine Weltgeschichte des Tanzes* (Berlin, 1933), p. 182 and *World History of the Dance*, trans. Bessie Schönberg (London, 1938), p. 269.

[27] Walter Salmen, 'Ikonographie des Reigens im Mittelalter', *Acta Musicologica*, 52 (1980), 15.

[28] Sibylle Dahms, 'Tanz. I, Mittelalter', *MGG 2*.

[29] Ann Harding, *An Investigation into the Use and Meaning of Medieval German Dancing Terms*, Göppinger Arbeiten zur Germanistik, No 93 (Göppingen, 1973), p. 9.

[30] Harding, p. 6.

[31] Harding, pp. 155 and 274.

[32] Harding, p. 180.

[33] Godefroy, 'Carole'.

> *gauche*, puis on se balance un peu, on rapproche le pied droit du gauche, ensuite on détache le gauche, et ainsi de suite.[34]
>
> (... men and women take hands and make a chain; the steps are simply performed in time with three steps *to the left*, then you balance a little; you join your right foot to the left, next you separate your left [from your right] and so on).

Although Paris describes a chain here, he subsequently states that the figure could be a circle. Bédier gives an approximation of the foregoing description of what he calls 'cette sorte de branle' (this kind of branle).[35] Paris, in addition to comparing the *carole* to a dance of the Faeroe Islands, also finds a close similarity with dances in the sixteenth-century dance manual, *Orchesographie*, by Thoinot Arbeau:

> Les branles du Poitou, si célèbres au moyen âge, étaient de danses pareilles; Jehan Tabourot, qui les décrit dans son *Orchesographie*, remarque que le mouvement en est toujours dirigé de droite à gauche.[36]
>
> (The 'Branles of Poitou', so famous in the Middle Ages, were similar dances, Jean Tabourot who describes them in his *Orchesographie*, notes that the movement is always from right to left.)

Verrier considers the steps of the *carole* to be the same as those of the 'Branle double', and he gives a paraphrase of Arbeau's description.[37] Rimmer affirms that 'among dances of much later origin in both areas [the Faeroe Islands and southern Brittany], there are some of the type known in medieval western Europe as *carole*, in the fifteenth century as *branle* and from the sixteenth century onwards as specific kinds of *branle*'.[38] The specific *branles* that she has in mind are Arbeau's 'Branle double', his 'Branle simple' and his *branle* 'Cassandra'.

Contrary to the statements of Paris and Rimmer, there was no medieval dance called the *branle*. In the late fifteenth century the steps of the *basse danse* included one called a *branle*. No dance type of that name, however, existed until the early sixteenth century. Late in the same century, a large number of *branles* are described by Arbeau.[39] His 'Branle double', 'Branle simple' and 'Branle coupé nommé

---

34 Paris, rev. of Jeanroy, p. 594.

35 Bédier, p. 398.

36 Paris, rev. of Jeanroy, p. 594.

37 Paul Verrier, *Le Vers français: formes primitives, développement, diffusion* (Paris, 1931), I, 34.

38 Joan Rimmer, 'Dance Elements in Trouvère Repertory', *Dance Research*, 3/2 (1985), 26–7 and p. 34, n. 18.

39 For the three dances named in the following sentence in my text, see Thoinot Arbeau [pseud. Jean Tabourot], *Orchesographie par Thoinot Arbeau: réimpresssion precédée d'une notice sur les danses du XVIe siècle par Laure Fonta* [facsimile of the

Cassandre' moved both to the left and to the right, whereas authors contemporary with the *carole*, as we shall see in the next chapter, clearly imply that the dance moved only to the left. The strictures of some moralists about the supposed evils of a dance moving to the left would be pointless if the dance also moved to the right. Arbeau gives the choreography for just one 'Branle de Poictou'; it indeed moves only to the left, but consists entirely of *pieds en l'air*. No evidence exists that these steps were used in the *carole*.

Finally there have been those who have taken the *carole* to be simply a round dance. In the eighteenth century, La Curne de Sainte-Palaye had defined it as *danse en rond* (round dance): 'danse ancienne en forme de ronde accompagnée de chants' (old dance in the form of a round accompanied by songs), and the phrase, *danse en rond*, is repeated subsequently in the French dictionaries of Godefroy, Huguet and the FEW, albeit with additions and qualifications.[40] Translated into German as 'Reigentanz mit Gesang' (round dance with singing), into Italian as 'danza popolare in tondo (round folk dance)' or into English as 'round dance (accompanied by singing)', it remains in these definitions essentially a circular dance.[41] Gérold who had earlier confidently asserted that the form of the dance could be either a circle or a chain, later decided on a circular form alone: 'c'était une sorte de ronde dont les pas et les mouvements des danseurs étaient plus ou moins réglés et guidés par le chant' (it was a kind of round in which the steps and the movements of the dancers were more or less regulated and guided by the singing).[42]

In countering Sahlin's argument for a processional form of the dance Falk noticed that, while she is willing to admit to there being only a single example of the *carole* as a round dance, she unwittingly quotes throughout her book a large

---

edition of 1589], Biblioteca Musica Bononiensis. II, No 102 (Bologna, 1981), fols 68^{v}–71^{r}, 71 $^{r-v}$, 74^{v}–75^{r}.

[40] *Trésor de la langue française: dictionnaire de la langue du XIXe et du XXe siècle (1789–1960)*, ed. Paul Imbs (Paris, 1971–94) 'Carole'; *Dictionnaire historique de l'ancien langage françois ou glossaire de la langue françoise depuis son origine jusqu'au siècle de Louis XIV*, compiled by Jean-Baptiste de la Curne de Sainte-Palaye, ed. L. Favre and M. Pajot (Niort, 1875–82), 'Carole'; Godefroy, 'Carole'; Huguet, 'Carole'; *FEW*, 'Choraula'.

[41] Tobler-Lommatzsch, 'Carole'; *Enciclopedia della musica*, ed. Claudio Sartori (Milan, 1963–64),'Carola'; *Old French–English Dictionary*, ed. Alan Hindley, Frederick W. Langley and Brian J. Levy (Cambridge, 2000), 'Carole'.

[42] Théodore Gérold, *Histoire de la musique des origines à la fin du XIVe siècle* (Paris, 1936), p. 304. Conversely, Christopher Page, in his earlier book, *Voices and Instruments of the Middle Ages: Instrumental Practice and Songs in France, 1100–1300* (London, 1987), described the dancers who, having linked hands, 'began to move in a circle to the left' (p. 79), but later in *The Owl and the Nightingale: Musical Life and Ideas in France, 1100–1300* (London, 1989), p. 116, revised his view of the formation of the dance to that of a line, ring or chain.

number of examples where the dance takes just such a form, and he goes on to cite a few examples of his own.[43]

One statement about the *carole*, often made in connexion with some of the foregoing pronouncements, is that the dance was widespread. Greene writes of 'its wide dissemination in various countries of Europe'.[44] Stevens opines that it was 'the principal dance form of courtly societies in western Europe during the 12th and 13th centuries'.[45] Verrier is likewise all-embracing, and, at the same time more detailed:

> Dès le XIIe siècle, au plus tard, notre carole avait passé à l'étranger, la chanson comme la danse, d'abord dans l'aristocratie, et bientôt dans toutes les classes. Ce n'est pas seulement dans les autres contrées gallo-romanes, –Wallonie, Suisse romande et Suisse roumanche, Piémont, Catalogne (y compris la province de Valence), Galice et Portugal, – qui forment bloc à ce point de vue, comme à d'autres, avec la France d'oui et d'oc: c'est aussi dans le reste de l'Italie et de l'Espagne, dans la Gaule germanisée, en Hollande, en Angleterre, en Scandinavie, en Allemagne.[46]

> (By the twelfth century, at the latest, our *carole* (both the song and the dance) had spread abroad, first among the aristocracy, and soon after among people of every class. This happened not only in other lands of the Romance languages – Wallonia, French-speaking Switzerland and Romansh-speaking Switzerland, Piedmont, Catalonia (including the province of Valencia), Galicia and Portugal – which, from this point of view, form a block with the France of the Langue d'Oil and the Langue d'Oc. It is the same in the rest of Italy and Spain in German-speaking Gaul, in Holland in England, in Scandinavia, and in Germany).

Salmen, as we have seen, starting from a linguistic starting point, not only implies the extensive dissemination of the *carole* by grouping together supposedly related terms, also inferred that this same dance was practised over a period stretching from the early thirteenth to the late sixteenth century.[47]

This line of argument, however, is difficult to sustain. First, there is no evidence that the *carole* closely resembled more recent folk dances. Second, the conviction that the *carole* was widely diffused throughout Europe relies on the resemblance between supposed cognates of the French word; but again no evidence been adduced to show that the dance was widely performed all over Europe during the

---

[43] Falk, p. 136.

[44] *The Early English Carols*, ed. Richard Leighton Greene (1935; 2nd ed., Oxford, 1977), p. xlviii.

[45] Stevens, 'Carole'.

[46] Verrier, *Le Vers français*, I, 30.

[47] Salmen, 'Ikonographie', 15–16.

Middle Ages. The cognates, in fact, appear to be all borrowings from the French, as we have already seen.

We are left, then, with a circular dance, and this view represents the consensus of opinion. All the authorities citing this view, however, simply repeat endlessly at different times and in different languages the same general point, namely that the dance was circular. No other information, based on primary sources, is provided. The question remains, therefore, whether any further details might be discovered among the extensive French literature of the Middle Ages.

Chapter 5
A Reconstruction of the Choreography

As no dance manual is extant from before the middle of the fifteenth century, any extant information has to be gathered from a wide variety of primary sources. To date these have provided only the most meagre of details. Yet the *carole* is one of the most frequently mentioned dances particularly in French literature. Taking the term 'literature' in its widest sense, sources abound. References, citations and allusions are to be found in prose including prose romances, chronicles, collections of anecdotes, moral treatises, a treatise on poetry, the life of a saint and even in a treatise on astronomy! Similar details are to be found in verse including verse romances and other narrative poems, a play in verse, lyrical poems, a historical poem, a satirical poem, a fable and a moral treatise in verse. The texts are not only in French, but also in Latin, Italian and English. Some citations, it is true, are merely passing references; but among the myriad occurrences, such as those just mentioned, there is a wealth of facts to be discovered.

If we are to investigate the various aspects of a dance, we must first consider the distribution of the sexes participating in the dance. A *carole* consisting entirely of men is possible, but is all but unknown. In the *chanson de geste*, *Gaydon*, the warriors stand around the wounded hero, and hold hands just as if they had been carolling: 'As mains se tiennent li baron alosé / Tout autressi com aient carolé' (The bold worthies hold hands just as if they had been carolling).[1] Of course the language here is figurative: but even in a literal sense the only *carole* to consist entirely of men is the second one in a fictional source, namely in the romance of *Guillaume de Dole*.[2]

Much more usual, however, is a *carole* comprising exclusively female dancers. In the *Conte du Graal*, the queen has her girls dance: 'ses puceles avoit fet prandre / ... chantent et querolent et dancent' (she ordered her girls to take hands ... they sing and carol and dance).[3] If the girls here both carol and dance, there are other instances where the noun *carole* or the verb *caroler* are employed alone: 'Et les dames se deportoient, / A Chauvenci, joieusement / Et karolent mout cointement / Une karole si tres noble ... ' (and the ladies disport themselves joyfully at

---

[1] *Gaydon: chanson de geste*, ed. F. Guessard and S. Luce (Paris, 1862), ll. 1889–90.

[2] Jean Renart, *Le Roman de la Rose ou de Guillaume de Dole*, ed. Félix Lecoy (1962; rpt Paris, 1979), ll. 2360–94.

[3] Chrétien de Troyes, *Le Conte du Graal (Perceval)*, Les Romans de Chrétien de Troyes, V, ed. Félix Lecoy (Paris, 1972–75), ll. 8718, 8722.

Chauvency, and carol very elegantly in a very noble *carole* ...).[4] The participants in the dance are not necessarily upper class either: 'Ches meskines siervans et toutes ches garcettes / voellent ... Karoler par les rues as tamburs, as musettes' (These serving wenches and all these young girls ... want to carol through the street with drums and bagpipes).[5] What appears to be unusual in the composition of dancers is the *carole* in *Méraugis de Portlesguez* where there is only one man in a dance otherwise consisting entirely of girls:

> Avoit puceles qui chantoient
> As caroles qu'eles fesoient
> N'avoit qu'un tot sol chevalier.[6]
>
> (There were girls singing for the *caroles* that they were performing, but there was only one knight.)

Frequently, as one might expect, the sexes are mixed. Indeed it is one of the aspects of dancing that was regarded as evil by moralists. The anonymous author of the *Mireour du monde*, for example, refers repeatedly in a disapproving manner to the participation of both sexes as, for instance, when he denounces the dancers 'quer tous ceus et toutes celes qui carolent font péchié de tous leurs membres' (because all those men and women who carol sin with every member of their bodies).[7] The *carole* in *Guillaume de Dole* mentioned above is composed entirely of men, but another in the same poem is made up of men and women.[8] Likewise in Froissart's poem, *La Prison amoureuse*, there are two *caroles*, one consists exclusively of ladies, but in the other the sexes are mixed.[9] Indeed in romances a situation in which knights and ladies join in a *carole* is commonplace.

The fact that both men and women could take part in the same *carole* leads one to consider their relative number and disposition in the dance. In the *Roman de Laurin* a lady, Dyogenne, directs the knights to take the ladies out to dance: 'Seigneur chevaliers, venez avant, et faites prendre ces dames et ces damoiselles

---

[4] Jacques Bretel, *Le Tournoi de Chauvency*, ed. Maurice Delbouille, Bibliothèque de la Faculté de Philosophie et Lettres de l'Université de Liège, 49 (Liège, 1932), ll. 3094–7.

[5] Gilles le Muisit, 'Li Complainte des dames', ll. 192, 194 in *Poésies de Gilles li Muisis*, ed. Baron Joseph Kervyn de Lettenhove, (Louvain, 1882), II.

[6] Raoul de Houdenc, *Méraugis de Portlesguez*, ll. 3675–7 in *Raoul von Houdenc: sämtliche Werke nach allen bekannten Handschriften*, ed. Mathias Friedwagner (Halle, 1897), I.

[7] *Le Mireour du monde: manuscrit du XIVme siècle découvert dans les archives de la Commune de la Sarra*, ed. Félix Chavannes, Mémoires et documents publiés par la Société d'Histoire de la Suisse Romande, No 4 (Lausanne, 1845), p. 164.

[8] *Guillaume de Dole*, ll. 505–50.

[9] Jean Froissart, *La Prison amoureuse*, ed. Anthime Fourrier, Bibliothèque française et romane, Série B, No 13 (Paris, 1974), ll. 402–60, 360–63.

toutes a la querolle, et les commençons de par Dieu en santé et en joie' (Gentle knights, come forward, and invite all these ladies to join in a *carole*, and let us begin, in Heaven's name, in joy and happiness.)[10] This suggests that the sexes are more or less evenly divided. Indeed a situation in which this is not the case seems to call for comment as in the lines from *Méraugis de Portlesguez* quoted above where it is emphasized that among the girls there was only one knight. Attention is also drawn to the unequal number of men and women in the *carole* in the *Prose Lancelot*: 'Et teuls y ot qui ne tenoi[en]t ne dame ne damoisele. ains tenoient cheualiers dont il y auoit asses plus que de dames ne de damoiseles' (And there were those who did not hold a lady young or old, but held another knight of whom there were rather more than the number of ladies.)[11] From the emphasis laid on the distribution of the sexes one might be inclined to infer with Sahlin that the *carole* was a couple dance, but this was not the case.

There is ample evidence that the dance was indeed circular. First, a number of sources employ the word *tour* as, for example, referring to the *carole* in the *Roman de la Rose*, 'et meint biau tor sor l'erbe fresche' (and many a fair round on the fresh grass) or 'Alons .i. tour a la querole' (Come let us make a round in the *carole*) or 'Yde vient carolant au tour' (Yde comes carolling in a round) or, referring to a *carole* in *Le Tournoi de Chauvency*, 'ainsi s'en vont faisant le tor' (thus they go making a round).[12] The notion that the dance was circular is underlined in some texts by statements that the dance is performed around an object: 'entor le pin por caroler' (to carol around the pine) and, describing the *carole* in the *Prose Lancelot*, 'et tout entour lez pins auoit cheualier & dames' (and all around the pines were knights and ladies); likewise in the *carole* in a *pastourelle* by Froissart, 'En carolant tout autour vont / De la fontainne' (they go right around the spring carolling).[13] Possibly the same idea is conveyed by the term *rondel*, which is also to be found, if in rare instances: 'karolle font et reondeiz' (they make *caroles* and

---

10 *Le Roman de Laurin, fils de Marques le Sénéchal*, ed. Lewis Thorpe, University of Nottingham Research Publication, No 2 (Cambridge, 1960), p. 134.

11 LBL, Additional, 10293 (c.1316), edited in *Le Livre de Lancelot del Lac*, ed. H. Oscar Sommer, The Vulgate Version of the Arthurian Romances, V, Carnegie Institution of Washington, Publication, No 74 (Washington, 1912), p. 123. The text quoted here appears on fol. 292^{v} of the manuscript. Sommer's edition is more relevant to the present study than Micha's more recent one, for which see below.

12 Guillaume de Lorris and Jean de Meun, *Le Roman de la Rose*, ed. Félix Lecoy (Paris, 1965–70), l. 744; *Roman de Laurin*, p. 94; *Sone von Nausay*, ed. Moritz Goldschmidt, Bibliothek des Litterarischen Vereins in Stuttgart, No 216 (Tübingen, 1899), 10545, *Le Tournoi*, l. 3105.

13 *Méraugis*, l. 3674; *Le Livre de Lancelot del Lac*, p .123; Jean Froissart, ' Pastourelle XI', ll. 76–7 in *The Lyric Poems of Jean Froissart: A Critical Edition*, ed. Rob Roy McGregor, Jnr, North Carolina Studies in the Romance Languages and Literatures, No 143 (Chapel Hill, NC, 1975).

rounds), 'la sont li rondel, les caroles' (there are rounds and *caroles* there).[14] Here one assumes that that *rondel* and *caroles* are synonyms.

From the foregoing statements it might be inferred that the dance was merely sometimes, or even frequently, executed in a circle, but that on other occasions, as some have maintained, it could be performed in a chain. Certain texts, however, make it clear that this was not the case; the circular form was not simply a typical feature of the dance; it was its defining element. Objects or persons forming a circle are said to be arranged in the manner of a *carole*. Guibert's *caraula* almost certainly signifies a *carole,* so that 'circulatim in modum caraulae' (in a circle in the manner of a *carole*) means that the dance to which he refers is characteristically circular.[15] More obviously Geoffrey of Monmouth refers to Stonehenge, a circular construction, as the *chorea gigantum*, which Wace translates as *carole as gaianz*.[16] Again Jean de Vignay, in his translation of Gervase of Tilbury, states that Stonehenge was erected 'en manere d'une karolle' thus clarifying that this circular arrangement is typical of the dance.[17] The warriors in Gaydon surround him as if they had been carolling.[18] Nicole Oresme, in *Le Livre du ciel et du monde*, a work expounding heliocentric motion and written between 1370 and 1377, and long before Copernicus, compares the movement of the earth to a wheel, which is 'comme des personnes en une carole' (like people in a *carole*).[19]

The idea of the *carole* as a kind of wheel is one that had been taken up by Dante. Postponing until a later chapter the question of whether the dance itself was actually performed in Italy, an Italian form of the word (*carola*, pl. *carole*) first appears in Italian in Dante's *Divine Comedy*. Dance had long been considered in Italy as symbolic of happiness, as we shall see. In addition to this concept, Dante wished, in the *Paradiso*, the third and last book of his great work, to evoke the symbol of the eternal happiness of the blessed in heaven. A ring is the symbol of eternity. The poet therefore conjures up the image of a circular dance:

> E come cerchi in tempra d'orïoli
> si giran si, che'l primo a chi pon mente
> quïeto pare, e l'ultimo che voli;
> così quelle carole, differente-

---

[14] Herbert, *Le Roman de Dolopathos*, ed. Jean-Luc Leclanche (Paris, 1997), l. 2884; *Floriant et Florete*, ed. Harry F. Williams, University of Michigan Publications, Language and Literature, No 23 (Ann Arbor, MI, 1947), l. 6227.

[15] See p. 20.

[16] See pp. 9–10.

[17] See p. 25.

[18] See p. 41.

[19] Nicole Oresme, *Le Livre du ciel et du monde*, ed. Albert D. Menut and Alexander J. Denomy, CSB, trans. Albert D. Menut (Madison WI, 1968), p. 340. In all the quoted translations from this edition, I have retained 'carole' from the original text instead of Menut's 'round dance' or 'dance'.

mente danzando, della sua richezza
mi facieno stimar, veloci e lente.[20]

(And as wheels in the structure of a clock revolve so that, to one watching them, the first seems at rest and the last to fly, so those choirs dancing [*carole*] severally fast and slow, made me gauge their wealth.)

The blessed in Heaven revolve in circles of different speeds in the *carole* like the wheels of a clock. Francesco da Buti, in his commentary on Dante, has the following note: '*quelle carole*; cioè quelli beati spiriti, che seguitavano come fanno le persone nel ballo tondo' (those *carole*, that is those blessed spirits who followed as people do in the round dance.)[21] He adds succinctly, 'carole è ballo tondo' (the *carole* is a round dance).[22] This simile of the blessed in Heaven as dancers of a *carola* returns as a metaphor in the next canto where, however, there is a shift in the meaning of the word *carole*: they are no longer primarily group of dancers but a choir:

E prima, appresso al fin d'este parole,
'*Sperent in te*' di sopr'a noi s'udì;
a che rispuoser tutte le carole.[23]

(And first, immediately I had finished speaking, *Sperent in te* [Let them hope in Thee] was heard above us, to which all the choirs [*carole*] responded.)

Buti once again explains the significance of these lines (II, 678): '*Rispuoser tutte le carole*: cioè tutti li cerchi de' beati' ('all the choirs responded', that is, all the circles of the blessed.)[24] These two passages in Dante are rich in symbolism, but the point at issue here, however, is that, as in French, the *carole* is established as a closed circle. Any reference that appears to indicate that it was also a linear dance will be considered in the next chapter.

The circle is a closed circle, not an arc of couples radiating from a central point, although Sahlin was misled by a number of texts into thinking that this, on

[20] Dante Alighieri, *The Divine Comedy of Dante Alighieri*, ed. and trans. John D. Sinclair (1939, rpt New York, 1961), *Paradiso*, XXIV, 13–18.

[21] Francesco di Bartolo da Buti (b. 1324–d. 1406), *Commento di Francesco da Buti sopra la Divina Comedia di Dante Allighieri*, ed. Crescentino Giannini (Pisa, 1862), III, 651.

[22] Francesco da Buti, *ibid.* Of course Francesco may have derived his knowledge, not from the dance itself, but from Dante's description.

[23] Dante, *Paradiso*, XXV, 97–9. The biblical quotation in Latin, identified by Sinclair, is from Psalm 9:10.

[24] Francesco da Buti, III, 679.

occasion, could be the case.[25] Several references in the context of the *carole*, such as the following quotations, might appear to support the idea: 'Synador la tint par la main' (Synador held her by the hand) and 'Cascuns prist par la main s'amie / S'ont la carole commenchie' (each man took his girl by the hand, and they began the *carole*).[26] But, as Falk commented, there is nothing to prevent the dancers from gathering in couples and then forming a circle.[27] The *carole* in the *Roman de la Rose* has also been cited as a procession of couples. Yet what is described is rather a number of individuals linked together; Deduit stands between Leesce and the Dieu d'Amour; beside him is Douz Regard. The poem continues with descriptions of other personifications.[28] The arrangement of the dancers is neither a procession of couples nor a line but a circle since two girls are said 'en mi la querole baler' (to dance in the middle of the *carole)*.[29] The purpose, then, of the dancers joining together as couples before dancing a *carole* seems to be that when they make a circle the sexes will alternate.

The dancers, having formed a circle, took hands. We saw that such an action is implied in *Gaydon*.[30] Froissart, in his narrative poem, *La Prison amoureuse*, relates that 'Les dames pas ne se lassoient, / Ains caroloient main a main / Tout le soir jusqu'a l'endemain' (the ladies did not tire, but carolled hand in hand all night until the following day).[31] The communal nature of the dance is illustrated in other texts as, for example, in the biography of William the Marshal, Earl of Pembroke, where the assembled men and women dance a *carole* 'Lors s'entrepristrent par les mains' (So they took one another by the hand).[32]

Occasionally citations refer to the dancers holding fingers rather than hands. In the *Roman de la Rose*, for instance, 'Deduit la [Leesce] tint par mi le doi / a la querole et ele lui (Pleasure held her [Joy] by the fingers in the *carole,* and she him), and in *Méliador*, a monumental narrative poem by Froissart, 'tout en carolant par le doy' (holding fingers while carolling).[33] It is unlikely, however, that a different manner of holding hands is indicated by these variants; more probably we are dealing with examples of synecdoche. Furthermore, in the *Roman de la Rose*,

---

[25] Sahlin, pp. 23–8.

[26] *Laurin*, p. 94, *Sone*, ll. 2029–30. See also, for example, the *Le Livre de Lancelot del Lac,* p. 123; Froissart, 'Pastourelles' [No] XI, ll. 68–9.

[27] Paul Falk, rev. of Sahlin, *Studia Neophilologica*, 13 (1940–41), p. 137.

[28] *Le Roman de la Rose*, ll. 745–1276.

[29] For the full description of the two girls' performance, see *Le Roman de la Rose*, ll. 757–69.

[30] See p. 41.

[31] Jean Froissart, *La Prison amoureuse*, ll. 402–4.

[32] *History of William Marshal*, ed. A. J. Holden, trans. S. Gregory, [historical notes, by D. Crouch], Anglo-Norman Text Society, Occasional Publications Series No 4 (London 2002-) I, 3474.

[33] *Le Roman de la Rose*, ll. 834–5; Jean Froissart, *Méliador par Jean Froissart*, ed. Auguste Longnon, (Paris, 1895–99), l. 17125.

variation in description is characteristic of the literary style of the work. In any case in both the foregoing citations *doi* forms a rhyme.

The question now arises whether the circle moved in a clockwise or in an anticlockwise direction. Most secular texts are silent on this point. It simply is of no concern to their authors as it is irrelevant to their purpose. But for one group of people it was a cause of the utmost concern—moralists of a strict persuasion. They condemned in no uncertain terms dances that moved to the left, and they drew on the Bible for support. Thomas de Cantimpré, refers to the account of the Last Judgement in the Gospel of Matthew in the New Testament when those about to be damned forever will be placed on the left hand of God. He expresses his displeasure in the following manner:

> Signum in choreis est evidentissime manifestum quod ad sinistram circumeuntes in qua parte die maledicti ponentur regnum perdituri sunt quod benedictis ad dexteram a Judice conferetur.[34]
>
> (Most obviously in dances the performers move to the left, on which side on the day of the damned those who are about to lose the kingdom [of Heaven] will be placed, because the Judge will place the blessed on his right.)

The word used here is *chorea*, which, as we saw in an earlier chapter, can simply mean *dance*. The stricture, however, could equally well apply to the *carole*. In fact the moralist author of *Le Mireour du monde*, in an Old Testament reference, is equally censorious, and mentions the *carole* specifically:

> Que les caroles sont les processions au déable, il apert parceque on tourne au senestre costé. De quoy la Sainte Escripture dist: 'Les voies qui tournent à destre connoist Dieu; celes qui tournent à senestre sont perverses et mauvaises, et les het Dieu'.[35]
>
> (It is obvious that *caroles* are processions to the Devil, because they turn to the left. Of which Holy Scripture says: 'God approves the ways that turn to the right; those that turn to the left are perverse and bad, and God hates them'.)

Although it is mainly moralists who refer to the direction in which the *carole* moved, we can find at least one other author who draws upon this feature of the dance. Nicole Oresme, writing about heliocentric motion, makes the following statement in the course of explaining the movements of the planets:

---

[34] Thomas de Cantimpré, *Liber Qui Dicitur Bonum Universale de Proprietatibus Apum* [Cologne, 1480?], sig. N1^{r}. This work was composed between 1256 and 1261. The biblical reference is to Matthew, 25: 32–34.

[35] *Le Mireour*, p. 163. The biblical reference is apparently to Proverbs, 4:27.

> … mais chascune des autres .iiii. differences peut estre signee equalment et samblablement par toute la circumference de la roe sanz quelconque difference fors en relacion de l'une a l'autre et quant au mouvement, car la partie qui va devant <est senestre et devant> ou resgart de celle qui vient apres elle, aussi comme des personnes en une carole. [36]
>
> (… and each of the other four positional differences can be assigned equally in the same manner throughout the entire circumference of the wheel with no distinction, save with relation to one another and to the motion of the wheel, because the part which moves forward is left and in front with regard to the part which follows, just like people in a *carole*.)

From our point of view what is at issue here is that the author is saying that the planets moving in a clockwise direction are like people in a *carole* where any one individual is, so to speak, in front of the person who is immediately to the right of him or her. And if, for moralists, right and left have a theological significance, for Nicole Oresme, the two sides have a social significance. The right hand side is more noble than the left; but if people are seated at a round table, then all are equally nobly seated.[37]

If the circle moves to the left, then the dancers must be stepping to the left. Very few sources mention the steps and then only in general terms. In the description of the *carole* in Jean Brisebarre's narrative poem, *Li Restor du Paon*, it is said of the heroine Elyot 'En ce point qu'Elÿos aloit la pietant …' (At that point when Elyot was dancing with a lively step …).[38] The precise significance of *pietant* here is not obvious. But the word that is most frequently used in relation to the steps, and which comes a little closer to describing the step involved, is the verb, *ferir* (to strike). Thus when, in *Méraugis de Portlesguez*, the eponymous hero joins an enchanted *carole*, 'il chante avant et fiert dou pié' (he leads the singing, and strikes with his foot).[39] Of Leesce, in the *Roman de la Rose*, we are told 'ainz se savoit bien debrisier, / ferir dou pié et envoisier' (thus she knew well how to sing agreeably, strike with her foot, and be lively.)[40] In the latest editor's preferred manuscript of the *Prose Lancelot*, the narrator states '… et se prent a la premiere damoisele qu'il encontre. Et lors conmance a chanter et a ferir del pié ausi conme li autre' (and he takes the first young lady whom he meets. And then he begins to sing and strike with his foot like the others.)[41] But the verb *ferir* does not give us

---

[36] Nicole Oresme, p. 340.

[37] Nicole Oresme, p. 348.

[38] For a full description of the *carole*, see Jean Brisebarre, *Jean Brisebarre: Li Restor du Paon*, ed. Enid Donkin (London, 1980), ll. 1159–77.

[39] *Méraugis*, l. 3744.

[40] *Le Roman de la Rose*, ll. 735–6.

[41] *Lancelot: roman en prose du XIIIᵉ siècle*, ed. Alexandre Micha (Paris, 1979), IV, 235.

a precise explanation of the step. Do the dancers stamp their feet as they move around? Fortunately the corresponding passage in another manuscript of the same text provides us with the required detail: 'si prent le premiere damoisele que il encontre. & lors commence a canter & a ferir lun pie encontre lautre' (he takes the first young lady whom he meets, and then he begins to sing and to strike one foot against the other.)[42] The dancers strike one foot against the other. In other words they step to the left, and then join the right foot to the left. No other kind of step is mentioned in the sources, so we must infer that no other kinds of steps were involved.

Yet there remains the question of whether this step repeated over and over again was performed on the toes or *à terre*. In a translation and commentary on the *Ars Amatoria* by Ovid, the *Art d'Amours*, the earlier part of which dates from the first third of the thirteenth century, the aspiring lover is advised 'en dance et en karole peut on sans blasme touchier a celle c'om veult amer. Illuec fait on les bonnes entrees d'amours par estraindre les dois, par marchier sus le pié …' (in dances and *caroles* you can, without blame, touch the girl with whom you wish to fall in love. Here you can make a good advance in love by squeezing her fingers or stepping on her foot …).[43] As it is easier to step on a flat foot, it would seem that steps performed *à terre* are more likely.

Thus we now possess the *carole* fully restored. It is a very simple dance consisting of women, or men and women generally alternating, stepping sideways to the left in a circle. The whole performance seems to be neatly summarized by another moralist, Jacques de Vitry, in a Latin version of one of his sermons when he denounces the *chorea*, by which he undoubtedly means the *carole*:

> Chorea enim circulus est, cuius centrum est diabolus; et omnes vergunt in sinistram, quia omnes tendunt ad mortem eternam. Dum autem pes pede comprimitur vel manus mulieris manu viri tangitur, ignis dyaboli succenditur.[44]
>
> (The *chorea* is a circle whose centre is the Devil, and in it all turn to the left, because all are heading towards everlasting death. When foot is pressed to foot or the hand of a woman is touched by the hand of a man, there the fire of the Devil is kindled.)

Little information exists either on the general character of the dance, so that explicit references are hard to find. We have, nevertheless, a few indications.

---

42 *Le Livre de Lancelot del Lac,* ed. Sommer, p. 123.

43 *L'Art d'amours: traduction et commentaire* de l'Ars Amatoria *d'Ovide*, ed. Bruno Roy (Leiden, 1974), I, 80.

44 Jacques de Vitry, 'Sermones Vulgares', PBN, fonds lat. 17509 (s. xiii), fol. 146v. The quotation will be found in Etienne de Bourbon, *Anecdotes historiques, légendes et apologues tirés du recueil inédit d'Etienne de Bourbon*, ed. Richard Albert Lecoy de la Marche (Paris, 1877), p. 162, n. 1.

Marcien in the *Restor du Paon* moves gracefully (*affaitiement*).[45] In the *Tournoi de Chauvency*, it is said of the ladies 'et karolent mout cointement' (and they carol very elegantly).[46] The author of the *Mireour du monde* seizes on the manner of performance, and expatiates on this elegant character as being an example of the performers sinning in all the bodies: 'quer tous ceus et toutes celes qui carolent font péchié de tous leurs membres: en passer cointement, en bras démener et hochier, en chanter, en paroler deshonètement … (because all those men and women who carol sin in every member of their bodies by turning elegantly and by moving and shaking their arms, by singing, and by speaking dishonourably).[47] The latter part of this quotation probably refers to the dancers' arms moving up and down as they step sideways. From such references we may take it that the dance was performed gracefully and elegantly.

We may conclude, then, from details garnered from texts extending over three centuries, that the features of the *carole* can be described quite precisely. For each element of the dance we are able to cite fictional and non-fictional sources to establish its choreography. There is nothing to suggest that this extremely simple dance contained features other than those cited, or that it changed in any way in the course of its existence as a dance in fashion. It was a circular dance for Wace in the middle of the twelfth century as it was for Nicole Oresme in the late fourteenth century. The dancers held hands in the works of Chrétien de Troyes as they did in those of Froissart. Early in the thirteenth century, Jacques de Vitry's *chorea* (which in this context is certainly the *carole*) moved to the left as it did for Nicole Oresme. The very simplicity of the dance explains why no written choreography or dance manual was required.

Thus *carole* was not a vague term for dance, or, as has been stated, one that that might cover a variety of choreographic forms including dances with elements of a more theatrical kind. It was a dance that existed on its own terms. It had a very specific choreography, and so differed from other kinds of communal dance to which it has been compared, notably to the *branle*. At the same time one question remains: the *carole* was only one of a number of dance terms current in the period under review. Were these synonyms of *carole* or discrete terms? This is a question that now needs to be answered.

---

[45] *Li Restor du Paon*, l. 1167.

[46] *Le Tournoi*, l. 3096.

[47] *Le Mireour*, p. 164.

Chapter 6
Carole, Bal, Danse, Tresche

We have seen that the Latin word *chorea* could sometimes signify *carole*. One may wonder whether other dance terms in the French of our period also bore some relation to the term. Those most frequently found in collocation with *carole* are *bal, danse* and *tresche*. Enumerations of terms are a characteristic literary device in medieval French literature, particularly in poetry. They lend emphasis to the event being described. We find the enumeration of musical instruments even as early as Wace in the middle of the twelfth century.[1] The actual number of instruments mentioned increased as time went on until, in the early fourteenth century, Machaut can cite over two dozen instruments in two of his works.[2] We can be sure, at least as regards most of the items named, that the instruments are different. Is the situation the same with dance terms? They are less easily defined and more difficult to illustrate. To understand their meaning we must study the literary contexts in which they occur. We must examine the way in which different terms are juxtaposed to arrive at a more precise appreciation of their similarity or difference. While the enumeration of musical instruments can be quite lengthy, that of dance terms is limited to two or three. Here we need only consider collocations that include the term *carole*.

Very few contexts involve the juxtaposition of *carole, bal* and *tresche*. It does, however, appear in the *chantefable*, *Aucassin et Nicolette* and in the *Roman de la Rose*.[3] The same three terms with the addition of *danser* occur in collocation in the works of Christine de Pizan.[4] Unfortunately little can be learnt from the point of view of the dance from these meagre examples.

Slightly more common is the combination of *carole, danse* and *tresche*. These three terms are loosely associated in the anonymous French version of the account of the celebrations following the coronation of King Philip III of France in 1271, quoted in Chapter 3, in which we have 'tresches et quaroles' and 'manieres de

---

1 Wace, *Le Roman de Brut de Wace*, ed. Ivor Arnold (Paris, 1938–40), ll. 10543–52.

2 Guillaume de Machaut, *Le Remède de Fortune*, ll. 3959–88, in *Le Jugement du roy de Behaigne* and *Remède de Fortune*, ed. James I. Wimsatt and William W. Kibler, music ed. Rebecca A. Baltzer (Athens, GA, 1988), and *La Prise d'Alixandrie (The Taking of Alexandria)*, ed. and trans. R. Barton Palmer (New York, 2002), ll. 1146–75.

3 *Aucassin et Nicolette: édition critique*, ed. and trans. Jean Dufournet (Paris, 1973), laisse XXXIII, 7; Guillaume de Lorris and Jean de Meun, *Le Roman de la Rose*, ed. Félix Lecoy (Paris, 1965–70), ll. 741–4.

4 Christine de Pizan, 'Le Dit de la Pastoure', ll. 160–68, in *Oeuvres poétiques de Christine de Pisan*, ed. Maurice Roy (Paris, 1891), II.

danser'.[5] They are also loosely connected in Jean Le Fevre's French translation of the *Lamentationes Matheoli*: 'Venés sça a nostre carole! … Ceux de la dance … faisoient leur treche et leur dance … (Come join in our *carole* … those in the *danse* performed their *tresche* and their *danse*).[6] The problem of elucidating the meaning of the terms is illustrated by lines from *Floriant et Florete*:

> Ces dames et ses damoiseles
> Courtoises, avenanz et beles,
> Ces varlés et cil bacheler
> Dancier, treschier et caroler;
> Tuit se poinent de joie fere,
> Nus n'i a anui ne contrere,
> Li .I. tumbent, li autre saillent,
> De joie fere se travaillent.[7]

> (These ladies, noble, charming and beautiful; these young men and squires are all eager to perform *danses*, *tresches* and *caroles*, and to enjoy themselves. There is no one who is troubled or upset. Some hop, some leap, and all are bent on merry-making.)

Are the dance terms synonyms? Does the hopping and leaping take place in one or more of the dances or is it just another aspect of the merry-making? The same terms, with the addition of *festier*, are found in a poem by Gilles le Muisit: 'caroler, et danser, treskier et festyer' (to perform *caroles* and *danses* and *tresches* and to celebrate).[8] As for the terms themselves, in examples such as these, the accumulation seems to be made for effect. Choreographically as they are set out in these texts we cannot distinguish between them.

The same is true of *carole*, *bal* and *danse*. This grouping appears as early as Chrétien de Troyes' *Chevalier de la Charrette*, where again much physical activity is involved:

> Li autre, qui iluec estoient,
> redemenoit lor anfances,
> baules, et quaroles et dances;

---

[5] See p. 27.

[6] Jean Le Fevre, *Les Lamentations de Matheolus et le Livre de Leesce de Jehan le Fevre de Resson*, ed. Anton-Gérard van Hamel (Paris, 1892–1905), ll. 2919, 2930, 2933.

[7] *Floriant et Florete*, ed. Harry F. Williams, University of Michigan Publications, Language and Literature, No 23 (Ann Arbor, MI, 1947), ll. 6055–62.

[8] Gilles le Musit, *Poésies de Gilles li Muisis*, ed. Baron Joseph Kervyn de Lettenhove (Louvain, 1882), II, 32.

> et chantent et tunbent et saillent
> et au luitier se retravaillent.[9]
>
> (The others who were there relived the *bals* and *caroles* and *danses* of their youth, and sing and hop and leap and engage in wrestling).

At this point one may wonder whether, when *tresches*, *bals* and *danses* are cited as forming part of the activity, much physical exertion was an essential part of it. Yet one can hardly believe that wrestling was a requirement.

We are cautioned against thinking that all the exertion mentioned in passages concerning dance terms are, in fact, connected with dancing by a citation such as the following from Guillaume de Machaut bringing together *carole*, *bal* and *danse*:

> S'en y avoit qui renoier
> Le jouster, ne le tournoier,
> Le dancier, ne le caroler
> Ne pooient, ne le baler.[10]
>
> (There were those who refused to take part in jousting, in the tournament, and could not perform *danses*, *caroles* or *bals*.)

No one could possibly believe that jousts and tournaments were components of any dance. What is surprising in this quotation is that the poet is saying that there were those who could not perform *danses*, *caroles* or *bals*. It seems beyond belief that there were those who could not perform a *carole*, the simplest of dances.

In all the foregoing examples of three dance terms juxtaposed, it is impossible to discern any difference between them. The terms seem to be chosen arbitrarily, and are merely intended to convey a high degree of activity.

We may now enquire whether any better result would be obtained if the number of terms were reduced to two. We find *carole* and *tresche* paired in such early instances as the *Roman de Renart*: 'Les damoiseles font caroles / Et treschent envoisement' (the young ladies perform *caroles* and *tresches* enthusiastically).[11] From the middle of the fourteenth century, in *Li Romans de Bauduin de Sebourc*, we encounter the statement 'Mais dames et puchelles i aloient souvent / Caroler et trechier et canter douchement' (but ladies and girls often went there to take part in

---

[9] Chrétien de Troyes, *Le Chevalier de la Charrette*, Les Romans de Chrétien de Troyes, III, ed. Mario Roques (Paris, 1958), ll. 1644–8.

[10] Guillaume de Machaut, 'Le Dit dou Lyon', ll. 216–19, in *Oeuvres de Guillaume de Machaut*, ed. Ernest Hoepffner (Paris, 1911), II.

[11] *Le Roman de Renart*, ed. Ernest Martin [i.e. Ernst Martin] (Strasbourg, 1882–87), I, 2708–9.

caroles and *tresches* and in singing sweetly).[12] The inference that one is inclined to draw from these citations is that we are dealing here with two different dances. On the other hand, on the showing of collocations of three terms, we cannot be sure that we are not being presented with two synonyms.

The problem becomes even more complicated with *carole* and *danse*. A definition in the *Lexicon latino-gallicum* defines *corea* as 'querole, dance'.[13] This might suggest that the two French terms are synonymous. Yet we saw in Chapter 4 that a tradition of German scholarship contrasts *carole* and *danse*, the *carole* being considered as a communal dance, the *danse* as a dance for couples. It will be recalled that advocates of the theory cited phrases such as 'puceles querolent et dancent' and 'li uns dance, l'autre querolle'. The question seems even more intractable when we discover that the phrase *danses et caroles* became something of a set expression, and occurs in authors of our period ranging from Chrétien de Troyes in the late twelfth century to Froissart and Deschamps in the late fourteenth.[14] It turns up both in prose and verse. As a collocation the following example from Froissart's chronicle, describing an event that took place in 1390, illustrates the point:

> Quant on eut dansé, joué et carolé assés ou chastel de Windesore, et la royne d'Angleterre eut donné de beaulx dons aux chevalliers et escuiers d'honneur du royaulme de France ... on l'en print congié au roy et à la royne.[15]
>
> (When people had danced, played and carolled enough at Windsor Castle, and the Queen of England had given fine gifts to the knights and squires of honour of the Kingdom of France ... they took their leave of the King and Queen.)

To complicate matters still further a construction such *dancer une carole* is possible, as we discover in *Renart le Contrefait*, where we find the phrase 'an

[12] *Li Romans de Bauduin de Sebourc, IIIe roy de Jhérusalem: poème du XIVe siècle*, [ed. Louis-Napoléon Boca] (Valenciennes, 1841), ll. 661–2. The more recent edition, *Baudouin de Sebourc*, ed. Larry S Crist (Abbeville, 2002), although using a base manuscript of c. 1350, does not include the relevant passage.

[13] The 13th-century manuscript is edited by (...) Hofman under the title 'Das zweitälteste unedirte altfranzösische Glossar', *Sitzungberichte der Königlichen Bayerischen Akademie der Wissenschaften zu München*, 1 (Munich, 1868), p. 129, [No] 330.

[14] Chrétien de Troyes, *Eric et Enide*, l. 1993, in Les Romans de Chrétien de Troyes, I, ed. Mario Roques, (Paris, 1952); Jean Froissart, *Chroniques de J. Froissart*, ed. Siméon Luce *et al.* (Paris 1869–1975), I, 76, XIII, 161, XIV, 133 and below in my text; Eustache Deschamps, *Oeuvres complètes de Eustache Deschamps*, ed. Auguste Henri Edouard marquis de Queux de Saint Hilaire and Gaston Raynaud, (Paris, 1887), V, 35. For a later use of the phrase *danses et carolles*, see p. 2.

[15] Jean Froissart, *Oeuvres de Froissart*, ed. Baron Joseph Kervyn de Lettenhove (Brussels, 1872), XIV, 265.

une querole dancier' (to dance in a *carole*).[16] Likewise in the translation of the *Lamentationes Matheoli* the expressions 'dancer a tele karole' (to dance in such a *carole*) and 'dancer a sa karole' (to dance in his *carole*) occur.[17]

In the end all these juxtapositions add nothing to our understanding of the dance terms. There is no significance in their number, in the actual choice of terms, or in their order. The purpose of the enumerations is clearly for the literary effect that such an accumulation provides. It should be noted, however, that while *bal* appears in triple citations, it almost never appears in duple ones. What significance this might have remains to be seen. Otherwise the only course remaining is to examine the terms where they occur singly.

If *bal* is less frequently found in collocation with the other terms, it is because it is less common. It appears as early as 1135–40 in Gaimar's poem in Anglo-Norman, *L'Estoire des Engleis*, although the citation cannot be definitely ascribed to earlier than the beginning of the thirteenth century – the date of the earliest manuscript: 'Wlstanet un naim aveit / Ki baler e trescher saveit'(Wulstanet had a dwarf who knew how to perform *bals* and *tresches*).[18] Clearer evidence is provided a century later, for example, in the *Art d'amours*: 'quant elle balera, si di que tu es tout emerveillé de la beauté de ses bras' (when she performs a *bal*, and you say that you are quite struck with the beauty of her arms).[19] The implication here is perhaps of a girl dancing on her own. This sense is more evident in one of the *pastourelles* in the Douce lyrics:

> 'E Marot, par cortoisie
> je te prie,
> mon meffait pardone moi.
> Je ferai une estampie
> si jolie:
> balle un petit, je t'an proi.'

---

[16] *Le Roman de Renart le Contrefait*, ed. Gaston Raynaud and Henri Lemaître (Paris, 1914), II, 199.

[17] *Le Lamentations*, ll. 175 and 1836.

[18] Gaimar (Geffrei), *L'Estoire des Engleis*, ed. Alexander Bell, Anglo-Norman Texts, Nos 14–15 (Oxford, 1960), ll. 3985–6. *Baler*, in the edition, is supplied from two 13th-century manuscripts. As for the graph *w*, E. J. Dobson explains that it was introduced into England in the 13th century replacing the native English graph *wynn*. There was at first some uncertainty about its use. As it is a 'double u' it was thought unnecessary to write another *u* after it (see *Medieval English Songs*, ed. E. J. Dobson and F. Ll. Harrison (London, 1979), p. 145, n. 18). The name, therefore, in the early 13th-century manuscript of Gaimar's Anglo-Norman text on which Bell's edition is based, although written 'Wlstanet', is, in fact, 'Wulstanet'.

[19] *L'Art d'amours: traduction et commentaire de l'Ars Amatoria d'Ovide*, ed. Bruno Roy (Leiden, 1974), I, 187.

('And Marion, I ask you as a favour, forgive me my misdeed. I'll play a nice estampie, so please perform a *bal*').[20]

The same sense of an individual female performer is present in Deschamps: '… fille joliete / Qui scet baler du talon' (… a lively girl who knows how to perform a *bal* with her heel.)[21] The idea of appropriate footwork signalled in the foregoing quotation is also explicit, together with other special movements, in *Renart le Contrefait*, where, nevertheless, the suggestion is of dancers of both sexes either in a group or in couples.[22] The singular gestures involved in a *bal* are further underlined in Guillaume de Machaut's *Dit dou Lyon*:

Le dos li tournast et l'espaule
Et s'en alast penre a la baule,
Pour li moustrer comme il baloit
Et comment contremont il saloit.[23]

(He turned his back and his shoulder away from her, went and took part in the *bal* to show her how well he danced, and how high he could jump.)

All these citations, dating mostly from the fourteenth century, represent comprehensively the isolated uses of *bal*. Together they give a somewhat clearer idea of the meaning of the term. It generally seems to indicate a more theatrical kind of dance with movements and steps quite distinct from those of the *carole*. Perhaps this fact explains why there is a reluctance to combine it with terms for purely social dances.

Although it occurs earlier, the term *danse*, became increasingly common in the fourteenth century. It, too, can imply a dance with special features or one performed for the entertainment of others as, for example, the 'Dance robardoise' in the *Tournoi de Chauvency*.[24] Elsewhere in this narrative poem, however, *gieu* and *tour* are used of such performances, one of which, the 'Tour du Chapelet', is described in some detail.[25] A similar diversion is called 'un poi de feste' in the play *Le Jeu de Robin et de Marion*.[26] Deschamps employs *dancier* and *dancerie*

---

20 OBl, Douce MS 308 (s. xiv[1]). The lyric cited here will be more conveniently found in *Pastourelles*, ed. Jean-Claude Rivière (Geneva, 1974), I, 103.

21 Eustache Deschamps, IV, 233.

22 *Renart le Contrefait*, II, 176.

23 'Le Dit dou Lyon', ll. 1567–70.

24 Jacques Bretel, *Le Tournoi de Chauvency*, ed. Maurice Delbouille, Bibliothèque de la Faculté de Philosophie et Lettres de l'Université de Liège, No 49 (Liège, 1932), ll. 2533–613.

25 *Le Tournoi*, ll. 4190–300.

26 Adam de la Halle, *Le Jeu de Robin et de Marion*, ed. Kenneth Varty (London, 1960), ll. 183–210.

for the performance of the daughter of Herodias when she requests the head of John the Baptist.[27] At the same time *danse* can also indicate a social dance as is implied, for instance, in *Guillaume d'Angleterre*: 'Chevaliers, dames et pucelles / Toute nuit dancent et anvoisent' (knights, ladies and young girls dance all night, and enjoy themselves.)[28] The application of the term is explicit in the *Tournoi de Chauvency* where the ladies dance 'une *carole* tres noble' (a very noble *carole*), but are interrupted by a herald arriving on a horse, who dismounts, and shouts 'Laciez! Laciez!' (Stop! Stop!). The poet then comments 'Tantost fu li dansiers lassiéz' (the dancing was stopped at once).[29] Here *dansiers* is synonymous with *carole*.

A particularly interesting case is to be found in the works of Froissart. In his chronicles he records the festivities given in 1368 by Amadeus VI, comte de Savoie in honour of Lionel, Duke of Clarence:

> Et passa li dessus dis dus parmi le royaume de France et vint en Savoie, où li gentilz contes de Savoie le rechut très honnerablement en Chambéri, et fu là deux jours en très grans reviaus de danses, de caroles, de tous esbatemens.[30]
>
> (And the aforementioned duke passed through the kingdom of France, and came to Savoy where the noble comte de Savoie received him very honourably at Chambéry, and he spent two days there with great rejoicing and *danses* and *caroles* and entertainments of every kind.)

There is nothing in this passage to assist us in differentiating the two terms. It might be inferred, then, that *danses* and *caroles*, joined together in so many sources, as previously mentioned, are being used as synonyms, or at least without much distinction in meaning. Such a conclusion, however, does not necessarily follow. In recalling the above event in *La Prison amoureuse*, a work composed in both verse and prose in 1372/73, Froissart clearly distinguishes between the two terms:

> La estoient li menestrel,
> Qui s'aquitoient bien et bel
> A piper, et tout de nouvel,
> Houes danses teles qu'il sceurent.
> Et si trestost que cessé eurent
> Les estampies qu'il batoient,
> Chil et chelles qui s'esbatoient
> Au danser, sans gaires atendre,

---

[27] Eustache Deschamps, IX, 93. The biblical account is given in the Gospel of Matthew, 14: 3–12.

[28] *Guillaume d'Angleterre*, ed. A. J. Holden (Geneva, 1988), ll. 1304–05. This work is doubtfully attributed to Chrétien de Troyes.

[29] *Le Tournoi*, ll. 3097, 3123–4.

[30] Jean Froissart, *Chroniques*, ed. Luce, VII, 64.

Commenchierent leurs mains a tendre
Pour caroler. La me souvint
D'un tamps passé: ja il avint
En Savoie, en le court dou conte
De qui on doit bien faire compte,
Car il est nobles et vaillans,
D'onneur faire aigres et taillans;
Celle grasce li portent tuit.
L' an mil .CCC. sissante et uit
Fu que passa parmi sa terre
Li uns des enfans d'Engleterre,
Lions, fils Edouwart le roi,
En tres noble et poissant arroi.[31]

(There were minstrels there who acquitted themselves well and truly in piping, and all in the latest fashion, for the hove dances that they knew so well. And as soon as they had finished the estampies that they were playing rhythmically, men and women who delighted in dancing, hardly waiting at all, began to join their hands to carol. Then I remembered a time past when someone came to the court of the comte de Savoie who ought to be held in high esteem, for he is noble and valiant, and he is brave and ardent, and all grant him these qualities. In the year 1368 one of the young sons of England, Lionel, the son of King Edward, passed through that land in very noble and great array.)

Here the *hove danse* is clearly differentiated from the *carole*. It is implied that the hove dance is a couple dance accompanied by instruments, specifically wind instruments. The *carole*, on the other hand, is explicitly a communal dance accompanied by singing without instrumental accompaniment. Yet the verb *danser* can also be applied to the *carole*. Indeed Machaut, in a passage in his *Remede de Fortune*, describes a circular dance that has every appearance of being a *carole*, but the term that he uses throughout is *danse*.[32] The sense of the term *danse* that is now beginning to emerge is that, at least in the second half of the fourteenth century, although *danse* could be a specific term, it could be used, throughout the whole period under review, as a general term for *dance*. In fact, in the late fourteenth century and moving into the beginning of the fifteenth century, the term *danse* is used in particular for dancing with instruments, more especially wind instruments, notably shawms, and this becomes the norm as exemplified in the works of Deschamps, Christine de Pizan and *Les Echecs amoureux*.[33] The notion,

[31] Jean Froissart, *La Prison amoureuse*, ed. Anthime Fourrier, Bibliothèque française et romane, Série B, No 13 (Paris, 1974), ll. 354–74.

[32] Guillaume de Machaut, *Remede de Fortune*, ll. 3349–516.

[33] Eustache Deschamps, V, 127–8, Christine de Pizan, *Le Livre du duc des Vrais Amans*, ll. 768–5 in *Oeuvres poétiques*, III. The relevant passage from *Les Echecs amoureux*

therefore, that *danse* and *carole* were two contrasting terms, a view maintained by some scholars, as stated in the last chapter, only holds good in the second half of the fourteenth century.

Finally we come to the term *tresche*. The word dates at least from the beginning of the thirteenth century as it is found in the passage from Gaimar cited above. Usage in some English translations indicates that it meant a circular dance, thus inviting us to believe that it was in some sense a synonym of *carole*. Thus an Anglo-Norman writer, Walter de Bibbesworth, in *Le Trétiz*, a guide to French vocabulary composed for an English lady, opines 'Quant povre femme mene la tresche, / Plus la vaudreit en mein la besche ...' (when a poor woman leads the *tresche*, it would be better if she had a spade in her hand ...).[34] But a contemporary gloss in the manuscript gives 'ring' as the equivalent of 'tresche'. A later text, the *Nominale* of c. 1340, provides an identical translation of the term: 'F[emme] treche mene pur deduyt / W[oman] the ryng leduth for ioye' (a woman leads the tresche for joy).[35] Indeed in Jean le Fevre's translation of the *Lamentationes Matheoli*, the same performance first called a *carole* is subsequently named a 'dance' and then a 'treche'.[36] Sahlin drawns attention to a particularly striking example of this synonymous usage in *Meraugis de Portlesguez*:

> Einsi li covient oblïer
> S'amie; lors vet caroler
> L'escu au col et chante avant.
> Li autre qui chantoit devant
> Guerpi la tresche, si monta
> Sor son cheval, lors s'en ala
> Fors la porte.[37]

> (So he must forget his love. Then, with his shield slung around his neck, he goes to take part in the *carole*, where he leads the singing. The other man, who had been singing previously, leaves the *tresche*, mounts his horse, and departs through the gate.)

---

is quoted in Herman Abert, 'Die Musikästhetik der Echecs Amoureux', *Sammelbände der Internationalen Musikgesellschaft*, 6 (1904–05), p. 355.

[34] Walter de Bibbesworth, *Le Trétiz*, ed. William Rothwell, Anglo-Norman Text Society, Plain Texts Series, No 6 (London, 1990), ll. 297–8.

[35] *Nominale sive Verbale*, ed. Walter W. Skeat, Transactions of the Philological Society, 1903–06 (London, 1906), ll. 213–14.

[36] *Les Lamentations*, ll. 2919, 2930, 2933.

[37] Sahlin, p. 7; Raoul de Houdenc, *Méraugis de Portlesguez*, Il, 3701–07, in *Raoul von Houdenc: sämtliche Werke nach allen bekannten Handschriften*, ed. Mathias Friedwagner (Halle, 1897–1909), I.

The foregoing citation would seem to confirm that the *tresche* is a circular dance. Yet it would be wrong to draw this conclusion. With the Anglo-Norman examples quoted above, the verb *mener* or *to lead* is employed. This collocation is frequent with *tresche*, but is all but unknown with *carole*. Evidence for this can be gathered from two separate passages in *Le Jeu de Robin et de Marion*, from one in the anonymous *Suite* to Matthieu le Poirier's *Le Court d amours* as well as later in the works of Deschamps and Christine de Pizan.[38]

We must also take into account the prepositional phrases used in conjunction with *tresche*. For although Gilles le Muisit speaks of 'karoler par les rues' (to carol through the streets), *par* and other prepositions are more commonly found with *tresche*.[39] Robin in *Le Jeu de Robin et de Marion* leads a *tresche* 'le sentele lès le bos' (along the path by the wood).[40] Watriquet de Couvin has a character say, 's'irons treschier parmi la rue' (and we shall dance a *tresche* through the street).[41] This kind of construction occurs even when *tresche* is collocated with *carole*. Thus, in Jean Renart's *L'Escoufle*, we find 'Aprés mangiers, fu grans la tresce / Par la maison, et les karoles' (after eating there were great *tresches* and *caroles* performed through the house).[42] Likewise in the *Livre d'Artus*, we are told 'ces dames & ces puceles comencent les queroles & les tresches parmi les rues de ioie & font la plus grant feste que il onques poeent' (these ladies and young girls begin the *caroles* and *tresches* through the streets for joy, and celebrate as much as they can).[43]

People or objects arranged in a circle are said to be in the form of a *carole*, and this formation is characteristic of the dance. On the other hand, the *tresche* is led along by a wood, through a house or through streets, and therefore must be linear in form. The *tresche*, unlike the *carole*, is not indicated as being circular except in the English translations mentioned above. The implication, therefore, is that the term refers essentially to a linear dance as Paris surmised.[44]

At the same time we are confronted with the fact that *tresche* can appear to be a synonynm of *carole*, and *carole* itself can, on occasion, be considered as a

---

38 Adam de la Halle, *Le Jeu*, ll. 211, 737; Matthieu le Poirier, *Le Court d'Amours de Mahieu le Poirier et la Suite anonyme de la* Court d'Amours, ed. Terence Scully (Waterloo, Ontario, 1976), ll. 3649–52; Eustache Deschamps, VII, 126; Christine de Pizan, 'Le Debat des deux amans', ll. 110–13 in *Oeuvres Poétiques*, II.

39 Gilles le Muisit, II, 193.

40 Adam de la Halle, *Le Jeu*, l. 736.

41 Watriquet de Couvin, 'Des Trois Dames de Paris', l. 157, in *Dits de Watriquet de Couvin*, ed. Auguste Scheler (Brussels, 1868).

42 Jean Renart, *L'Escoufle: roman d'aventure*, ed. Franklin Sweetser (Geneva, 1974), ll. 3652–3.

43 *Le Livre d'Artus*, p. 106 in The Vulgate Version of the Arthurian Romances, ed. H. Oskar Sommer (Washington, 1913), VII.

44 Gaston Paris, rev. of *Les Origines de la poésie lyrique en France au Moyen Age*, by Alfred Jeanroy, in *Mélanges de littérature française du Moyen Age*, ed. Mario Roques (Paris, 1912), 594, n .4.

linear dance. This interchangeability of the two terms suggests that the two dances, although not actually identical, were nearly so. This would explain why both terms can be used synonymously in *Meraugis*, why a linear dance can, on occasion, be called a *carole*, why conversely, *tresche* can be translated into English as 'ring', and possibly why *tresche* and *carole* can both translate the Latin *choreas* in the accounts of the celebrations of Philip III. What the evidence, taken as a whole, seems to suggest is that, while the *carole* was strictly speaking a circular dance, and the *tresche* a linear one, in all other respects they were identical, that is to say, the dancers held hands, made steps sideways to the left, or in other words both dances moved to the left. The two dances, although essentially distinct, resembled each other so closely that their names could be used synonymously. This possibly explains why *carole*, which is metrically more suitable, is used where *tresche* would have been more choreographically accurate in *La Manekine*.[45]

Thus the names of dances found in French literature of the twelfth to the fourteenth centuries, like the names of musical instruments, have distinct meanings. *Danse* is a general term for choreographic performance, except when, in the later fourteenth century, it can signify the hove dance. *Bal* designates an activity of a more theatrical nature. *Carole* and *tresche* both refer to social dances, but the former is essentially circular, the latter linear. Yet clearly some latitude is observable in the usage of these two terms.

When, however, two or three of these terms are applied to the same performance, as in some enumerations, they cannot mean different things. In fact it seems likely that in the enumeration of dances, like the enumeration of musical instruments, nothing more is intended than a generalized reference to dancing or music-making. In poetry it is the effect of the accumulation of terms that is important. Stylistic considerations or the requirements of prosody may also play a part. Hence the synonymous use of *carole* and *tresche* in *Meraugis* or of *carole*, *bal* and *tresche* in the *Roman de la Rose* may be ascribed to elegant variation. Likewise, it is possible that the number of syllables or the requirements of rhyme might determine a poet's choice a particular term.

The term *carole*, then, can be isolated from other dance terms. Its choreographic features can be gathered from a wealth of sources, so much so that we can reconstruct the dance. Yet a performance of the dance is not possible unless we have the required music. Readers may have noticed that, among the many texts cited so far, many of them show that the *carole* was accompanied by singing. There are, of course, two aspects involved in singing, the lyrics and the music. The obvious course to pursue, therefore, is to search out and examine these lyrics first.

---

[45] See p. 33.

Chapter 7
The Lyrics

Among the contributions of literary historians and literary critics to the lyric verse of the Middle Ages, some have inevitably devoted special attention to dance lyrics as being an important genre. Too often, however, they have been rather subjective in deciding what a dance lyric is. They do not provide any evidence why any one lyric is to be so considered, and, *a fortiori*, they do not relate any particular lyric to any particular dance or dance type. The result is an inevitable vagueness about what constitutes such a lyric. The approach adopted here is consequently different, and only lyrics that are explicitly identified in the primary sources as dance lyrics, and more particularly *carole* lyrics, are considered.

Dance lyrics associated with the *carole* first appear in the *Roman de Guillaume de Dole*, the composition of which dates from the first third of the thirteenth century although the unique manuscript that contains it dates from the end of the century.[1] Unfortunately this manuscript lacks the requisite music, and many of the lyrics are in a garbled form. The work, nonetheless, had a great influence on subsequent writers, and French works with lyric insertions, either in prose or in verse or in a combination of both, appeared throughout the remainder of the thirteenth and fourteenth centuries. Characters in *Guillaume de Dole* perform the *carole* twice in the course of the romance, and four lyrics are provided for the first *carole*, three for the second. These songs belong to two different categories. One type consists simply of a number of lines arranged in triplets; the other of lines arranged to form a stanza.

Of the first kind only one example appears as a *carole* lyric in *Guillaume de Dole*. This lyric is copied with word division lacking, and is written as prose in the manuscript, but the pointing makes it clear that it is composed of three assonating lines, which can be transcribed thus:

> Renaus et s'amie chevauche par un pré,
> tote nuit chevauche jusqu'au jor cler.
> Ja n'avrai mes joie de vos amer.[2]

[1] See Jean Renart, *Le Roman de la Rose ou de Guillaume de Dole*, ed. Félix Lecoy (1962; rpt Paris, 1979), p. iii. This is the edition used here unless otherwise stated.

[2] A facsimile of this and the other two lyrics for the second carole will be found in Hendrik van der Werf, 'Jean Renart and Medieval Song' in *Jean Renart and the Art of Romance: Essays on* Guillaume de Dole, ed. Nancy Vine Durling, (Gainsville, FL, 1997), p. 161, Fig. 4. The lyric is edited in *Guillaume de Dole*, ll. 2389–91.

(Renaus and his lady friend ride through a meadow. All night they ride until the break of day. I shall never have the joy of loving you.)

A lyric consisting of only three lines may seem unbelievably short, and in fact a number of commentators have considered that, as with many other lyrics of the kind, the quoted lines were merely part of a much longer composition. This, however, is not the case, as we shall see. For the moment, we need only note another instance in the narrative although it is not represented as a dance song in the text. After a picnic the ladies and a knight sing a lyric consisting of a rhymed couplet; then a girl sings another song in the same form.[3]

In fact lyrics of no more than three lines make up the seven pieces for a *carole* in what is chronologically the next romance to contain lyric insertions, *Le Roman de la Violette*.[4] This was followed by several other works (both fictional and non-fictional) during the rest of the thirteenth century. Lyrics of the kind also accompany performances of the *tresche* in the play *Le Jeu de Robin et de Marion*, where a lyric of two lines ends the play.[5] A similar lyric for a *tresche* is to be found in the continuation of the narrative poem *Le Cour d'Amours*.[6] Lyrics of the same type accompanying both the *carole* and the *tresche* are another indication that the two dances were closely related.

Jeanroy was the first notable literary historian to make a detailed study of medieval French lyrics, and he, together with others following him, has called such short pieces 'refrains'.[7] Yet the term, whether in French or in English, is more properly applied to the repetition of the same words to the same music (where it exists) within the same piece.[8] For *carole* lyrics as a whole, the word most commonly used in the sources is simply *chanson* or occasionally *chansonette*. Where no dancing actually takes place in a particular context, such lyrics can, nevertheless, be cited as being associated with the *carole*. Thus in *Li Prisons d'Amours* by Baudouin de Condé we have a lyric followed by a defining comment:

---

3 *Guillaume de Dole*, ll. 291–2.

4 Gerbert de Montreuil, *Le Roman de la Violette, ou de Gérart de Nevers par Gerbert de Montreuil*, ed. Douglas Labaree Buffum (Paris, 1928), ll. 104, 110–11, 119–20, 126–8, 134–5, 141–2, 152–3.

5 Adam de la Halle, *Le Jeu de Robin et de Marion*, ed. Kenneth Varty (London, 1960), ll. 762–3. Varty prints BNF f. fr. 25566 (La Vallière) the most complete and accurate MS, and this contains many two-line lyrics, which therefore must be complete in themselves.

6 Matthieu le Poirier, *Le Court d'Amours de Mahieu le Poirier et la Suite anonyme de la* Court d'Amours, ed. Terence Scully (Waterloo, Ontario, 1976), [Lyric No] XXXIII.

7 Alfred Jeanroy, *Les Origines de la poésie lyrique en France au Moyen Age* (1889, 3rd ed. Paris, 1925), pp. 102–26.

8 *Le Grand Robert de la langue française*, ed. Paul Robert, 2nd ed. rev. Alain Rey (Paris, 1985), 'Refrain'; *OED*, 'Refrain'.

> 'Sa biele boucete, par un très douc ris
> A mon cuer en sa prizon mis.'
> Ceste prizons dont ci parolle
> Iceste cançon de carolle,
> C'est la prizons d'amors sans doute … .[9]
>
> ('Her beautiful little mouth with her very sweet laugh has put my heart in prison'. The prison of which this *carole* song speaks, is, without doubt, the prison of love … .).

Yet if the word used in the sources to designate these lyrics is overwhelmingly *chanson*, other terms are occasionally found. One of these is *rondet*. If Baudouin de Condé, in the passage cited above, calls his lyric a 'cançon de carolle' he had, in the line immediately preceding it, called the same piece a 'rondet'.[10] The two terms are therefore synonymous. In *Renart le Nouvel*, a lyric comprising a single couplet, and actually used in the context to accompany a *carole*, is described as 'che rondet joli'.[11] Later in the same poem the term 'ce rondet a carole' occurs where there is no dancing.[12]

The word *rondet*, then, referring to a lyric of a couple of lines, can also indicate a song for a *carole*. Why such a short piece not beginning and ending with the same words, and therefore not circular in form, is called a *rondet* is not immediately obvious. Probably the explanation is that it is so called because it accompanied a round dance. Baudouin de Condé appears to have been the first to use the term. Later in the thirteenth century it was to take on the forms *rondel* and *rondiaus* in a manuscript of the works of Adam de la Halle.[13] By that time its application was different in that it now referred to an eight-line lyric of a particular structure to be examined below.

Another unusual term is *motet*, which is found in the *Art d'Amours*:

> Et pour ce dient elles en leurs chançons et en leurs karoles ce motet:
> 'Chappel de hous ne d'ortie
> Ne point tant comme jalousie'.[14]

---

[9] Baudouin de Condé, 'Li Prisons d'Amours', ll. 126–30, in *Dits et contes de Baudouin de Condé et de son fils Jean de Condé*, ed. Auguste Scheler (Brussels, 1866), I.

[10] Another couplet, later in 'Li Prisons d'Amours' (ll. 168–70), is also called a 'rondés'.

[11] Jacquemart Gielée, *Renart le Nouvel*, ed. Henri Roussel (Paris, 1961), ll. 2555.

[12] *Renart le Nouvel*, l. 6884.

[13] PBN, f. fr. 25566 includes in the list of contents headed, 'ses rondiaus', and a heading on fol. 32^{v} reads 'li rondel adan'.

[14] *L'Art d'amours: traduction et commentaire de l'*Ars Amatoria *d'Ovide*, ed. Bruno Roy (Leiden, 1974), I, 108.

(And for this reason they sing in their songs and in their *caroles* this motet: 'A chaplet of holly or nettles does not sting as much as jealousy'.)

The word *motet* here evidently means 'motto'; pithy phrases are common in such short lyrics. *Motet* is collocated with *conduit* and *chançonnete* in the later part of the *Roman de la Rose*, where Genius speaks of the blessed in Heaven:

chantant en pardurableté
motez, conduiz et chançonnetes,
par l'erbe vert, seur les floretes,
souz l'olivete querolant.[15]

(Singing throughout eternity *motets*, *conducti* and little songs, on the green grass, on the flowerlets, carolling under the olive tree.)

Chançonnete, as we have seen, is occasionally used of songs for *caroles*. The *conductus* was a purely musical form, and was never associated with secular dancing. What we have here is simply three synonyms for *song*. Jean de Meun may be mingling terms in a kind of elegant variation, or he may wish by the accumulation of terms to impart a sublime vision of a heavenly dance.

The second type of lyric associated with the *carole* is, as stated above, one that consists, not of an arbitrary number of lines, but one in which the lines are ordered in the predetermined form of a stanza. To return to the second of the two *caroles* in *Guillaume de Dole*, the second lyric of the group is set out in the manuscript as follows:

Mauberion sest main leuee.dioree.
buer .i.vig a la fontaine est alee or
en ai dol.Diex diex or demeure.mau
berions a leue trop.[16]

The lyric as it stands is without meaning or form. Yet is is clear that it is intended to have three lines rhyming in 'ee'. Gennrich's reconstruction of the piece, therefore, seems plausible:

---

[15] Guillaume de Lorris et Jean de Meun, *Le Roman de la Rose*, ed. Félix Lecoy (Paris, 1965–70), ll. 20626–9.

[16] Hendrik van der Werf, p. 161, Fig. 4, *Guillaume de Dole*, ll. 2379–85. The lyrics in the layout in which they appear in the manuscript are conveniently reproduced together in Jean Renart, *The Romance of the Rose or of Guillaume de Dole (Roman de la Rose ou de Guillaume de Dole*), ed. and trans. Regina Psaki, Garland Library of Medieval Literature, No 92A (New York, 1995), pp. 269–80; 'Mauberjon' is on p. 275.

Mauberjon s'est main levée
buer i vig ... diorée,
a la fontaine est alee:
    or en ai dol.
Dieus, Dieus, or est demeurée
    a l'eve trop.[17]

(Mauberjon got up one morning to wash a decorated [vig ...]. She went to the spring.) Now I am sorry for it. Dear! Dear! She stayed too long at the water!)

The piece can thus be seen as a development of 'Renaus', the last lyric for the second *carole* discussed above. In 'Renaus' there are three assonating lines. In the version of 'Mauberjon', as edited, the lyric begins with three rhyming lines, which are extended by the addition of three more lines. This extension does not simply add three further lines with a new rhyme or assonance, which would, in effect, constitute a second stanza, but retains the original rhyme in a line enclosed by two lines introducing a new rhyme. Thus the whole presents an integrated stanza, with a readily recognizable rhyming or assonating scheme: aaabab.

One lyric for this *carole*, the first of the three pieces, remains to be considered. This is written as follows in the manuscript:

La ius desouz loliue
Ne vos repentez mie
Fontaine i sourt serie puceles carolez
Nevos repentez mie deloiaument amer.[18]

At first sight this presentation might seem acceptable. But l. 4, extending what is evidently a refrain, seems questionable, and the internal rhyme in ll. 4 and 5 also raises suspicions, as it seems unlikely in a dance song at this period. Gennrich's realignment of the stanza offers a more comprehensible rhyming scheme:

La jus desouz l'olive,
–ne vos repentez mie!–
fontaine i sourt serie.
    Puceles, carolez!
Ne vos repentez mie
    de loiaument amer.[19]

---

[17] *Rondeaux, Virelais und Balladen*, ed. Friedrich Gennrich, Gesellschaft für romanische Literatur, No 43 (Dresden, 1921), No 12.

[18] Hendrik Van der Werf, p. 161, fig. 4; *The Romance*, ed. Psaki, p. 275; *Guillaume de Dole*, ll. 2369–74.

[19] *Rondeaux*, ed. Gennrich, No 11. The refrains of the lyrics are not, however, italicized in Gennrich's edition.

(Down there under the olive tree, *do not repent*. There the clear spring rises. Girls, dance the *carole*! *Do not repent* of loving faithfully).

The emended form is more plausible because it can be seen as fitting into a developing pattern of the *carole* lyric. As before, the lyric comprises six lines, but ll. 2 and 5 are now identical, and introduce the concept of a refrain: aAabAb.

Turning to the first of the four lyrics for the first *carole* in *Guillaume de Dole*, it, too, is set out in the manuscript in four lines, each with a different number of syllables, so there can be little doubt that this arrangement is incorrect, and that the lyric actually in six lines:

C'est tot la gieus enmi les prez,
Vos ne sentez mie les maus d'amer!
Dames i vont por caroler.
  Remirez vos braz!
Vos ne sentez mie les maus d'amer
  Ausi com ge faz![20]

(It's all a game there in the meadows. *You do not feel the pains of love*. Ladies go there to dance the *carole*. Look at your arms! *You do not feel the pains of love* as I do!)

The general acceptance of this disposition confirms that the rhyming scheme proposed for the previous lyric is the correct one, and one, moreover, that establishes it as relatively fixed in a continuing development of the *carole* lyric.

The second lyric for this first *carole* was also copied out in the manuscript in four lines:

Cest la ius desoz lolive
robinsenmaine samie
lafontaine i sort serie desouz lolivete
Enondeu robins enmaine bele mariete.[21]

Here ll. 1 and 2 assonate, and have seven syllables each; ll. 3 and 4 rhyme, and have 13 syllables each. This might appear to offer a satisfactory lyric, but for the fact that we have what seems to be a refrain with the words 'Robins enmaine' (ll. 2 and 4), and an internal rhyme with 's'amie' and 'serie'. Furthermore, with this example, the prosody is not improved if the four lines are simply written as six, because the lines would no longer rhyme or assonate. If, however, one retains the

[20] *The Romance*, ed. Psaki, pp. 269–70; *Guillaume de Dole*, ll. 514–19; *Rondeaux,* ed. Gennrich, No 5.

[21] *The Romance*, ed. Psaki, p. 270; *Guillaume de Dole*, ll. 522–7.

six lines, but accepts Gennrich's emendation of making l. 5 identical to l. 2, on the model of the two previous examples, the difficulty is overcome:

> C'est la jus desoz l'olive,
> *Robins enmaine s'amie*;
> la fontaine i sort serie
> desouz l'olivete.
> *Robins enmaine s'amie*,
> bele Marïete.[22]

> (It's the game under the olive tree. *Robin leads his lady love*. There the clear spring rises under the olive tree. *Robin leads his lady love*, the fair Marion.)

Leaving aside, for the moment, the third lyric, the fourth is arranged differently in the manuscript from the previous ones:

> main se leva la bien fete aeliz
> p[ar] ci passe li bruns li biaus robins
> biause para et plus biause vesti
> marchiez la foille et ge qieudrai la flor
> parci passe robins li amorous
> encor enest li herbage plusdouz [23]

Here we actually have six lines, and l. 5 appears to reproduce l. 2 in some measure, as we might expect from previous examples, but the rhyming scheme is faulty. Three assonating lines (aaa) are followed by three more lines with a different assonance (bbb) constituting two stanzas. This defect is remedied by emending l. 5 to bring it into conformity with l. 2, as Gennrich proposes:

> Main se leva la bien fete Aëliz,
> –*Par ci passe li bruns, li biaus* Robins–
> biau se para et plus biau se vesti.
> Marchiéz la foille, et ge qieudrai la flor;
> *par ci passe li bruns, li biaus Robins;*
> encor en est li herbages plus douz.[24]

---

[22] *Rondeaux*, ed. Gennrich, No 6.

[23] *The Romance*, ed. Psaki, p. 270. It is possible that a scribe did not understand the form, and therefore recomposed the fifth line. For a version edited differently, see *Guillaume de Dole*, ll. 542–7.

[24] *Rondeaux*, ed. Gennrich, No 8. For a version edited differently, see *Guillaume de Dole*, ll. 542–7.

(The lovely Aelis got up in the morning – *this way passes the dark, the handsome Robin* – beautifully she adorned herself, and more beautifully she dressed herself. Step on the leaf, and I'll gather the flower. *This way passes the dark, the handsome Robin.* The grass is sweeter still because of it.)

To return to the remaining lyric, the third one, this is copied in the manuscript as three lines:

main selevoit aaliz.iai non enmelot
biau se para et vesti soz la rocheguion
cui lairai ge mes amors amie sa vosnon[25]

(Aelis got up one morning. My name is Emmelot. Beautifully she adorned and dressed herself under Roche Guyon. To whom shall I give my love if not to you?)

This is one of a number of Aelis lyrics, all with very similar subject matter. Unlike all the other *carole* lyrics this one cannot be resolved into some sort of semantic or prosodic sense, particularly as, in common with several other lyrics, *Guillaume de Dole* is the sole source. The reference to Emmelot is out of place. The prosody is also highly questionable. As Gaston Paris and Delbouille point out, *-ot* cannot assonate with *–on*.[26] Gennrich, as one might expect, reconstructs the lyric as a six-line stanza, but his solution is unsatisfactory, as it produces a rhyming scheme (aBacBc) that, in effect, divides what obviously should be a single stanza into two stanzas, and has all the appearance of being a form of his own devising unrelated to any that we have encountered so far, or are yet to meet.[27] There seems to be no way of restoring the piece. As for the reference to Emmelot, Lejeune plausibly suggests that this may be the result of contamination with another lyric in which Emmelot is also named.[28]

If most of Gennrich's editorial interventions have been accepted here, his approach has not met with universal critical approval. Spanke, for example, considered that it was possible for lyric forms to diverge.[29] Le Gentil, while admitting that the manuscript does not always present the lyrics in an intelligible way, questions Gennrich's emendations, and argues in respect of the divergent

[25] *The Romance*, ed. Psaki, p. 270, *Guillaume de Dole*, ll. 532–7.

[26] Gaston Paris, 'Bele Aaliz' in *Mélanges de littérature française du Moyen Age*, ed. Mario Roques, (1896; rpt Paris, 1912), p. 621; Maurice Delbouille,'Sur les traces de "Bele Aëlis"', *Mélanges de philologie romane dédiés à la mémoire de Jean Boutière (1899–1967*), ed. Irénée Cluzel and François Pirot (Liège, 1971), I, 211.

[27] *Rondeaux*, ed. Gennrich, No 7.

[28] Jean Renart, *Le Roman de la Rose ou de Guillaume Dole*, ed. Rita Lejeune (Paris, 1936), p. 137.

[29] Hans Spanke, 'Zum Thema "Mittelalterliche Tanzlieder"', *Neuphilologische Mitteilungen*, 33 (1932), 18–19.

forms in which the lyrics are found in the manuscript that 'elles montrent simplement que les trouvères entendaient jouer de la forme avec le maximum de souplesse' (they simply show that the trouvères were intending to play with the form with the greatest possible flexibility.)[30] Likewise Van den Boogaard opposes the uniformity of Gennrich's rhyming schemes, and opines that:

> Notre but est au contraire de faire voir la richesse des formes, de montrer que beaucoup de poètes du XIIIe siècle ont essayé de rompre le cadre trop rigide du rondeau ou que les règles n'étaient pas encore aussi strictes qu'au XIVe siècle et que le rondeau était une forme expérimentale vivante.[31]
>
> (My aim, on the contrary, is to reveal the richness of the forms, to show that many thirteenth-century poets tried to break the all too rigid structure of the rondeau or to show that the rules were not yet as strict as in the fourteenth century, and that the rondeau was still a living experimental form.)

Thus the tendency has been to stress the diversity of poetic composition.

Such a viewpoint, however, seems to overlook the nature of the pieces under review. The dance lyrics are not the inspired work of poets or trouvères; they are simply lyrics of a popular nature in which stereotyped phrases are strung together to achieve some kind of meaning. There is no evidence of a striving for originality, but rather of numerous scribal errors. Some lyrics as set out in the manuscript imply no formal pattern, and some even fail to make sense. Those who have paid careful attention to the texts have been obliged to concede the inadequacies of the source. This fact is tacitly accepted by editors who, while rejecting most of Gennrich's emendations, nevertheless choose to accept some of them in a purely arbitrary way. It must also be remembered that the lyrics under consideration are intended as dance songs, and, as such, adherence to a predetermined form is to be expected; indeed predictabalility is a requirement.

It will have been noticed that Van den Boogaard, in common with others, calls the six-line pieces 'rondeaux'. This appellation is not used in the sources, where, as has been already stated, the lyrics are generally called *chanson* or *chansonette*. As noted above the term, in the form *rondet*, appeared in the middle of the thirteenth century about the same time that the form itself, to which the term *rondeau* was later applied, first appeared. A text that provides some of the earliest examples of the form, as distinct from the name, is the *Roman de Laurin*. The narrative involves the performance of two *caroles*, for which two lyrics are provided for the first *carole*, and one for the second. Although all three pieces consist of eight lines

---

30 Pierre Le Gentil, 'A propos du Guillaume de Dole', *Mélanges de linguistique romane et de philologie médiévale offerts à M. Maurice Delbouille*, ed. Madeleine Tyssens (Gembloux, 1964), II, 391–2.

31 *Rondeaux et refrains du XIIe siècle au début du XIVe*, ed. Nico H. J. van den Boogaard, Bibliothèque française et romane, Série D, No 3, (Paris, 1969), p. 12.

of a particular pattern, each piece is simply called in the text a 'chançon'. The lyric for the second *carole* is set out as follows:

Se j'ai amours servie loiaument,
Il est bien droiz que j'aie mon ami:
Pour ce fait bon esploitier sagement.
Se j'ai amour servie loiaument,
Elle est si large qu'elle a cent doubles rent
Celui qui sert de loial cuer ami.
Se j'ai amours servie loiaument,
Il est bien drois que j'aie mon ami.[32]

(*If I have served love faithfully, it is right that I should have my lover.* To this end it is good to act prudently. *If I have served love faithfully*, it has been so generous that it repays him a hundredfold who serves his love with a true heart. *If I have served love faithfully, it is right that I should have my lover.*)

Both in content and form the lyric here is more complex. There is a greater coherence in the development of the theme. At the same time the simple form aAabAb that we encountered in *Guillaume de Dole* is expanded by making a refrain of the last two lines which are then added to the beginning of the piece, resulting in a total of eight lines rhyming ABaAabAB, thus giving the standard form of the rondeau.[33]

The two lyrics for the first *carole* in the *Roman de Laurin* are obviously intended to have the same pattern, so that the first should read as follows:

Se j'ai grant joie enz enz mon cuer
Ne demandez dont elle vient!
Gallyenne, tres douce suer,
Se j'ai grant joie ens enz mon cuer
Ne veul que nuls en sache fuer!
Que j'aing du cuer, vous savés bien.
Se j'ai grant joie enz enz mon cuer
[Ne demandez dont elle vient!][34]

---

32 *Le Roman de Laurin, fils de Marques le Sénéchal*, ed. Lewis Thorpe, University of Nottingham Research Publication, No 2 (Cambridge, 1960), pp. 134–5.

33 The standard rondeau in the vernacular remained throughout our period a single stanza form. Latin versions, however, regularly consist of several stanzas, for which see *Notre Dame and Related Conductus: Opera Omnia*, Collected Works, X, Part 8, The Latin Rondeau, ed. Gordon A. Anderson Repertoire (Henryville, UT, 1979).

34 *Roman de Laurin*, p. 94.

(*If I have great joy in my heart, do not ask whence it comes!* Galyenne, my sweet sister, *if I have joy in my heart*, I do not want anyone at all to know about it! That I love with all my heart, you know full well. *If I have joy in my heart, [do not ask whence it comes!]*)

This is not, it seems, how the lyric appears in the manuscript sources, nor indeed, how it appears in the edition. The editor has emended the patently incorrect manuscript *suer* to *fuer* in l. 5. He has not, however, inverted the phrases in l. 6 as required by the rhyming scheme, or noted the omission of the eighth line, which the rondeau form demands. The curtailment of the repetition of the refrain may be a scribal convention, but some indication of this should be given in editing the piece, which otherwise will appear to be defective.

If we bear in mind the vigilance required in noting such scribal conventions and shortcomings, the second rondeau would read:

Amis, on me destraint pour vous
Mais ne m'en chaut quant vous m'avez:
Celui avez mis au dessous.
Amis, on me destraint por vous!
Si est bien drois que moi et vous
Aienz joie a nos volentez.
Amis, on me destraint por vous,
[Mais ne m'en chaut quant vous m'avez.][35]

(*My love, they torment me because of you, but I am not worried since I am yours.* You have vanquished that fellow. *My love they torment me because of you!* It is right that you and I should have all the happiness we want. *My love they torment me because of you, [but I am not worried since I am yours.]*)

Here the editor has restored *m'en* l. 2 for the *vous* found in four manuscripts, but he retains a redundant line after l. 4, and again omits the eighth line.

The creators of rondeaux clearly understood that the form had a standard rhyming scheme. In particular, the same eight-line form with the same rhyming scheme was subsequently specified as accompanying *caroles* in, for instance, *Le Castelain de Couci, Li Restor du Paon* and *Méliador*.[36] Deviations from the pattern can, for the most part, be attributed to scribal error. Nevertheless, voluntary departures from the form most certainly exist; but in such cases it is obvious

---

[35] *Roman de Laurin*, p. 95.

[36] Jakemes, *Le Roman du Castelain de Couci et de la Dame de Fayel*, ed. from notes by John E. Matzke by Maurice Delbouille (Paris, 1936), ll. 3857–64; Jean Brisebarre, *Jean Brisebarre*: *Li Restor du Paon*, ed. Enid Donkin (London, 1980), ll. 1170–73; Jean Froissart, *Méliador par Jean Froissart*, ed. Auguste Longnon (Paris, 1895–99), ll. 13305–11. For the text of the rondeau, 'Ensi va' in *Li Restor du Paon*, see Appendix A, Ex 2.

what the lyricist is doing. As an example of an exceptional rondeau cited as accompanying a *carole* we can turn to the second *carole* in *Le Castelain de Couci*:

Toute nostre gent
Sont li plus joli
Dou tournoiement.
S'aimment loiaument.
Toute nostre gent.
……………………
Et pour cou le di
Qu'il ont maintien gent.
Toute nostre gent
Sont li plus joli
Dou tournoiement.[37]

(*All our people are the happiest at the tournament.* They love one another faithfully, *all our people* […]. And for that I say that they have a noble bearing. *All our people are the happiest at the tournament.*)

The number of lines in the refrain has been increased to three, resulting in a rondeau consisting of 11 lines, although one line is missing in both manuscript sources. The word missing would have had a rhyme in *a*, because the lines between the partial internal repetition of the refrain and the final full repetition always anticipate the rhyming scheme of that full repetition. Thus, the form of the foregoing piece is *A*BAa*A*[a]ba*A*BA. Here the extension and development of the rondeau form is patently obvious.

The rondeau, of course, did not exist solely as an accompaniment to the *carole*; it had an independent existence. Adam de la Halle, in the late thirteenth century, composed 16 pieces entitled 'rondel' and 'rondiaus' in their principal manuscript source.[38] Half of these are in the standard eight-line form discussed above (Nos 2, 3, 6, 10, 11, 13, 14 and 15).[39] No 8, although in eight lines, is in monorhyme. On the other hand Nos 7 and 12 have 11 lines (the latter having the rhyming scheme that I conjecture is that of 'Toute nostre gent'). No 5 has 13 lines; Nos 1 and 9 have 14 lines; No 16 has 18 lines and No 4 has 24. Adam achieves this development by increasing the number both of the refrain lines and the non-refrain lines. Furthermore, in No 16 and No 4, he radically alters the structure although the form of the two pieces still adheres to the essential idea of the rondeau in his use of the refrain. No 16 has the rhyming scheme AAbcbccaAAbcbccaAA, and No 4 the rhyming scheme ABAccaABAddaABAeeaABA. All repetitions of the refrain are

---

[37] *Le Castelain de Couci*, ll. 989–9.

[38] See p. 65.

[39] The numbering of the lyrics is from Adam de la Halle, *The Lyric Works of Adam de la Halle*, ed. Nigel Wilkins, Corpus Mensurabilis Musicae, No 44 (n.p., 1967).

now complete repetitions, and the intervening non-repeated lines form complete 'stanzas', so to speak, which are linked to the refrain only by their last line. Another important aspect of these pieces is that, unlike the music for dancing of the period, which, as we shall see in the next chapter, was monophonic, all these rondeaux are for three voices. In short, here indeed we see the poet and composer at work. The changes wrought in the form are demonstrably intentional, not pointless deviations that destroy rather than create any semblance of an artistic form.

Adam's two longest rondeaux relate the form to the virelai because they are divided into 'stanzas' with the refrain stated at the beginning of the piece and after each of these 'stanzas', and with the rhyme of the last line of each connecting it to the refrain. The virelai is, in fact, a development of the rondeau. It begins with the refrain, which has the first section of the music. This is followed by two or three stanzas with the refrain and its music repeated after each. Each stanza is divided into three sections: the first is called the *ouvert*, and has the second section of the music; the second section of the stanza repeats the rhymes and music of the first section of the stanza, and is called the *clos*. This is followed by the third section, which repeats the rhymes and music of the refrain and is called the *tierce*. In the rondeau the rhymes between the internal partial statement of the refrain and the full final restatement of the refrain anticipate the rhyming scheme of that full restatement. Thus, for example, in the standard form of the rondeau, ABaAabAB, ab is followed by the final AB. This characteristic is reflected in the virelai, where the rhyming scheme of the *tierce* anticipates the return of the refrain (as in the following example from Froissart) consisting of two stanzas:

AABAAB||ccd|ccd|aabaab||A[ABAAB]|| ccd|ccd|aabaab||A[ABAAB][40]

(Refrain || *ouvert* | *clos* | *tierce* || Refrain || *ouvert* | *clos* | *tierce* || Refrain).

If there were music for this virelai the sections would be:

I || II | II | I || I || II | II | I || 1.

The 'rondeaux' of Jean de Lescurel, although not dance lyrics, include three pieces that are actually virelais of the type just described.[41] The term virelai itself dates from the thirteenth century when it was first applied to a meanlingless refrain, then to a song, then to a dance song.[42] It was not, however, used to designate a specific

40 Jean Froissart, 'Je ne sui onques si lie', in *La Prison amoureuse*, ed. Anthime Fourrier, Bibliothèque française et romane, Série B, No 13 (Paris, 1974), ll. 429–60.

41 Jean de Lescurel, *The Works of Jehan de Lescurel*, ed. Nigel Wilkins, Corpus Mensurabilis Musicae, 30 (n.p., 1966). Of the five pieces called virelais by Wilkins, Nos 20, 21 and 29 are virelais; Nos 10 and 32 are not.

42 On the development of the virelai, see Robert Mullally, 'Vireli, Virelai', *Neuphilologische Mitteilungen*, 101 (2000), 451–63.

form until the fourteenth century when Guillaume de Machaut appears to have been the first to use it in this sense.

The compositions of Adam de la Halle and Jean de Lescurel represent an art music development of the rondeau. But dance music itself was to become more sophisticated in the fourteenth century, or so the sources would seem to suggest. Pieces consisting of short groups of lines are no longer found; the rondeau, however, is still associated with the *carole* as performed by the upper echelons of society. But it may have been the case that the upper strata of society often preferred the virelai. Johannes de Grocheo, in his musical treatise in Latin, although he refers to the *rotundellus* (rondeau) does not relate it to dancing. Instead he reserves that function for the *ductia*, which, from his description, appears to be the virelai.[43] Another music theorist, Robertus de Handlo, writing in 1326, also seems to differentiate between rondeaux, ballades and dance songs when he makes a passing reference to 'rundelli, balade, coree'.[44] Guillaume de Machaut, in his *Remede de Fortune*, employs a virelai (which he would rather call a 'chançon balladee') to accompany a 'danse' which seems to be a *carole*, and the example from Froissart cited above of a virelai is specifically for a *carole*.[45]

If the rondeau and the virelai were lyrics associated with the *carole*, one might assume that the other *forme fixe*, the ballade, was also related to it, or at least to dancing in general. Its very derivation (Late Latin, *ballare*, to dance) might encourage us in this view, and many literary historians and critics have confidently assumed that this was the case. Yet evidence to support this assumption is all but impossible to find. What seems to be a unique exception is to be found in *Le Romans de la Dame a la Licorne et du biau Chevalier au Lyon*:

Apres disner sont en la voie
De dansser et de karoler.
Lors doucement prist a chanter
La Dame a la Lycorne et dist
Unne canchon et li souvint.[46]

[43] On Johannes de Grocheo's treatment of secular monophony in general and of dance music in particular, see Robert Mullally, 'Johannes de Grocheo's "Musica Vulgaris"', *Music & Letters*, 79 (1998), pp. 1–26.

[44] Robertus de Handlo, *Regule / The Rules, and* Johannes Hanboys, *Summa / The Summa*, ed. and trans. Peter M. Lefferts (Lincoln, NE, 1991), p. 15. Lefferts suggests, rightly I believe, that 'coree' here might mean virelais.

[45] Guillaume de Machaut, *Remede de Fortune*, ll. 3451–96, in *Le Jugement du roy de Behaigne* and *Remede de Fortune*, ed. James I. Wimsatt and William W. Kibler, music ed. Rebecca A. Baltzer (Athens, GA, 1988); Jean Froissart, *La Prison amoureuse*, ll. 429–60.

[46] *Le Romans de la Dame a la Lycorne et du biau Chevalier au Lyon: ein Abenteuerroman aus dem ersten Drittel des XIV. Jahrhunderts*, ed. Friedrich Gennrich, Gesellschaft für romanische Literatur, No 18 (Dresden, 1908), ll. 5267–71.

(After dining they are off to dance and carol. Then the Lady of the Unicorn began to sing, and sweetly perform a song that she remembered.)

These lines are followed by the rubric 'Conment la Dame a la Lycorne chante et mainne la dansce et y est son ami' (How the Lady of the Unicorn sings, and leads the dance, and takes part in it with her lover.) A lyric in the form of a ballade follows. The exceptional inclusion of this form as a dance lyric may possibly be due to the fact that most of the twenty-six lyric insertions in this romance are ballades, and are sometimes named as such in the text.

In summary, then, particular forms of lyric were associated with the *carole*. The simple groups of lines developed into the more sophisticated, and perhaps more aristocratic, forms of the rondeau and the virelai. The earlier, shorter pieces, popular in style, were subject to vagaries in their transmission, no doubt because they were less valued than other kinds of verse. Only the later rondeaux and virelais, the work of poets and composers, fared better. Although we can now identify the lyrics for the *carole* and even for the *tresche*, it remains to be seen how these pieces related to the dance in performance, in other words, how they were set to music, and how that music was related to the dance.

Chapter 8
The Music

The situation regarding the music of the *carole* stands in parallel to the lyrics. Not sufficient attention has been paid to pieces denominated 'dance music' to ascertain whether in fact they justify the term, and still less as to whether the piece or pieces in question relate to any particular dance or dance form. Even if a composition could be so described, what is important from the dance historian's point of view is whether such a piece could actually be represented as being intended for dancing. There is a difference between art music and *Gebrauchsmusik*. Composers have frequently taken up dance forms and elaborated on them, sometimes to the extent that they are hardly recognizable any longer as dance music. An indication of the way in which a piece of music can be transformed was given in the last chapter where we saw that the standard monophonic rondeau employed for dancing could become the varied polyphonic rondeau unrelated to dancing. Compositions in a dance form, whether intended for dancing or not, often bear the the title of a dance form. With the *carole*, however, we are confronted with a seemingly intractable difficulty: there is no piece of music called a *carole*.

This extraordinary circumstance has led some musicologists to conclude that no music for this dance exists. Gérold, for example, writing about 'les caroles et les tresques' of the later Middle Ages, laments that 'malheureusement, pour cette époque comme pour la précédente, les documents musicaux manquent' (unfortunately for this period, as for the previous one, documented music is lacking).[1] Indeed the opinion has even been expressed that neither lyrics nor music for the *carole* is extant. Stevens in his entry in an earlier edition of the standard English dictionary of music states that 'no single *carole*, so designated, survives as a complete text, literary or musical'.[2] In a later study on medieval music he concluded that 'the *carole* must surely have been not *a* single form but a potential form, a dance-*idea*, waiting to be realized in various forms' (his italics).[3] It is true that no lyric or piece of music entitled 'carole' exists; but the French term refers exclusively to the choreography, while the lyrics, and by implication their tunes, were generally, as we have seen, called *chanson* or *chansonette*.

---

1 Théodore Gérold, *La Musique au Moyen Age* (Paris, 1932), p. 301.

2 John Stevens, *New Grove 1*, 'Carole.

3 John Stevens, *Words and Music in the Middle Ages: Song, Narrative, Dance and Drama 1050–1350* (Cambridge, 1986), p. 175.

Neither of the earliest sources that contain *carole* lyrics, *Guillaume de Dole* or the *Roman de la Violette*, include the required music.[4] This fact notwithstanding, music for the phrases 'ne vos repentez mie / de loiaument amer' in the song in ' La jus desouz l'olive' in *Guillaume de Dole* is quoted in a different song in the manuscript known as the 'Chansonnier de Noailles' as well as in other sources.[5] As the lyric bears some similarity to the rondeau, the music for these two lines contains all that is required to reconstruct the music of the whole piece. In the same manner the same chansonnier preserves all the music needed, for example, for 'Ja ne mi marïerai' in the *Roman de la Violette*.[6] Unfortunately the notation in all such sources is non-mensural, and as dance music is essentially mensural, any transcription depends on the transcriber's own rhythmic interpretation.

There are, however, a considerable number of dance tunes notated mensurally in other manuscripts. The system of mensuration used in this period was based on rhythmic patterns known as modes. These were generally counted as being six in number, and dance music, as will become evident, was in Mode 1. This mode has a trocaic rhythm in which a note called a Longa is twice as long as the Brevis that follows it, thus indicating a trocaic rhythm. Music in this mode is to be found in a piece specifically named a 'cantilena de chorea', 'Nobilitas ornata moribus', a musical insertion based on a French dance tune, which is found in the closet drama in Latin, *Ludus super Anticlaudianum*.[7] There are two especially valuable sources of dance music. One is the La Vallière manuscript, which contains the music for the *carole* 'Ja ne lairai' (*Le Roman de la Violette*), 'An si bone conpaignie' (*Le Tournoi de Chauvency*) and the 'canchon a carole' 'J'ai pensee a tel i a' (*Renart le Nouvel*).[8] More interestingly, the manuscript provides the four tunes for a *carole* that is actually performed by the animal characters in *Renart le Nouvel*: 'Vous

[4] Jean Renart, *Le Roman de la Rose ou de Guillaume de Dole*, ed. Félix Lecoy (1962; rpt Paris, 1979); Gerbert de Montreuil, *Le Roman de la Violette ou de Gérart de Nevers par Gerbert de Montreuil*, ed. Douglas Labaree Buffum (Paris, 1928).

[5] *Guillaume de Dole*, ll. 2373–4; 'Chansonnier de Noailles', fol. 122v. For this latter source and others, see Maria Vedder Fowler, 'Musical Interpolations in Thirteenth- and Fourteenth-Century French Narratives', PhD. Diss., Yale University, 1979, p. 359.

[6] *Le Roman de la Violette*, ll. 119–20, 'Chansonnier de Noailles', fol. 191v.

[7] Adam de la Bassée, *Ludus super Anticlaudianum*, ed. Abbé Paul Bayart (Tourcoing, 1930), with a facsimile of the music on p. 250 and an edition of it on p. 323.

[8] PBN, fonds fr. 25566 (1291–97), (MS W), fols 167r, 164v, 146r. The lyric will be found respectively in *Roman de la Violette*, ll .152–3; Jacques Bretel, *Le Tournoi de Chauvency*, ed. Maurice Delbouille, Bibliothèque de la Faculté de Philosophie et Lettres de l'Université de Liège, No 49 (Liège, 1932), l. 3118; Jacquemart Gielée, *Renart le Nouvel*, ed. Henri Roussel (Paris, 1961), following l. 4411.

n'ales mie', 'Ja ne serai sans amour', 'Tres douche dame jolie' and 'Hé, Dieus' (See Plates 1 and 2, and also Appendix A, Ex. 1).[9]

Another important source is the Montpellier Codex, a vast collection of polyphonic motets. Incorporated into some of these works are the melodies of monophonic dances. Apart from the *carole* tune 'Je tien par la main m'amie' (*Art d'Amours*), it furnishes one of the two rare examples of tunes for a *tresche*, 'Fui te gaite' (*Court d'Amour: Suite anonyme*).[10] The other *tresche* tune is 'Venés apres moi' in *Le Jeu de Robin et de Marion*, and is to be found in the principal source of that play.[11] The tune of this latter piece is in two sections, the second of which is concordant with the *carole* tune 'Vous ne li sariés' as Fowler notes.[12] Thus music for the *tresche* can be seen to be the same as that of the *carole*, lending further support to the idea that the two dances were almost identical.

The music considered so far, with the exception of 'Nobilitas ornate moribus', does not include any setting of a rondeau to accompany dancing. In fact the only example, apart from the one just cited, is the setting in one of the 16 manuscripts of *Li Restor du Paon*. In this manuscript the music for the *carole* performed in the course of the narrative is to be found almost fully notated (See Plate 3 and Appendix A, Ex. 2).[13]

---

[9] La Vallière MS, fols 128^{v}-129^{r}: for the context, including the lyrics, see *Renart le Nouvel*, ll. 2535–61. There are three other manuscripts of *Renart le Nouvel*: PBN, fonds fr. 372 (MS Cangé, s. xiv^{int}), PBN, fonds fr. 1593 (MS Fauchet, s. xiii^{ex} or s.xiv ^{int}), PBN fonds fr. 1581 (MS Lancelot, s. xiii^{ex}). The first two of these contain music but Fowler points out (p. 331) that 'Manuscript W … is the most reliable source for the melodies of *Renart le Nouvel*'. For a study of the relationship between all the tunes in the three manuscripts, see Anne Ibos-Augé, 'Les Insertions lyriques dans le roman de Renard le Nouvel: éléments de recherche musicale', *Romania*, 118 (2000), 375–93.

[10] See Montpellier, Faculté de Médicine, MS H 196, fols. 256^{v} and 315 $^{r-v}$ for the tunes cited here. For an edition with facsimiles, see *Polyphonies du XIIIe siècle: le manuscrit H. 196 de la Faculté de Médecine de Montpellier*, ed. Yvonne Rokseth (Paris, 1935–39), with facsimiles in Vol. I and with editions in Vol. III, 50 and 140–41, respectively. A more recent edition without facsimiles is *The Montpellier Codex*, ed. Hans Tischler, Recent Researches in the Music of the Middle Ages and Early Renaissance, (Madison, WI, 1978), III, 40 and 115, respectively. For the lyrics, see *L'Art d'amours: traduction et commentaire de l'*Ars Amatoria *d'Ovide*, ed. Bruno Roy (Leiden, 1974), II, 161: Matthieu le Poirier, *Le Court d'Amours de Mahieu le Poirier et la Suite anonyme de la* Court d'Amours, ed. Terence Scully (Waterloo, Ontario, 1976), [Lyric No] XXXIII.

[11] For the text and music of 'Venés après moi', see Adam de la Halle, *Le Jeu de Robin et de Marion*, ed. Kenneth Varty (London, 1960), ll. 762–3. The musical transcription [p. 37] is by Eric Hill.

[12] Fowler, p. 335.

[13] The manuscript is Oxford, Bodleian Libarary, Bodley MS 264, and the rondeau appears on fol. 181^{v}. See Jean Brisebarre, *Le Restor du Paon*, ed. Richard J. Carey (Geneva, 1966), pp. 210–12, for a reproduction of the music, his transcription of it (different from mine) and a discussion of both the music and the lyric. Carey, however, uses as base

Before going any further it must be mentioned that there are three dance pieces that do not present a clearly defined trocaic rhythm throughout and seem, therefore, to be exceptions to the rule. The trocaic rhythm is evident in the second of the two sections of the music for the *tresche* 'Venes après moi', but not in the first section in Adam de la Halle's play *Le Jeu de Robin et de Marion*.[14] The characteristic dance rhythm is not to be found at all in the short dance song. 'Onques mes n'amai' quoted in Jehannot de l'Escurel's *dit enté* 'Gracieus temps est', and cited as a dance song in Jacques Bretel's narrative poem, *Le Tournoi de Chauvency*.[15] Again there is no sign of a defining trocaic rhythm in the virelai 'Dame, a vous sans retollir', for the 'danse' in Guillaume de Machaut's *Remede de Fortune*.[16] It will have been noticed that composers had a hand in all three pieces, and, as observed at the beginning of this chapter, composers noted for their art music tend to bring their own interpretations to dance music.

Music for both the *carole* and the *tresche*, then, survives. A problem, however, arises when this music is transcribed into modern notation. It is possible to transcribe a given mode into different modern time signatures. It might seem obvious that the Longa-Brevis of Mode 1 would easily translate into a basic minim–crochet rhythm, namely into 3/4 time, and that is, in fact, what many transcribers have done. Gennrich, with some exceptions, adopts this triple time in his transcriptions and reconstructions of dance songs.[17] Stevens approves of this: 'subsequent discussion will show, I think, that Gennrich's triple-time transcription is more likely to be right than a transcription based on the isosyllabic principle'.[18] Certainly an isosyllabic transcription can be ruled out. Fowler, with one or two exceptions, transcribes the dance pieces into 3/4 time. Transcriptions in triple time, however, even if widely used, are not invariably used. Indeed Van der Werf doubts whether any mensural transcription is appropriate: 'furthermore, since nothing is known about the meter of medieval dances, there is no reason to take

---

manuscript for his text, PBN, fonds, fr. 12565. *Jean Brisebarre; Li Restor du Paon*, ed. Enid Donkin (London, 1980) uses the Bodleian manuscript, but does not reproduce or transcribe the music. The unnamed scribe of the Bodleian copy (which includes *The Romance of Alexander*) finished his work on 18 December 1338, and the illustrator, Jean de Grise, finished his on 18 April 1344. For these dates and a facsimile of the whole manuscript see, *The Romance of Alexander: A Collotype Facsimile of MS Bodley 264*, with an introduction by M. R. James (Oxford, 1933), p.1. The scribe has not left space above the last two lines of the lyric for the music, but this can be supplied from the first two lines.

[14] See note 11 above.

[15] Jehannot de l'Escurel, *The Works of Jehan de Lescurel*, ed. Nigel Wilkins, Corpus Mensurabilis Musicae, No 30 (n.p., 1966), p. 30; Jacques Bretel, *Le Tournoi*), l. 2462.

[16] Guillaume de Machaut, *Remede de Fortune* in *Le Jugement du roy de Behaigne* and *Remede de Fortune*, ed. James I. Wimsatt and William W. Kibler; mus. ed. Rebecca A. Baltzer (Athens, GA, 1988). ll. 3451–70.

[17] See, for example, *Rondeaux, Virelais und Balladen*, ed. Friedrich Gennrich, Gesellschaft für romanische Literatur, No 43 (Dresden, 1921), Nos 5, 7, 11 and 309.

[18] Stevens, *Words and Music*, p. 188.

it for granted that all dancing songs were performed in a ternary meter'.[19] He therefore transcribes the famous Occitan song, 'A l'entrada del tens clar', which he, in common with others, believes to be a dance song, although there is no evidence for this, into non-mensural notation.[20] Rimmer makes the following prescient observation on Van der Werf's pronouncement: 'while his conclusion is undoubtedly true, the premise on which it was based is not'.[21]

Following what was said above about transcriptions, it is not surprising to find that those who have transcribed dance music do not choose the same time signature even when transcribing the same piece. 'Nobilitas ornata moribus' appears in 6/8 time but also in 3/4 time.[22] Rokseth transcribes the motet that incorportates the *carole* song 'Je tiens' in 3/8; Tischler transcribes the same music in 6/8.[23] Gennrich has a time signature of 3/8 for 'Vous n'alés mie' (*Renart le Nouvel*); Stevens and Fowler have it in 3/4.[24] Gennrich employs 6/8 for the rondeau, 'Ensi va', which Carey transcribes in 12/8.[25] Similarly with the *tresche* pieces: Rokseth, of course, puts 'Fui te gaite, in 3/4 time, Tischler in 6/4.[26] The *tresche* in *Le Jeu de Robin et de Marion* is found both in 3/4 time and in 6/4 time.[27]

Editors may reasonably differ in their transcription of pieces and arrangements of pieces that are not intended for dancing as in the Montpellier insertions, but music for dancing must have a specific rhythm. The choreography of the *carole*, and almost certainly the *tresche*, consists of two steps – a step to the left followed by joining the right foot to the left. This requires the music to be in duple time, which, taking into account the trocaic rhythm of Mode 1, means that tunes for both the dances should be transcribed in 6/8 time. The only variation in the tunes that seems to be permissible is that in some pieces there is evidence of anacrusis, that is to say they are in what Roesner calls 'mode I with an upbeat'.[28] Examples of dance songs where this feature has been actually applied in transcription

---

[19] *The Chansons of the Troubadours and Trouvères*, ed. Hendrik van der Werf (Utrecht, 1972), pp. 98–99.

[20] *The Chansons*, p. 98.

[21] Joan Rimmer, 'Dance Elements in Trouvère Repertory', *Dance Research*, 3/2 (1985), p. 26.

[22] *Ludus* (p. 323) and Fowler (p. 523) in 6/8 time; *Rondeaux*, ed. Gennrich, I, No 345 and Stevens, *Words and Music* (p. 194) in 3/4 time.

[23] *Polyphonies*, ed. Rokseth, III, 50 [No 225]; *The Montpellier Codex*, ed. Tischler, III, 40 [No 225].

[24] *Rondeaux*, II, 156; Stevens, *Words and Music*, p. 195; Fowler, p. 465.

[25] *Rondeaux*, ed. Gennrich, I, No 353; *Le Restor*, ed. Carey, p. 212.

[26] *Polyphonies*, ed. Rokseth, III, 140–41 [No 279]; *The Montpellier Codex*, ed. Tischler, III, 115 [No 279].

[27] Adam de la Halle, *Le Jeu de Robin et de Marion*; the musical transcription in this edition [p. 37] is in 3/4 time as in Fowler (p. 463); Gennrich, II, 89, chooses 6/4.

[28] *Le Magnus Liber Organi de Notre-Dame de Paris*, ed. Edward H. Roesner (Monaco, 1993), I, lxxxvii.

include the *cantilena de chorea* 'Nobilitas ornate moribus', the *carole* songs 'Vous n'ales mie' and 'Avec tele conpaignie'. It might also be applied in the *tresche* song 'Venés après moi'.[29]

If one major question concerning the music of the *carole* is its rhythmic interpretation, the other is the actual performance of the music. Here literary texts are more helpful than exclusively musical manuscripts.

As we saw in the last chapter, the *carole* and the *tresche* were always accompanied by songs sung by the dancers themselves. Our first task, therefore, is to discover who sang these songs, how many songs were sung and how they were distributed among the performers. Male participants are occasionally named as singers. The eponymous character himself is the singer in *Guillaume le Maréchal*, and he is followed by a herald.[30] Three men sing one song each for the second *carole* in *Guillaume de Dole*.[31] The singers are women in several romances, and where only one singer is named it is usually a woman. The singers of the seven songs for the *carole* in the *Roman de la Violette* are all women, although men are evidently taking part in the dance.[32] Of course, just as the dancers can be mixed, so the singers can be mixed in which case the sexes do not necessarily seem to sing alternately.

The record of the number of songs sung for a *carole* varies. In some descriptions the author simply states that singing took place. In other accounts only a single song is cited as in *Li Restor du Paon*.[33] Such brief performances may be due to demands of the narrative. In the second *carole* in the *Tournoi de Chauvency* the dancing is cut short when a herald enters the hall, and orders the dancing to stop, which obviously indicates that not only the dancing, but also the singing is curtailed.[34] On the other hand many narratives suggest the involvement of a succession of singers, each singing one song, as, for example, in both performances in *Guillaume de Dole*, the seven songs sung in the *Roman de la Violette* (the largest number quoted for a single *carole*) and *Renart le Nouvel*.[35] Even where all the songs are not actually quoted, a sequence of songs is indicated. For the second *carole* in the *Roman de Laurin*, Dyogenne sings a quoted rondeau, but a number of unquoted songs follow: 'la querolle si dura moult longuement et si y ot moult dites de chançons'

[29] For example, in Fowler, pp. 523 and 465 and *Le Jeu, ibid.*

[30] *History of William Marshal*, ed. A. J. Holden, trans. S. Gregory, [historical notes by D. Crouch], Anglo-Norman Text Society, Occasional Series Publication No 4 (London, 2002–) I, ll. 3471–94.

[31] *Guillaume de Dole*, ll. 2360–94.

[32] *Roman de la Violette*, ll. 92–155.

[33] *Li Restor*, ed. Donkin, ll.1159–73.

[34] *Le Tournoi*, ll. 3094–128.

[35] *Guillaume de Dole*, ll. 505–50 and ll. 2360–94; *Roman de la Violette, ibid.*; *Renart le Nouvel*, ll. 2534–56.

(the *carole* lasted a very long time, and many songs were sung).[36] Similarly in the *Castellain de Couci* 'Ma dame de Faiiel' sings a rondeau, then another lady sings, and the poet adds 'Dire ne compter ne vous sai / Les cancons que on y canta' (I cannot say or tell you the number of songs that were sung there).[37] The conclusion, to which this evidence seems to point, is that several songs were usually sung in the performance of a *carole*.

If the songs were sung in succession, and the individual singer is indicated, then one might infer that each of these performances was a solo. Many of these songs had no refrains. There are, however, several exceptions, most obviously the eight-line rondeaux. In such cases Jeanroy proposed that a soloist sang the non-repeated lines of the lyric, and the other participants in the dance joined in the refrains as a chorus, and this theory has been widely accepted. As evidence, a passage in *Méraugis de Portlesguez* has been cited:

> Entor le pin por caroler
> Avoit puceles qui chantoient.
> As caroles qu'eles fesoient
> N'avoit qu'un tot sol chevalier.
> Iluec por la joie esforcier
> Chantoit avant.[38]
>
> (There were girls singing around the pine for *caroles*. In the *caroles* that they were performing, there was only a single knight. There, to add to the enjoyment, he led the singing.)

But the knight, Outedotez, does not lead a chorus here. 'Chantoit avant' means that the knight sang first, and the girls sang individually in succession after him. This seems more likely because more than one *carole* was danced. Later Méraugis joins the dance: '... lors vet caroler / L'escu au col et chante avant' (... then he joins the *carole* with his shield slung around his neck, and he leads the singing.).[39] The implication is that when Méraugis joins the *carole*, he takes over the singing. Similar ambiguous passages occur in other narrative poems.

On the other hand the case for choral involvement may seem to be reinforced by the use of the verb *respondre* (literally 'to answer'). In the general context of singing, examples where people 'answer' in a song are not hard to find. But when

---

[36] *Le Roman de Laurin, fils de Marques le Sénéchal*, ed. Lewis Thorpe, University of Nottingham Research Publication, No 2 (Cambridge, 1960), pp. 134–5.

[37] Jakemes, *Le Roman du Castelain de Couci et de la Dame de Fayel*, ed. from notes by John E. Matzke by Maurice Delbouille (Paris, 1936), ll. 3869–70.

[38] Raoul de Houdenc, *Méraugis de Portlesguez*, ll. 3674–79 in *Raoul von Houdenc: sämtliche Werke nach allen bekannten Handschriften*, ed. Mathias Friedwagner, (Halle, 1897–1909).

[39] *Méraugis*, ll. 3702–03.

these examples are examined closely it is by no means clear that choral singing is taking place. Confining ourselves to instances applicable to dance songs, we can cite, for example, the following lines from Froissart's *Méliador*:

> On ne fu mies longement
> En sejour que la Luciienne
> Ala ossi dire le sienne,
> Qui fu liement respondue,
> Car elle fu bien entendue ...[40]
>
> (One had not to wait long before Lucienne also began her [song], which was joyfully received, because she was heard with great attention ...)

The idea conveyed by *respondue* here is that Lucienne's song is well received by the other participants in the dance, not that the others joined in the singing. A similar impression is imparted in another of Froissart's narrative poems, *La Prison amoureuse*, describing the celebrations at Chambéry in 1368: 'Mainte canchon bonne et nouvelle / On y chanta et respondi' (many a good new song was sung, and 'answered'), but then 'L'un apriés l'autre sans detri / Chantoient sicom par estri' (one sang after the other without a pause, and they sang to their hearts' content).[41] Froissart's virelai 'Je ne sui onques si lie' is sung and

> Tout chil et chelles qui oïrient
> Che virelay s'en resjoïrent
> Et fu moult grandement prisiés.[42]
>
> (All those men and women who heard this virelai were delighted by it, and it was greatly appreciated.).

The singers sing one after the other; they do not join in the refrain of the virelai, but respond enthusiastically to it. In the *Tournoi de Chauvency*, a lady sings for dancing, and the passage continues:

> Jehans d'Oiseler la menoit,
> Qui cortoisement la tenoit.
> En chantant li a respondu,
> Si haut que tuit l'ont entendu,
> A clere vois, cette chanson:

---

[40] Jean Froissart, *Méliador par Jean Froissart*, ed. Auguste Longnon (Paris, 1895–99), ll. 22876–80.

[41] Jean Froissart, *La Prison amoureuse*, ed. Anthime Fourrier, Bibliothèque française et romane, Série B, No 13 (Paris, 1974), ll. 410–11, 417–18.

[42] *La Prison amoureuse*, ll. 461–3.

'Améz moi, blondete, améz,
Et je n'amerai se vos non!'[43]

(Jehan d'Oiseler led her, and courteously held her by the hand. He 'answered' her by singing the following song so loudly, and in a clear voice that everyone could hear: 'Love me, my sweet blonde, love me, and I shall not love anyone but you'.)

In this instance, quite obviously, 'Jehan d'Oiseler' 'answers' simply by singing another song; no other singer takes part. All these examples make choral participation seem highly unlikely. Rather the implication is of a succession of solo singers, that *respondre* means in these situations 'to respond', and denotes the reaction of the other dancers as, in the *carole* in *Le Roman du comte d'Anjou*: 'chacun lez respond liement' (everone responds joyfully).[44] It is this reaction that is constantly emphasized. The observation made by several medieval French authors on the favourable reception of the singing of a song suggests, perhaps, that it was this aspect that constituted the chief pleasure of the performance, rather than that of the dance itself, which could not have been simpler. Yet it was the performance of the dance that provided the motivation for the singing of a succession of songs by different performers, and therefore it had a critical social importance.

As with the lyrics, dance songs are to be found in contexts in which there is no dancing. They can be incorporated into both monophonic and polyphonic motets. Even as independent monophonic songs, they can be performed in different ways. 'Une dame de Normendie' sings 'Ja ne lairai' for the *carole* in the *Roman de la Violette*, but a lady also sings it when there is no dancing in *Renart le Nouvel*.[45] More significantly 'madame de Lucembour' sings 'An si bone conpaignie' for a *carole* in *Le Tournoi de Chauvency*, but it reappears slightly varied as a lyric sung in its own right by a character in *Renart le Nouvel*, and as a monophonic choral number (the only one in the play) in *Le Jeu de Robin et de Marion*.[46] The 'princhesse de Tarente' sings 'Fui te, gaite' for the 'treske' in the *Cours d'Amours: Suite*, and several young gentlemen sing it, slightly varied and obviously in unison, in another example from *Le Tournoi de Chauvency*.[47] These citations show not only that a song sung in one context for a *carole* or a *tresche* can be sung in another without dancing, but also that it can be sung by a singer of a different sex or by a group of people in a unison chorus, again without dancing.

The *carole*, then, like the *tresche*, was invariably accompanied by the singing of the dancers themselves. The question arises, however, whether instruments

43 *Le Tournoi*, ll. 2485–90.

44 Jean Maillart, *Le Roman du comte d'Anjou*, ed. Mario Roques (Paris, 1931), l. 2880.

45 *Roman de la Violette*, ll. 152–4, *Renart le Nouvel*, l. 6841ff.

46 *Le Tournoi*, l. 3115–18; *Renart le Nouvel*, l. 6630ff; *Le Jeu de Robin et de Marion*, [p.37].

47 *Le Court d'Amours*, ll. 3649–56 and No XXXIII; *Le Tournoi*, ll. 2340–51.

also took part, even if only on some occasions, in the performance of these two dances. Some scholars incline to the view that instruments might sometimes have been used. Gérold concludes that 'un instrument marquant le rythme, tel que le tambour, accompagnait parfois le chant' (an instrument marking the rhythm, such as a drum, sometimes accompanied the singing).[48] Sahlin tentatively arrives at the same conclusion: 'il arrivait aussi, mais rarement, qu'on s'accompagnait d'instruments aux caroles' (it also happened, although rarely, that *caroles* were accompanied by instruments), and she quotes lines from the *Roman de la Rose* and other texts (to be discussed presently) as possible instances.[49] Fowler, while agreeing about the use of instruments for dancing in general, is more circumspect about their use in the *carole*. 'Dancing', she affirms, 'is frequently accompanied by instruments', but she later points out, in relation to a passage in Froissart's *Méliador*, that 'it would seem here that the caroling was not accompanied, or at least did not need to be accompanied'.[50]

The problem with some of the examples cited in support of the employment of instruments is that carolling appears to be only one of a number of activites taking place in the passages cited. Gérold, as evidence for the use of instruments, cites a couplet from the *Roman des Sept Sages*: 'Li jougleour vont vielant / Et les borjoises karolant' (the minstrels go about playing the vielle, and the citizens go carolling).[51] Yet there is no reason to assume that, in contexts like this, the jongleurs are accompanying the dancing rather than that the instrumental music and the dancing are two separate activites.[52] In this connexion Sahlin's citation of the *Roman de la Rose* calls for further comment.[53] In the romance we first have the *carole* for which Leesce sings. Next there is the music of the 'fleüteors' and the other instrumentalists. Then there are the 'tableteresses' and the 'timberesses' who juggle with their 'timbres'. Finally there are the two girls whom Deduit makes 'em mi la querole baler' (dance in the middle of the *carole*). The performance of the two girls is explicitly not part of the dance. Neither is juggling essential to it. It cannot be assumed, therefore, that the instrumentalists are necessarily involved either. Indeed the *carole* and the instrumental music seem to be separated by the rhetorical effect of the syntax; 'Lors veïssiez quarole aler … La veïssiez fleüteors / et menestreus et jugleors' (there you might see a carole being performed …

---

48 Gérold, *La Musique*, p. 299.

49 Sahlin, pp. 20–21.

50 Fowler, pp. 214–16.

51 *Le Roman des Sept Sages*, ed. Jean Misrahi (Paris, 1933), ll. 697–8; Gérold, *La Musique*, p. 299.

52 Neither is there any reason to assume that the 'dance a vïele' (*Le Tournoi*, l. 2403) is a *carole*. There are passages in other texts in which the dancing of *caroles* and the playing of instruments are mentioned in the same general context, but in which the two activities should be construed as distinct.

53 Sahlin, pp. 20–21 and Guillaume de Lorris and Jean de Meun, *Le Roman de la Rose*, ed. Félix Lecoy (Paris, 1965–70), ll. 741–56, for what follows in my text..

there you might see minstrels and *jongleurs*). Here, then, it would appear that instruments are not accompanying the *carole*, but rather that four separate activities are taking place. It is, perhaps, significant that Gui de Mori, in this passage in his *remaniement* (completed in 1290) of the *Roman de la Rose*, although he made several excisions in the text, includes the *carole*, but omits all reference to the 'menéstrels' and the 'jongleurs'.[54]

Yet examples can be cited where, in the performance of both the *carole* and the *tresche*, instruments are unambiguously involved. In the thirteenth-century poem, *La Court de Paradis*, the four evangelists play horns, and in one of the manuscripts of the work, a rubric reads 'la Feste de Touz Sainz et la Querole de Paradis' (the Feast of All Saints and the *Carole* in Paradise)[55]. In Jean le Fèvre's French version of the *Lamentationes Matheoli*, many a citole, many a vielle and many a harp are said to have provided the music for a heavenly *carole*.[56] But the manuscript cited here of *La Court de Paradis* is late and corrupt, and the so-called *carole* in the *Lamentationes* contains movements found in no other description of the dance.[57] We can, therefore, safely disregard these celestial performances.

Nevertheless accounts of more mundane dances are to be found in which instruments take part. In two thirteenth-century *fabliaux* this is clearly the case. In one, a cowherd plays the drum on Sundays for the *carole*.[58] In the other, a woman marries a thief, and the neighbours sing and lead the same dance to the sound of tambourines and vielles.[59] In a fourteenth-century poem, servant girls are rebuked for imitating their betters by carolling through the streets with drums

---

[54] This version of the *Roman de la Rose* remains unedited. Marc-René Jung, however, 'Gui de Mori et Guillaume de Lorris', *Vox Romanica*, 27 (1968), 106, gives the date of composition, and describes the manuscripts. He notes departures from the original version and, particularly relevant to the present context, the omission of 'le passage sur les ménéstrels et les jongleurs' (the passage on the minstrels and jongleurs), p. 117.

[55] *La Court de Paradis: poème anonyme du XIIIe siècle*, ed. Eva Vilamo-Pentti, Suomalaisen Tiedeakatemian Toimituksia, Series B, No 79/1 (Helsinki, 1953), p. 24. For the manuscripts, see p. 20.

[56] Jean Le Fèvre, *Les Lamentations de Matheolus et le Livre de Leesce de Jehan le Fevre de Resson*, ed. Anton-Gérard van Hamel (Paris, 1892–1905), ll. 2918–22.

[57] Of MS C of *La Court de Paradis* (the latest and the one cited here), the editor says (p. 24) 'le texte que ce manuscript donne de notre poème est le moins soigné de tous' (the text that this manuscript provides is the least correct of all).

[58] 'Le Flabel d'Aloul' in *Recueil général et complet des fabliaux des XIIIe et XIVe siècles imprimés ou inédits*, ed. Anatole de Montaiglon and Gaston Raynaud (Paris, 1872–90), I, 276.

[59] 'De la fame qui pris a mari lo larron', in the *Ysopet de Lyon*, reproduced in facsimile in *Bibliothèque de la Ville de Lyon: documents paléographiques, typographiques, iconographiques*, ed. R. Cantinelli (Lyon, 1923), II/I, Plate V. The piece is edited in *Lyoner Ysopet: altfranzösische Übersetzung des XIII. Jahrhunderts in der Mundart der Franche-Comté*, ed. Wendelin Foerster, Altfranzösische Bibliothek, No 5 (Heilbronn, 1882), p. 10.

and bagpipes.[60] *Le Jeu de Robin et de Marion* ends with Robin leading the other characters in a *tresche* with three fellow shepherds playing two horns and a bagpipe.[61] Such examples have been cited by Sahlin as evidence of instrumental involvement. What has not been noticed, however, is that all the participants in these cases are of low social status quite unlike the courtly dancers described in most texts.

One cannot ignore, however, the fact that a few sources actually describe courtly performances of *caroles* with instruments. A case in point is the *Chevalier du Papagau*:

> Quant ilz orent mengé a leur voulenté, a grant aise et a grant solas, et les tables furent levees, ilz ont commensé par la sale grant karoles et merveilleuses a son de viëlles et de arpes et d'autres estrumens que les jogleurs sonnoyent par le palais moult doulcement.[62]

> (When they had eaten all they wanted to their great pleasure and satisfaction, and the tables were removed, they began great and wonderful *caroles* throughout the hall to the sound of vielles and harps and other instruments that the musicians played very sweetly throughout the palace.)

An identical situation is found in *Perceforest*: the guests eat, then the tables are removed, and instruments lead the *caroles*.[63] Although both the *Chevalier du Papegau* and *Perceforest* were composed in the fourteenth century, all but one of the manuscripts of both texts date from the fifteenth century, and in all of them the language has been 'modernized'. Moreover the collocation of the instruments named in the *Chevalier du Papegau* ('viëles' and 'arpes') is something of a stereotyped phrase in this work, and is repeated at other places in the text. As for *Perceforest*, Flutre points out that all the sources are corrupt.[64] It should also be noted that in the fifteenth century the *carole* was replaced as the dance most in request by the *basse danse*, which was accompanied by instruments without voices. The revisers of the two texts, therefore, were probably influenced by the practice of their time. The performance, then, of the both the *carole* and the *tresche* did not involve the use of instruments except when these dances were executed by the lowest stratum of society.

---

60 Gilles le Muisit, *Poésies de Gilles li Muisis*, ed. Baron Joseph Kervyn de Lettenhove (Louvain, 1882), II, 192–3.

61 *Le Jeu*, ll. 736–69.

62 *Le Chevalier du Papegau*, ed. Ferdinand Heuckenkamp (Halle, 1896), pp. 41–2.

63 *Le Roman de Perceforest: première partie*, ed. Jane H. M. Taylor (Geneva, 1979), pp. 164–5.

64 Louis-Ferdinand Flutre, 'Etudes sur le Roman de *Perceforêt*: premier article', *Romania*, 70 (1948), 475.

In fact instruments are entirely absent in most descriptions of the *carole* so that their use in conjunction with either the *carole* or the *tresche* is exceptional. Thus even when instruments were available it was considered inappropriate to use them to accompany the *carole*. In Froissart's *La Prison amoureuse*, the wind players play 'estampies' to accompany the *hove danse*, but they stop playing when the *carole*, which follows it, begins. This is not only the situation in the fictional account but also apparently on the actual occasion of the celebrations at Chambéry in 1368.[65] It may be remarked in passing that Froissart's narration of the dancing in the poem is the earliest citation of the term *hove danse*, which, unlike the *carole*, seems to have been a couple dance accompanied by instruments, typically shawms.[66]

To conclude about the *carole* and its performance, more than sufficient evidence exists not only about the dance, but also about the lyrics and the music that accompanied it, and the same, to a lesser extent, may be said of the *tresche*. The choreography of the dance can be fully documented. The music for the dance exists, and we know the manner in which it was sung and played and by whom. The *carole*, then, is the earliest western European dance that can be performed with any degree of certainty. The evidence comes from the medieval manuscripts themselves. Some of these manuscripts, especially those of the *Roman de la Rose*, contain miniatures, and some of these purport, at least, to depict the *carole*. The question, therefore, is whether these illustrations add to our knowledge of the dance, confirm what we already know in whole or in part or even contradict it.

---

65 Jean Froissart, *La Prison amoureuse*, ll. 354–460 and *Chroniques de J. Froissart*, ed. Siméon Luce *et al.* (Paris, 1869–1975), VII, 64.

66 On the hove dance, see Robert Mullally, 'Houes Danses', *Neophilologus*, 76 (1992), 29–34.

Chapter 9

The Iconography

The representation of the *carole* in art has been the most neglected aspect of the subject. True, Fleming and Stones, in their separate studies, have commented briefly on the dance in the iconography of the *Roman de la Rose* and the *Prose Lancelot* respectively.[1] In two works more specifically concerned with dance (those by Sachs and by Sahlin) the authors refer in passing to individual works of art.[2] Salmen's essay, the one monograph that ostensibly examines the iconography of the *reigen* or *carole*, is, in fact, a broad study of circular dances in general in medieval and Renaissance Europe.[3] But no study has investigated in detail the features of the *carole* as depicted in miniatures, and related these to the written sources.

Representations of the *carole* are particularly numerous. It is, perhaps, one of the most widely illustrated of dances, thanks to the fact that a performance of the dance takes place in two of the most popular French texts of the Middle Ages, which are also the most frequently illustrated manuscripts, namely the *Prose Lancelot* and the *Roman de la Rose*. As a sample from the entire range of illustrations, 50 items have been chosen for consideration here, and these can be divided into four categories. First, there is a group drawn from miscellaneous manuscript sources. Second, there exists a number of almost identical small ivory caskets illustrating the entire narrative of the *Châtelaine de Vergy*, which include a depiction of the *carole*. Third, we have some miniatures from the *Prose Lancelot*. Finally, a selection is chosen from the vast number of illustrated manuscripts of the *Roman de la Rose*. All these illustrations date from before c. 1400, the date at which the *carole* went out of fashion.

---

[1] John V. Fleming, *The* Roman de la Rose: *A Study in Allegory and Iconography* (Princeton, NJ, 1969), p. 84; Alison Stones, 'The Illustrations of BN fr. 95 and Yale 229: Prolegomena to a Comparative Analysis' in *Word and Image in Arthurian Literature*, ed. Keith Busby (New York, 1996), pp. 211–13.

[2] Curt Sachs, *Eine Weltgeschichte des Tanzes* (Berlin, 1933), p. 183, *World History of the Dance* (London, 1938) trans. Bessie Schönberg, p. 272 – a fresco by Ambrogio Lorenzetti to be discussed in Chapter 10. Sahlin, p. 27, cites the miniature in LBL, Harley 4425 (c. 1500), fol 14^{r}, as evidence of the processional form of the *carole*, but the illustration in this manuscript is much more likely to show a *basse danse*, the principal dance in fashion in francophile regions in the late 15th century.

[3] Walter Salmen, 'Ikonographie des Reigens im Mittelalter', *Acta Musicologica*, 52 (1980) 14–26. Salmen maintains essentially the same position on dance in his more recent *Tanz und Tanzen vom Mittelalter bis zur Renaissance* (Hildesheim, 1999), for which, see especially pp. 138–46.

Of the miscellaneous pictures, among the earliest depictions of the *carole* is one from *Le Conte du Graal*, and it is found in a manuscript possibly dating from the end of the thirteenth century. In the text the queen orders her girls to welcome Gauvain, and so they dance: 'contre lui grant joie comancent, / chantent et querolent et dancent' (they rejoice in his honour. They sing and carol and dance).[4] Gauvain arrives on his horse, and dismounts among them. The miniature shows four girls close together facing forward, and holding their raised forearms so that their joined hands are at chin height. This representation fills the entire space of the miniature. Dating from slightly later is the miniature of a *carole* illustrating the *fabliau* cited in the previous chapter, in which a woman marries a thief and her neighbours celebrate: 'Il chantent et moinnent queroles / Sonant tambours, sonant violes' (they sing and lead *caroles*, playing tambourines and vielles).[5] Here a woman holds hands at shoulder height with the man on either side of her. All three are turned more or less towards the viewer. On the viewer's left a third man uses a stick to beat a tambourine with a snare. Again the figures fill the entire space. The last of the group comes from the Bodleian manuscript of *Li Restor du Paon* (completed in 1344) (see Plates 3 and 6).[6] In the episode in question, the king and his followers enter in a line the place where the *carole* is in progress. The *carole* opens up, and the newcomers join in. Elyot (the heroine) is holding an eagle on her gloved hand. She is placed between two male characters: Emenidus on one side and Marcien on the other, who supports her elbow (presumably the one holding the eagle). The trumpets fall silent (indeed they probably fell silent before the dance began). Elyot then sings to accompany the *carole*. This event is illustrated by two juxtaposed miniatures. The first (see Plate 6) shows a group of nine well-dressed people in a circle facing inwards, and holding hands at hip level. They are placed against a chequered background, the whole surmountd by a castellated arcade. The second miniature (see Plate 3) has a diamond-patterned background, and shows six people – a man between two ladies and a lady between two men all facing the viewer. The lady between the two men is holding a bird on her right hand, which is supported by the hand of the man on her right.

---

[4] For the text, see Chrétien de Troyes, *Le Conte du Graal (Perceval)*, Les Romans de Chrétien de Troyes, V, ed. Félix Lecoy (Paris, 1972–75), ll. 8716–23, Illustration No 1; this and subsequent reference numbers refer to the primary sources of the iconography cited in Appendix B.

[5] No 2. A facsimile of the text together with the miniature will be found in *Bibliothèque de la Ville de Lyon: documents paléogaphiques, typographiques, iconographiques*, ed. R. Cantinelli (Lyon 1923), II/I, Pl. V.

[6] No 3. The manuscript, in the Bodleian Library is reproduced in facsimile with an introduction by M. R. James under the title *The Romance of Alexander: A Collotype Facsimile of MS Bodley 264* (Oxford, 1933), where the miniatures appear on fol 181^{v}. An edition based on this manuscript is Jean Brisebarre, *Jean Brisebarre: Li Restor du Paon*, ed. Enid Donkin (London, 1980), ll. 1159–77. The miniatures, however, are not reproduced in this edition.

These few examples demonstrate that the iconography does not always give a coherent view of the dance. The examples from *Le Conte du Graal* and the *fabliau* do not even attempt to show the *carole* as a circle – the formation repeatedly stressed in textual references. It might be argued that the straight line of the dancers represents a related dance, the *tresche*, and the artistic technique of most early artists was not equal to representing people in a circle. Then again the illustrator may have been more concerned with depicting a dance of some kind, and was more anxious to complete his task of executing a large number of miniatures in a reasonable time than attending to choreographic verisimilitude. An obvious discrepancy exists between text and illustration in the manuscript of the fable: the 'violes' (vielles) mentioned in the text are not depicted in the accompanying miniature. The artist may have realized that a high-status instrument like the vielle was inappropriate in a low-status performance. The first of the two miniatures in *Li Restor du Paon* actually shows the dancers in a circle, and they all hold hands in the same position. The illustrator separates the performance of the dance from the carrying of the eagle by representing them in two different miniatures. Again, he may have been struck by the implausibility of people dancing while one of them is holding a large bird. If we were to judge from these three examples taken as a whole we could derive little or no information about the *carole* as a dance.

The *Châtelaine de Vergy* was composed about 1240. In the relevant part of the tale the chatelaine is lying dead in her chamber but, ignorant of this fact, her lover is below in the hall enjoying himself in a *carole*.[7] The dance, however, is not described in detail. The ivory caskets all date from the second quarter of the fourteenth century.[8] There are five complete caskets and one almost complete. Fragments of three others have also been located. These items appear to be unique in that they are the only *objets d'art* to illustrate an entire narrative, and this was possible because the narrative poem itself is relatively short. The group is also unique in that they are the only works of art in ivory that unquestionably depict a *carole*.

---

[7] Among several editions of the text is *La Châtelaine de Vergy*, ed. and trans. Jean Dufournet and Liliane Dulac (Paris, 1994), in which see especially ll. 840–52.

[8] No 4. An early study of the caskets is Karl Borinski, 'La Chastelaine de Vergy in der Kunst des Mittelalters', *Monatshefte fuer Kunstwissenschaft*, 2 (1909), 58–63, which gives a brief description of the representation of the *carole* (p. 61). Beate Schmolke-Hasselmann, '*La Chastelaine de Vergi* auf Pariser Elfenbein-Kästchen des 14. Jahrhunderts [etc.]', *Romanistisches Jahrbuch*, 27 (1976), 52–76, notes that, while the caskets are not identical, they have the same basic design (p. 62). She also points out (p. 65) that the setting for the scene in the text has been altered in the caskets. Laila Gross, '"La Chastelaine de Vergi" Carved in Ivory', *Viator: Medieval and Renaissance Studies*, 10 (1979), 311–21, gives a detailed list of the complete caskets and the fragments (p. 312, n. 7). She also cites a series of frescoes illustrating the *Châtelaine de Vergy* in the Palazzo Davanzati in Florence, but I can report that these do not depict the dance. All three studies focus on the example in the British Museum, which is reproduced in Borinski (p. 61), Schmolke-Hasselmann (Abb. 4) and Gross (Fig. 3).

As the caskets are said to be more or less identical, the exemplar in the British Museum is studied here. The left end panel shows a double row of dancers facing forwards and holding hands at hip level. At both the extreme right and at the extreme left, a trumpeter stands on a rostrum roughly indicated in the carving. Both musicians play long trumpets, which extend over the heads of some of the dancers. The whole is surmounted by a blind gothic arcade. The double line of dancers is undoubtedly intended to represent a circle. But a double line rather constrains the artist to show some (in this case all) the dancers facing the viewer when in reality they would all be in a circle facing inwards. Moreover, trumpets at this date were merely signalling instruments, and in any case, even if instruments were present, they would have stopped playing before the *carole* began. They may have been included as being proper to aristocratic festivities or simply as being emblematic of music.

The *Prose Lancelot* was composed about 1214, and illustrated manuscripts began to appear within a decade of its composition, but the earliest example considered here dates from the end of the thirteenth century.[9] In the episode involving the *carole*, as described in Sommer's base manuscript (see Plate 5), Lancelot and his squire come upon a field in which stand a tower and 30 tents. In the middle of the tents are four large pines, and in the middle of these is an ivory chair covered with red samite with a large, heavy, gold crown upon it. Knights (some armed) and ladies are compelled by magic to dance around the pines. Lancelot, too, is mysteriously forced to join in this enchanted *carole*, from which the dancers will be released only when someone, whom the crown fits, is found. Lancelot, giving his horse to his squire, throws his lance and shield to the ground, and takes part. Later it transpires that he is the person whom the crown fits.

Of the six miniatures examined here, three show a single line of dancers, two a double line and one a circle.[10] The sexes do not alternate in any of the representations, but are distributed arbitrarily with two or three men or women together. The hands are held at shoulder height in one example, at chest height in another, at waist level in two, at hip level in one and at various levels in the remaining picture.[11] The dancers have their feet apart with the toes pointing outwards in three depictions.[12] In two the feet are placed in a less precise manner.[13]

---

[9] For the text relevant to the present discussion, see *Le Livre de Lancelot del Lac*, ed. H. Oskar Sommer, The Vulgate Version of the Arthurian Romances, Carnegie Institution of Washington, Publication No 74 (Washington, 1909–16), V, 123; for the accompanying miniature see No 6.

[10] Single line in Nos 5, 8 and 10; double line in Nos 6 and 7; circle in No 9.

[11] Shoulder in No 10; chest in No 7; waist in Nos 5 and 9; hip in Nos 6; various in No 8.

[12] Nos 6, 8 and 9.

[13] Nos 5 and 10.

In one the feet are not clearly visible.[14] No instrumentalists are to be seen either inside or immediately outside the border in any of the miniatures.

Once again we find no agreement on any aspect of the dance other than the total absence of musicians, which, in any case, are not mentioned in the text. The double line may be taken, as in examples previously discussed, as a substitute for a circle. The various representations of the position of the hands offer no indication of how they were held in actual performance. The turned-out feet suggest an artist's interpretation rather than the parallel feet implied by text of Sommer's manuscript. On the other hand, the miniatures indicate, with varying degrees of detail, features actually described in the narrative: for example, the trees and the crowning of Lancelot are evident in some depictions. This suggests, as one might expect, that it was the features of the narrative, and not those of the choreography, that engaged the attention of the miniaturist.

The *carole* in the *Roman de la Rose* takes place in the first part of the work – the part written by Guillaume de Lorris between 1225 and 1230. The narrator is invited to join allegorical characters representing aspects of courtly love in the dance in the garden of Deduit (Pleasure).[15] They are accompanied by the singing of Leesce (Joy). Also present are 'fleüteors', 'menestreus' and 'jugleours' (indicating musicians), as well as a female jugglers, and two young girls who dance in the middle of the *carole*.

The present survey comprises 40 miniatures dating from the fourteenth century.[16] As a whole, they clarify the status of the illustrations better than the examples considered so far, no doubt because of the greater number available. Of the total of 40, 32 show the dancers in a straight line, one in an irregular line, four in a double line and three in a circle facing inwards.[17] The dancers are all men in three cases and possibly all women in one.[18] The sexes are unidentifiable in two because the detail of the dance is very small.[19] The sexes are mixed in

---

14 No 7.

15 For the text see Guillaume de Lorris and Jean de Meun, *Le Roman de la Rose*, ed. Félix Lecoy (Paris, 1965–70), ll. 725–1276, especially ll. 725–74.

16 Nos 11–50. Reproductions of a number of the miniatures cited here can be seen in a variety of sources notably Fleming, Figs 16, 19, 20 and 21 (Nos 38, 12, 42 and 23 respectively); Salmen, Abb 2, 4 and 8 (Nos 14, 25 and 45 respectively); Edmund A. Bowles, 'Instrumente des 15. Jahrhunderts und Ikonographie', *Basler Jahrbuch für historische Musikpraxis* [vol. for 1984], 8 (1985), Abb 6, 7, 8 and 9 (Nos 34, 38, 44 and 45 respectively); Lucien Fourez, '*Le Roman de la Rose* de la Bibliothèque de la Ville de Tournai', *Scriptorium: Revue Internationale des Etudes Relatives aux Manuscrits / International Review of Manuscript Studies*, 1 (1946–47), Pl. 21 (No 24).

17 Straight line, Nos 11, 12, 13, 14, 15, 16, 17, 18, 19, 20, 21, 22, 27, 28, 29, 30, 32, 33, 34, 35, 36, 37, 38, 39, 40, 41, 43, 44, 45, 48, 49 and 50; an irregular line, No 24; double line, Nos 23, 25, 26, and 42; circle facing inwards, Nos 31, 46 and 47.

18 All men in Nos 11, 17 and No 46, possibly all women in No 30.

19 Nos 22 and 24.

the remaining 34. As for the order of the sexes in these 34, men and women in no particular order are found in eight; while they alternate in the remaining 26.[20] In the grand total of 40 miniatures, hands are held at shoulder height in five miniatures, at chest level in two, at waist level in eight and at hip level in sixteen.[21] The position of the hands varies in seven, and this detail is unclear in two.[22] The feet are turned out in seven illustrations, they are separated in a less easily defined way in eight; they are parallel in five; they are in various positions in 11, but in nine others they are not clearly visible bringing the grand total to 40.[23]

As for the musicians, 21 of the 40 illustrations show none at all within their borders.[24] This absence of instrumentalists is especially noticeable in manuscripts dating from the first half of the century. Of the remaining 19 most show a single musician: three show a pipe and tabor, one a long trumpet, one a shawm, two a bagpipe and two a vielle.[25] Where more than one performer is depicted, two of the same kind are to be found in six examples; two long trumpets in four examples, two shawms in one and two bagpipes in another.[26] Two different instrumental combinations can be seen in four: a vielle and an unidentifiable wind instrument in one, a vielle and pipe and tabor another, one shawm and a bagpipe in a third and two shawms and a bagpipe in the fourth, thus accounting for the 40 miniatures.[27]

The same variety of instruments appears in the area outside the borders of the miniatures. Again the largest number (28 out of the 40) shows no musicians.[28] Seven, however, include them. Six of these have the following combinations: one has two shawms, one a pipe and tabor and a bagpipe, one shows two long

---

[20] Sexes in no particular order in Nos 13, 20, 23, 27, 31, 42, 47 and 48; sexes alternating in 12, 14, 15, 16, 18, 19, 21, 25, 26, 28, 29, 32, 33, 34, 35, 36, 37, 38, 39, 40, 41, 43, 44, 45, 49 and 50.

[21] Hands shoulder height in Nos 11, 12, 18, 23 and 33; chest height in Nos 16 and 29; waist height in Nos 14, 15, 25, 27, 30, 40, 41 and 44; hip height in Nos 13, 20, 28, 31, 32, 36, 37, 38, 42, 43, 45, 46, 47, 48, 49 and 50.

[22] Hands in varying positions in Nos 19, 21, 24, 26, 34, 35 and 39; position unclear in Nos 17 and 22.

[23] Feet turned out in Nos 11, 19, 32, 36, 41, 42 and 45; feet apart in Nos 14, 16, 25, 27, 29, 37, 47 and 49; feet parallel in Nos 28, 33, 34, 43 and 44; feet in various positions in Nos 15, 21, 23, 26, 31, 35, 38, 39, 40, 48 and 50; feet not visible in Nos 12, 13, 17, 18, 20 22, 24, 30 and 46.

[24] No musicians in Nos 11, 12, 14, 17, 18, 20, 21, 23, 24, 26, 27, 28, 29, 32, 33, 34, 40, 41, 45, 46 and 49.

[25] Pipe-and-tabor in Nos 30, 31 and 42; long trumpet in No 16; shawm in No 19; bagpipe in Nos 25 and 48; vielle in Nos 13 and 37.

[26] Two trumpets in Nos 15, 35, 36 and 43, two shawms in No 47; two bagpipes in No 38.

[27] Vielle and an unidentifiable wind instrument in No 22, a vielle and pipe and tabor in No 50; one shawm and bagpipe in No 39; two shawms and a bagpipe in No 44.

[28] No musicians in Nos 11, 12, 13, 15, 16, 17, 18, 19, 20, 22, 24, 27, 28, 29, 30, 31, 36, 37, 39, 40, 41, 42, 44, 46, 47, 48, 49 and 50.

trumpets, one a single bagpipe, one a pair of nakers, a bagpipe and a shawm, one a bagpipe and two shawms.[29] The seventh depiction brings together an ensemble of five instrumentalists playing what appear to be a bagpipe, a harp, a pair of nakers, a flute and a vielle.[30] No conclusion can be drawn about the remaining five illustrations as only reproductions of the miniatures were available for review.[31]

In the illustrations in the *carole* in the *Roman de la Rose*, certain features recur. There is a preference for showing the dance incorrectly as a straight line. One strongly suspects, once again, that technical shortcomings or haste to complete a commission played a part. It is observable that only in the most lavish and artistically accomplished depictions does the miniaturists represent the dance realistically as a circle, as, for example, in the *carole* in the Bodleian *Restor du Paon* or in the miniature of the 'danse' (probably a *carole*) in a famous manuscript of Guillaume de Machaut's *Remede de Fortune*.[32] Yet aspects sometimes plausibly reflect details of the choreography. Where the sexes are mixed, they often alternate. A number of examples show the hands held at hip level, which also seems likely. Sometimes even the feet are parallel. The absence of musicians in many of the miniatures is noteworthy. Yet in general, it must be said, the illustrations are an unreliable guide to the choreography.

The absence of musicians, especially in the earlier miniatures, is significant, and may be an indication that the artists were aware that instruments did not accompany the dance in the high-status performances being illustrated. Their presence, notably in the *Roman de la Rose*, may be seen as an attempt to give a more general impression of the garden scene where musicians are explicitly stated to have been present. Still, the choice of instruments seems arbitrary in the extreme. Trumpets, as already noted, were not musical instruments in the fourteenth century. Bagpipes, which turn up so frequently, are entirely out of place in high-status situations. Harps and vielles, it can be said, never accompany French social dances. Indeed, of the entire panoply of instruments only shawms participated in dancing and, in the present context, they only accompanied the hove dance in

---

[29] Two shawms, in No 21; pipe-and-tabor and a bagpipe in No 23; two long trumpets in No 26; a bagpipe in No 32; nakers, bagpipe and shawm in No 34; a bagpipe and two shawms in No 45.

[30] No 35.

[31] Nos 14, 25, 33, 38 and 43.

[32] François Avril, *L'Enluminure à la Cour de France* (Paris, 1978), Pl. 24, names the dance in PBN, fonds fr. 1586 (c. 1350–56), fol. 51ʳ, as a *carole*. Pl. 24 can also be seen in François Avril,. *Manuscript Painting at the Court of France: The Fourteenth Century (1310–1380)* trans. Ursule Molinaro and Bruce Benderson, (London, 1978) (English translation of the foregoing). While *carole* as an interpretation seems likely, the relevant passage of Guillaume de Machaut's *Remede de Fortune* uses only the word *danse* throughout, for which see Guillaume de Machaut, *Remède de Fortune*, ll. 3349–516, in *Le Jugement du roy de Behaigne* and *Remède de Fortune*, ed. James I. Wimsatt and William W. Kibler, mus. ed. Rebecca A. Balzer (Athens, GA, 1988).

the second half of the fourteenth century. It is possible, too, that the depictions of instruments outside the miniature were not intended to be seen in relation to the dance, but were merely additional decorations. In fact, the general impression that one has is that the artists allowed their fancy to roam free in deciding what instruments to represent on the page and where to represent them.

Illustrations added greatly to the beauty and value of manuscripts. From an aesthetic point of view their importance cannot be denied. As historical evidence, however, they are mostly unreliable. Whereas written sources generally give a coherent view of the *carole*, the iconography, while interesting, is varied and conflicting.

Chapter 10
Carola in Italian

The *carole* was a French dance, or at least a dance of regions under strong French cultural influence. The written sources are usually in French, the sources of the music are French, the iconography is French. One important exceptional use encountered so far is Dante's employment of an Italian form of the term, *carola*, in his *Divine Comedy*. His references denote an indisputable use of the word in a language other than French at a time when the dance was still in vogue. This fact prompts the suggestion that the *carole* was not only known, but also performed, in Italy. Moreover, two frescoes, also from the fourteenth century, show girls executing dances that many have judged to be dances of the *carole* type. Thus two questions arise: first, whether, and to what extent, the dance was known and practised in Italy, and second, if this is true, whether it is also represented Italian art. Answers to these questions are facilitated if we know what dances were in use in Italy before the fifteenth century. In this way we can tell how widespread the Italian form, *carola*, was. Also, if the dancing depicted in the frescoes is not a *carole*, we are better placed to know what kind of dance or dances it might be.

The most frequent citation of Italian dance terms occurs in verse, where by far the commonest is *danza*. The word appears at the dawn of Italian literature in a poem by Re Giovanni, and it is found thoughout our period and, of course, later.[1] The term is employed by poets of the thirteenth century such as Rinaldo d'Aquino and Jacopone da Todi.[2] It was used in the fourteenth century by Franco Sacchetti and Federico Frezzi.[3] For these poets the word has a general meaning exactly like the French *danse* or the English *dance*.

The non-specific nature of the term is particularly evident in sonnets by Francesco Ismera and Folgore da San Gemignano, since both poets qualify the word *danza*. Thus Francesco has the line 'donne et donzelle in danza gire a

---

1 Jean de Brienne (born c. 1148—d. 1234) acquired the title of King of Jerusalem, hence the soubriquet 'Re Giovanni'. The reference is to his *discordo*, 'Donna audite como' printed in *Le rime della scuola siciliana*, ed. Bruno Panvini, Biblioteca dell 'Archivum Romanicum', Serie 1, No 65, (Florence, 1962); for the citation see p. 86.

2 Rinaldo d'Aquino (fl. 1240–50), 'In amoroso pensare' in *Le rime* I, 115. Jacopone de' Benedetti (b. 1230/36–1306) is better known as Jacopone da Todi. The reference is to his 'Secreto Spirituale' in *Le poesie spirituali del B. Jacopone da Todi, frate minore*, ed. Francesco Tresatti (Venice, 1617), pp. 1024 and 1027.

3 Franco Sacchetti (b. 1332?–d. 1400), *Opere*, ed. Alberto Chiari (Bari, 1936–38), I, 106, 117, 256 and II, 45, 67; Federico Frezzi, *Il quadriregio*, ed. Enrico Filippini (Bari, 1914), pp. 6 and 386. *Il quadriregio* was begun in 1394 and completed in the years 1400–?03.

tresca' (ladies and girls dancing a round *tresca*).[4] Folgore, in his series of sonnets on the months of the year, enumerates among the joys of April 'cantar, danzar a la provenzalesca / con istormenti novi della Magna' (singing, dancing in the Provençal manner with new instruments from Germany).[5] The significance of *tresca* in the first quotation will be examined later; the import of 'danzar a la provenzalesca', however, remains unexplained.

But *danza*, and dancing in general, is the physical manifestation of joy. Rinaldo alludes to this in the poem cited above with the phrase 'danzar goiosamente'. A similar feeling is conveyed in a religious poem attributed to Jacopone da Todi, the 'Secreto Spirituale', in which the poet exclaims

> Nol mi pensai giamai
> Di danzar alla danza;
> Ma la tua innamoranza
> Jesu lo mi fe fare.[6]
>
> (I never thought to dance in the dance; but your love, Jesus, made me do it.)

Jacopone goes on to express the hope that he might be joined in the dance of the blessed in heaven. This idea of dancing expressing the joy of those in Heaven is taken up again in Dante's *Divine Comedy*, as we saw in Chapter 5.[7]

Although *danza* remained almost exclusively a poetic term, an important exception is its several appearances in the prose of Boccaccio's *Decameron* as, for example, in the following passage:

> E appressandosi l'ora della cena, verso il palagio tornatesi con diletto cenarono; dopo la qual cena, fatti venir gli strumenti, comandò la reina che una danza fosse presa e, quella menando la Lauretta, Emilia cantasse una canzone da' leuto di Dioneo aiutata. Per lo qual comandamento Lauretta prestamente prese una danza e quella menò, cantando Emilia la seguente canzone amorosamente [the lyric follows].[8]

---

4 This sonnet by Francesco Ismera is quoted in Folgore da San Gemignano, *Le rime di Folgore da San Gemignano e di Cene da la Chitarra d'Arezzo*, ed. Giulio Navone (Bologna, 1880), p. cxv.

5 Jacopo di Michele, better known as Folgore da San Gemignano, composed his series of sonnets on the months between 1309 and 1317. The quotation from 'D'aprile' appears on p. 11 of the edtion cited in n. 4.

6 Jacopone da Todi, p. 1024.

7 See p. 44.

8 The edition used here is Giovanni Boccaccio, *Decameron*, ed. Vittore Branca (1980; 6th ed, Turin, 1992), 2 vols paginated continuously throughout. The quotation is from *Giornata* I, *Conclusione*, [I] 125–6. The *Decameron* was completed between 1349 and 1351. The holograph, which is the base manuscript for this edition, was copied c. 1370.

(And with supper-time approaching, having returned to the elegant villa, they supped with pleasure; after which, having summoned instruments, the queen ordered that a dance should begin with Lauretta leading it, and that Emilia should sing a song accompanied on the lute by Dioneo. At this command, Lauretta promptly began a dance, and led it with Emilia singing the following song in an amorous manner.)

In this, as in other passages in the *Decameron*, *danza* seem to be, as in verse, a general reference to dancing.

Another commonly used term, both in prose and in verse, is *ballo*. An early citation is to be found in a reference to the arrival in Prato of the Cardinal of Florence on 9 May 1304, an event mentioned in the chronicle of Dino Compagni.[9] It is the only dance term employed by Francesco Barberino in his *Reggimento e costume di donna*, a work partly in verse and partly in prose, in which, among other topics, the author is preoccupied with the morality of women who dance.[10] Dante does not use the noun *ballo* at all, and rarely used the verb *ballare*. Boccaccio employs the verb, *ballare*, only once in the *Decameron*, where it is synonymous with *danza*.[11] But in his commentary on part of the *Divine Comedy*, he uses *ballo* exclusively, as does Franceso da Buti in his commentary on the relevant passages.[12] If Sacchetti and Frezzi often use the term *danza*, both have even more frequent recourse to *ballo*.[13] Taken as a whole these citations suggest that *ballo* was the usual Italian term for dance in the fourteenth century.

A word of more specific import is *tresca*, which is already found in the early thirteenth century in the prose of Guido Faba: 'ma per noi e la nostra gente se fa belli canti e tresche' (but for us and our people beautiful songs and *tresche* are performed.)[14] But this citation sheds little light on the sense of the term. Francesco

---

9 Dino Compagni (c. 1260–1324), *Cronica*, ed. Gino Luzzato, NUE, nuova serie, No 46 (1968; rpt Turin, 1978), p. 135.

10 Francesco Barberino, *Reggimento e costume di donna*, ed. Giuseppe E. Sansone, Collezione di 'Filologia Romanza', No 2 (Turin, 1957), pp. 13, 16, 25, 35, 84, 215, 220. The work was composed in the years 1318–20.

11 Decameron, *Giornata* VI, Conclusione, [II], 782.

12 Giovanni, Boccaccio, *Esposizioni sopra la comedia di Dante*, ed. Giorgio Padoan, in *Tutte le opere di Giovanni Boccaccio*, ed. Vittore Branca (Milan, 1965), VI, 385–6, 641. Boccaccio, in the first of these two passages, is commenting on *Inferno*,VII, ll. 23–5; Francesco di Bartolo da Buti (b. 1324–d. 1405), *Commento di Francesco da Buti sopra la Divina Comedia di Dante Allighieri*, ed. Crescentino Giannini (Pisa, 1858–62), I, 550, II, 233, 676, III, 226, 320, 651, 680.

13 Sacchetti, I, 68, 100, 106, 118, 121, 281, 326, 334, 345, 350, II, 20, 41, 45; Frezzi, pp. 9, 26, 61, 79, 80, 125, 189, 297, 383.

14 Guido Faba (b. before 1190–d. after 1243), 'Gemma purpurea', ed. M. Marti, in *La prosa del Duecento*, ed. Cesare Segre and Mario Marti, La letteratura italiana; storia e testi, No 3 (Milan, 1959), p. 16.

Ismera in the phrase already quoted ('donne e donzelle in danza gire a tresca') indicates that *tresca* had more restricted meaning than *danza*. Dante compares the *tresca* to the actions of the suffering in Hell:

> Sanza ripose mai era la tresca
> delle misere mani, or quindi or quinci
> escotendo da sè l'arsura fresca.[15]
>
> (There was no pause in the dance [*tresca*] of the wretched hands, now here, now there, beating off from them the fresh burning.)

Boccaccio, in his commentary, defines the dance thus: 'è la "tresca" una maniera di ballare, la quale si fa di mani e di piedi' (the *tresca* is a manner of dancing, which is performed with the hands and the feet).[16] Buti is a little more helpful in his explanation: 'tresca si chiama uno ballo saltereccio, ove sia grande e veloce movimento e di molti inviluppato' (*tresca* is the name of a hopping dance in which there is much fast movement in a dance involving many).[17] Barberino considers it very unseemly for ladies to hop, and Dante in his usage of the term *tresca* appears to imply that it is a less decorous dance more suitable for the inhabitants of the infernal regions.[18] Buti's hopping dance appears to be quite different from the French *tresche*, in which no mention is made of hopping steps.

Apart from a citation in a sonnet doubtfully attributed to Dante, the word *carola* is found during our period only in two works: the *Divine Comedy*, as previously noted, and no doubt under Dante's influence, in Boccaccio's *Decameron*.[19] In the passage from this work quoted above the term *danza* is used twice, but immediately following it we find the phrase 'dopo alcune altre carolette fatte' (after performing some more little *caroles*). Is *danza* being used as a general term, which is then particularized as *caroletta*, or are both terms synonymous? The usage in the following extract is ambiguous:

---

[15] The edition used here is Dante Alighieri, *The Divine Comedy of Dante Alighieri*, ed. and trans. John D. Sinclair (1939; rpt, New York, 1961). The quotation is from *Inferno*, XIV, ll. 40–42.

[16] Boccaccio, *Esposizioni*, p. 641.

[17] Buti, I, 380.

[18] Barberino, p. 25; Dante in the above quotation.

[19] The exception is in the 16-line sonnet, 'Iacopo, I' fui nelle nevicate alpi', which has the line, 'Donde non nacquer canti né carole'. This sonnet will be found in *Dante Alighieri: rime, 3 testi* in *Rime dubbie*, ed. Domenico de Robertis (Florence, 2002), VII, 516–17. For a comment on this sonnet, see Marco A. Cavallo, 'Carola', *Enciclopedia dantesca* (1970; 2nd ed., Rome, 1984).

> Dove con freschissimi vini e con confetti la fatica del picciol cammin cacciata via, intorno della bella fontana di presente furono in sul danzare, quando al suono della cornamusa di Tindaro e quando d'altri suon carolando.[20]
>
> (Where with the coolest of wines and with sweetmeats, the fatigue of the short walk was chased away, and around a beautiful fountain they began at once to dance, sometimes to the music of Tindaro's bagpipe, and sometime dancing *carole* to other kinds of music.)

Yet for Boccaccio *danza, ballo* and *carola* seem to be synonyms and therefore to be employed without distinction. This impression appears to be confirmed by a further reference to dancing where he passes from *carola* to *ballare* to *danza* without any obvious differentiation being made between them.[21]

Thus, although Dante may have been conscious of the fact that the *carole* was a circular dance, and Boccaccio likewise (since he refers in the passage quoted above to a dance around a fountain), for neither author does *carola* have the meaning of a precise technical term. For Dante it signifies not only a dance but its significance is extended to embrace the sense of a *choir*. Boccaccio, with one exception, avoids the usual word for dance, *ballo*, in his *Decameron*, preferring instead the poetic *danza* or *carola*. Yet *ballo* is the only term that he employs in his commentary on Dante. The conclusion that one inevitably draws from these observations is that, for both these authors, *carola* was simply an elegant term for *dance*, rather than a reference to a specific dance that was known and practised in Italy.

As to whether the French *carole* is depicted in Italian art, as many have stated or implied, two representations in particular come in for scrutiny. One is a fresco painted about 1365 by Andrea di Bonaiuto and his assistants in the Cappellone degli Spagnoli of the convent of Santa Maria Novella in Florence (see Plate 8).[22] In the relevant detail four girls hold hands in a circle; another three, in a straight line and separated from the others, link their little fingers. None of them is singing as the seven dancers have their mouths quite definitely closed. An eighth girl stands apart from them, and is no doubt the one singing, while at the same time she is beating a tambourine. The representation does indeed include dancers in a circle, but the fact that the other three are in a line, that none of the seven dancers is singing, that the singing seems to have been provided by a participant who is not dancing, and that she is playing an instrument eliminates the possibility that the dance depicted is a *carole*.

The other illustration is a fresco usually entitled *Gli effetti del buon governo* (The Effects of Good Government). It was painted by Ambrogio Lorenzetti in the years 1338–39 on a wall of the Sala della Pace in the Palazzo Pubblico in Siena

---

20 Boccaccio, *Decameron, Giornata* VII, *Conclusione* ([II], 883–4).

21 Boccaccio, *Decameron, Giornata* VI, *Conclusione*, ([II], 782).

22 Andrea di Bonaiuto is also known as Andrea da Firenze. The fresco is variously entitled by commentators.

(see Plate 9). A detail shows seven girls forming a U-shaped chain by holding hands. Two more face each other, and make an arch; the girl on the viewer's left by raising her right arm, the girl on the viewer's right by raising her left arm. The first girl in the chain of the seven dancers has already passed under the arch, and is more or less facing the viewer. The second girl in the chain is lowering her head ready to pass under the arch. The music is provided by a tenth girl, who is evidently singing since she is the only visible one with her mouth open, while at the same time she is beating a tambourine with jingles.

This painting is clearly not the *carole* as described by French writers although it has frequently been described a such.[23] The formation is not that of a circle; nor is an arch ever mentioned as a constituent of the French dance. Moreover the singing is not provided by the dancers themselves, but by another person. Nor are instruments involved in performances of the French *carole* when executed by persons of good social position as the young ladies in this dance evidently are.

Other evidence tends to support the view that the *carole* is not represented in either of the frescoes, but that another dance is being illustrated. In a Lombard drawing of the mid-fourteenth century (not reproduced here) a couple on the viewer's right face each other, and form an arch, the man (on the viewer's right) with his right arm, the woman (slightly to his left) with her left arm.[24] A second couple is about to pass under the arch. On the viewer's extreme left, a young man plays a lute using a plectrum. The details here are comparable to those in

---

[23] The painting is discussed in George Rowley, *Ambrogio Lorenzetti*, Princeton Monograph in Art and Archaeology, No 32, (Princeton, NJ, 1958), I, 99–122, with particular reference to the dance on pp. 110–11. The dates for the fresco are given on p. 127. The detail of the dance is reproduced in II, Plate 218. Among the many who have cited the dance is Vincenzo De Bartholomaeis, *Le origini della poesia drammatica italiana* (Bologna, 1924), p. 74 , who calls this dance, as well as the one in the Florence fresco, a 'ruota', which he equates with the *ridda, carola, tresca, ronda* and *rigoletto*. His statements, however, on the *carola* (p. 79) are derived from Jeanroy and Bédier (whose pronouncements on the dance were discussed in Chapter 4). Raimond van Marle, *Iconographie de l'art profane au Moyen-Age et à la Renaissance et la décoration des demeures: la vie quotidienne* (The Hague, 1931), Fig. 68, calls the dance a 'ronde'. Heinrich Besseler, *Die Musik des Mittelalters und Renaissance* (Potsdam, 1931), Tafel X, judges the dance to be a 'Reigentanz'. Likewise, Curt Sachs, *Eine Weltgeschichte des Tanzes* (Berlin, 1933), p. 183, trans. Bessie Schönberg, *World History of the Dance* (London, 1938), p. 272, refers to the dance as being of the *Reigen* type in which he includes the French *carole*. Ingrid Brainard, 'Medieval Dance', *International Encyclopedia of Dance: A Project of Dance Perspectives Foundation*, ed. Selma Jeanne Cohen *et al.* (New York, 1998), cites the painting as illustrating 'line dances of the *carole* type'; see also her article 'Dance 3 (i) *New Grove 2* [Pl.]. 4.

[24] New York, Pierpont Morgan Library. Van Marle reproduces the drawing (Fig. 71), but gives no catalogue number and, as with so many of his captions, the picture is merely entitled a 'ronde'. A small reproduction of the drawing is to be found in Karl Michael Komma, *Musikgeschichte in Bildern* (Stuttgart, (61, Fig. 140), but is assigned the wrong date (beginning of the fifteenth century).

the Siena fresco in that people, obviously dancing, are passing under an arch, and that the music is being provided by an instrumentalist. We can infer from this that the dance represented in both these pictures is not simply an inspiration of the respective artists, but that the depictions record an actual feature of an Italian dance of the period.

In fact Rowley, in his monograph on Ambrogio Lorenzetti, calls the dance in the Siena fresco a *ridda*, but without giving any reason for his choice of designation. The earliest occurence of this term is in the poem by Re Giovanni cited above: 'Or venga a rid <d>are, / chi ci sa [ben] andare' (Now let him come, and dance a *ridda* who can perform it well).[25] In the context *ridda* appears to be synonymous with *danza*. Yet Ser Gorello seems to differentiate between the two terms: 'con danze e con rida / giovani, donne con strumenti e canti' (with dances and with the *ridda* young men, ladies with instruments and songs).[26] Giovanni delle Celle similarly distinguishes the term from *ballo* when he asks rhetorically 'Peccano mortalmente coloro che menano il ballo e la ridda non lecita?' (Do those who lead the dance and the forbidden *ridda* commit a mortal sin?).[27] The inference that the *ridda* did not meet with everyone's approval can also be drawn from a reference in the *Inferno* of the *Divine Comedy*:

> Come fa l'onda là sovra Carriddi,
> che si frange con quella in cui s'intoppa,
> così convien che qui la gente riddi.[28]
>
> (As do the waves there above Charybdis, on breaking against another when they meet, so must the souls here dance their *ridda*.)

Dante compares the avaricious and the profligate in Hell to the two halves of the same circle of waves eddying around the legendary whirlpool of Charbydis, and then changing places. Both Boccaccio and Buti, commenting on these lines, explain the simile in terms of two waves of two different seas (Boccaccio) or the ends of a broken circle of dancers (Buti) which, in both cases, rush against each other.[29] Yet Dante's simile can only be intended to indicate quite vigorous movement, since one

---

[25] Re Giovanni, 'Donna audite como', ll. 37–8.

[26] Cited in Battaglia, 'Ridda'. Battaglia's definitions, both of the noun *ridda* and of the verb *riddare*, however, do not accord with literary descriptions of the dance.

[27] Cited in Battaglia, 'Ridda'.

[28] *Inferno*, VII, ll. 22–4. In Sinclair's translation given here I have substituted *ridda* for 'round'.

[29] Boccaccio, *Esposizioni*, pp. 385–6; Buti, I, 204. The usual interpretation is that *riddi* here derives from the verb *riddare*. On this verb, and also on M. d'Andria's dissenting view that dancing is not intended in this context, see Bruno Bernabei, 'Riddare', *Enciclopedia dantesca* (1973; 2nd ed. Rome, 1984) where Bernabei refutes d'Andria's interpretation of *riddare* as 'tornare indietro' (to turn back).

would suppose that dancers must do more than rush against one another. Moreover, the possibility of circular form for the dance is confirmed by two madrigal lyrics, one of which refers specifically to a 'tonda ridda' (a round *ridda*).[30]

Fazio degli Uberti, in his universal history in verse, *Il dittamondo*, likens the *ridda* to a river. In the passage in question, the poet and his companion, Solino, are travelling in Greece. They come upon a river, and Fazio asks Solino where it rises. He replies that it rises in Mound Ida, flows through Macedonia, and from there into the Aegean:

> A volte, come l'uom la ridda guida,
> passando se ne vien per Macedona,
> in fino che nel mar Egeo s'annida.
> Partus ha nome, del qual si ragiona
> che Io, per li poeti, fu sua figlia,
> per la quale Argus perdeo la persona.[31]

> (By turns, as one guides the *ridda*, it passes through Macedonia, and at last sinks into the Aegean Sea. Partus is its name, whose daughter, according to the poets, was Io, by whom Argus met his end.)

The bizarre conception of geography, and the myth to which the poet alludes, do not concern us here except for the river named. Fazio gives the name Partus to the River Inachus, so called from Inachus, the King of Argos, who was, according to some writers of the ancient world, the father of Io. There are three rivers in Greece called the Inachus, but the context of the poem clearly locates the one named in the poem in the Peloponnese.[32] This river rises in the region of Lyrkia, flows eastwards and then south to the west of Argos, and enters the Gulf of Argolis near Nea Kios. It follows a winding course. By comparing the river to the *ridda*, Fazio implies that the dance in this case also meandered, and did not form a straight line.

The *ridda*, then, could be a complete circle or a meandering line of dancers. These choreographic features correspond better with the scenes in the Siena and Florentine frescoes than with those of the French *carole*, although we cannot know for certain that the *ridda* is the dance represented in these paintings.

---

30 *Poesie*, pp. 19, 99.

31 Fazio degli Uberti, *Il dittamondo e le rime*, ed. Giuseppe Corsi, Scrittori d'Italia, Nos 206 and 207 (Bari, 1952), IV, 5, ll. 28–33. The poem was begun in 1345, but remained unfinished at the poet's death in 1367. There are two Mount Idas, one in Crete and one in Asia Minor (modern Turkey); neither is the source of the river mentioned here.

32 Corsi, in his edition of *Il dittamondo* (pp. 304–5), discusses at length the identification of the Partus. He suggests, *inter alia*, that the Inachus, to which Fazio alludes, is another river of the same name, a tributary of the Spercheios in southern Thessaly, which the poet mentions elsewhere in the poem. The text itself and the mythological context here, however, clearly place the river in the Peloponnese.

There appears to be a difference in the way in which French artists and Italian artists, or at least those two Italian artists under discussion, considered dancing. The French are generally more interested in illustrating a narrative, and consider any plausible representation of a dance acceptable. They tend to be less attentive to the choreographic detail of any particular dance mentioned in their accompanying text. The two Italians, on the other hand, were concerned with the realities of daily life, namely good government and good behaviour. The details of the dances in their frescoes therefore correspond to the descriptions of a dance as described by contemporary Italian writers.

If there is a marked difference between French and Italian dances and their depiction in art, the same is true of the music that accompanied those dances. As with French dances, singing is frequently mentioned with all kinds of Italian dances. The striking contrast between the two is that in Italy, even in polite society, instruments can participate. Several instances of this will have been noted in the examples cited so far.

Instruments in the Middle Ages were classed as either 'loud' (wind and percussion) or 'soft' (strings) but flutes could belong to either group. The kinds of instruments that accompanied the Italian dances are not socially divided. Dances designated *danza* or *carola* are usually accompanied by 'soft' instruments. Descriptions in the *Decameron* are the most enlightening here. Thus Emilia sings for a *danza* and is accompanied by Dioneo on the lute.[33] A lute and a vielle can actually take the place of singing for a *carola*.[34] The choice of these instruments probably reflects the intimate nature of the dances performed in the upper echelons of Italian society. On the other hand, in the *Decameron*, Tindaro accompanies dancing (*danzare*) on a bagpipe.[35] This rather exceptional use of a 'loud' instrument can probably be explained by the fact that the dancing is taking place outdoors.

The *ridda*, it seems, was usually accompanied by both singing *and* an instrument or instruments. Armannino Giudice recalls the story in Greek mythology when Achilles hid himself among women, but was discovered by Ulysses to be male in the way that he danced:

> Licomede comanda che debbino ballare e fare festa agli greci baroni; fatti ha venire gli stormenti usati; bacinetti, tamburi e fiauti. Quivi cominciano le donne a sonare e le donzelle fare loro ridda; quivi Ulisse maggiormente s'acorse al muovere delle braccia e de' piedi che Achille facea più tardi che l'altre, ch'egli era diritto maschio e per molti altri atti che gli vide fare. Secretamente lo monstra a Diomedes; quello lo guarda e pargli molto el vero.[36]

---

[33] Boccaccio, *Decameron, Giornata* II, *Conclusione* [I], 125–6.

[34] Boccaccio, *Decameron, Giornata* I, *Introduzione* [I], 46.

[35] Boccaccio, *Decameron, Giornata* VII, *Conclusione*, [II], 883–4.

[36] Armannino Giudice, 'La Fiorita' in *Testi inediti di storia trojana* [etc.], ed. Egidio Gorra, Biblioteca di testi inediti e rari, No 1 (Turin, 1887), pp. 545–6. The poem, containing

> (Lycomedes ordered that they should dance, and entertain the Greek lords. He had the usual instruments summoned: small cymbals, drums and flutes. The ladies began to play, and the girls to perform their *ridda*; then Ulysses noticed, particularly from the movements of arms and feet, that Achilles was slower than the other girls, and because of this, and many other gestures that he saw him make, that he was in fact male. He pointed this out covertly to Diomedes who looked at Achilles, and it seemed to him that this was indeed true.)

Similarly in the *Decameron,* following a reference to a certain Belcore, we have the comment 'e oltre a ciò era quella che meglio sapeva sonare il cembalo e cantare *L'acqua corre la borrana* e menar la ridda e il ballonchio, quando bisogno faceva' (and besides that, she was the one who knew how best to beat the tambourine, and the sing *L'acqua corre la borrana*, and lead the *ridda* and the *ballonchio* when need be).[37] From these two citations we may conclude that these two dances were associated with 'loud' instruments and particularly with percussion. Belcore's tambourine is precisely the instrument seen in Andrea di Bonaiuto's and Ambrogio Lorenzetti's frescoes, which may lend some weight to the conclusion that that the dance depicted in both paintings is the *ridda.*

The conclusion to be drawn from this survey is that there is no evidence for the existence of the *carole* in Italy, or even for an Italian version of it. Certainly Dante's description of a circular dance corresponds with those in French. On the other hand, he also used the term for a choir of blessed spirits. Boccaccio, in his *Decameron,* has a predilection for a recherché vocabulary of dance terms, and he avoids the common term for dance, *ballo.* It would appear that for both authors *carola* is nothing more than an elegant borrowing from the French. Conclusive proof that the dance was neither known nor practised in Italy is provided by the fact that Dante and Bocaccio were the only Italian authors in our period to use the term *carola,* which must mean that even the very word was not in general use in Italy, and therefore the dance is most unlikely to have been represented in Italian art.

---

many factual errors, was completed in 1325. According to the mythology, Achilles was nine years old when this incident took place, thus making the myth seem more plausible.

[37] Boccaccio, *Decameron, Giornata* VIII, *Novella* 2, [II], 896–7.

Chapter 11
Carole in Middle English[1]

French was the official language of England after the Norman Conquest. English did not start to regain its position in language and in literature until the middle of the thirteenth century. It is not surprising, therefore, that dance terms in Middle English do not occur with any frequency until after that date. It is only then that we find the term *ring*. Walter de Bibbesworth, a writer in Anglo-Norman of a verse guide to good behaviour for an upper-class lady for use by her daughter, censures the dancing of poor women: 'Quant povre femme mene la tresche, / Plus la vaudreit en main la besche' (when a poor woman leads the *tresche*, it would be better if she had a spade in her hand).[2] A contemporary gloss in English gives the equivalent of *tresche* as *ring*. A sermon of the same period comments on a song sung by 'wilde wimmen & gol me[n] i mi contereie wan he gon o þe ring' (wild women and lustful men in my region when they go into the ring).[3] The context makes it clear that he is referring to dancing. Similarly in the early fourteenth century the religious writer Richard Rolle employs the term in an English verse translation of his own Latin prose: 'sed uerum dicitur quia amor preit in tripudio, et coream ducit' (but truly it is said that love goes forward and leads the dance), which he translates into English as 'bot suth þan es it sayde þat lufe ledes þe ryng' (but truly then is it said that love leads the ring).[4] From citations such as these it is obvious that *ring* means a dance. But if it is a circular dance, it cannot be the equivalent of the French *tresche*, which was a linear dance; then again, as we have seen before, it is possible that the term is being used indiscriminately for a dance of the *carole* type.

Certainly the two terms are collocated in the anonymous fourteenth-century *Stanzaic Life of Christ*:

---

[1] In this chapter I have tried, as far as possible, to retain the spelling *carole* for the dance and *carol* for the English song or its lyric.

[2] Walter de Bibbesworth, *Le Trétiz*, ed. William Rothwell, Anglo-Norman Text Society, Plain Texts Series, No 6, (London, 1990), ll. 297–8.

[3] The complete sermon is quoted in Carleton Brown, 'Text and the Man: Presidential Address Given in London, June 30, 1928', *M.H.R.A.: Bulletin of the Modern Humanities Research Association*, 2 (1928), 106–7.

[4] Richard Rolle, *The Incendium Amoris of Richard Rolle of Hampole*, ed. Margaret Deanesly, Publications of the University of Manchester, Historical Series, No 26 (Manchester, 1915), p. 276. The translation will be found in *English Writings of Richard Rolle, Hermit of Hampole*, ed. Hope Emily Allen (Oxford, 1931), p. 68.

Thow in þo ryng of carolyng
Spredis þin armes furth from the,
And I on croice have hom spredyng
Schamely, as men movn see.[5]

(Thou stretchest out thy arms from thee in the ring of the *carole*, and I have stretched them on a cross shamefully, as anyone may see.)

These lines are a versification of a meditation on the Crucifixion in the *Legenda Aurea* by Jacobus de Voragine: 'tu in choreis brachia extendis in modum crucis in gaudium et ego ea in cruce extensa habui in obprobium' (thou stretchest thy arms as if on a cross joyfully in dances, but I have truly stretched them on a cross in shame.)[6] *Carolyng* not only indicates a dance, but one in which the arms are stretched, and perforce, the hands joined.

Yet it is impossible to establish whether *ring* was always the exact equivalent of *carole*. The term *carole* had been recorded in England since the early twelfth century, because, as we saw in Chapter 3, it is found in a number of Anglo-Norman translations of the Psalter. This suggests that the dance itself was probably known in England. In any case, the word *carole*, like the word *dance*, first appears in writings in English composed about 1300, but it is only preserved in manuscripts dating from the fourteenth century. One of the earliest of these works is Robert Mannyng's moral treatise in verse, *Handlyng Synne*, which repeats once more the legend of the dancers of Kölbigk:

Þese wommen ȝede & tolled here oute
Wyþ hem to karolle þe cherche aboute.
Beune ordeyned here karollynge:
Gerleu endyted what þey shuld synge.[7]

(These women went and enticed them out to dance a *carole* with them around the church. Beune directed their carolling. Gerleu composed what they should sing.)

The Cotton Manuscript of the universal history in verse called the *Cursor Mundi* describes women singing and dancing to celebrate David's victory over the

[5] *A Stanzaic Life of Christ Compiled from Higden's* Polychronicon *and the* Legenda Aurea, ed. Francis A. Foster, The Early English Text Society, Original Series, No 166 (London, 1926), l. 5936ff.

[6] The Latin quotation in *A Stanzaic Life of Christ* is attributed in this text (l. 5937) to St Bernard, but is actually by Jacobus de Voragine (1228/30–98); see *Jacobi a Voragine Legenda Aurea Vulgo Historia Lombardica Dicta*, ed. Theodor Graesse (Dresden, 1846), p. 227.

[7] Robert Mannyng of Brunne, *Handlyng Synne*, ed. Idelle Sullens, Medieval and Renaissance Texts and Studies, No 14 (New York, 1983), ll. 9045–8.

Philistines: 'þai karold wimmen be þe wai' (The women carolled on the way).[8] Other manuscripts of the text, some later, refer to 'dance'.

Even by the end of the fourteenth century, 'carole' could still signify a *dance*. Ranulph Higden, in his *Polychronicon*, recounts how Robert, Duke of Normandy, the father of William the Conqueror, fell in love with a skinner's daughter:

> Transiens aliquando iste Robertus per Phalesiam urbem Normanniae, vidit puellam Arlet nomine, pelliparii filiam, inter caeteras in chorea tripudiantem.[9]
>
> (This Robert passing on a certain occasion through Falaise, a city in Normandy, saw a girl, Arlette by name, the daughter of a skinner, dancing in a dance with other girls.)

Chorea in Latin here is translated by *carole* in John of Trevisa's English translation and augumentation made in 1387:

> Þis Robert somtyme passyinge þoruȝ Phalesiam, a citee of Normandy, he saw a mayden, Arlek [i.e. Arlette] by name, þe douȝter of a skynner, daunsynge in a caroll among oþer maydouns … .[10]

All the foregoing examples in English are, in one way or another, translations in which various words for dance are rendered in English as *carole*. Much early Middle English literature is, in fact, translation of this kind and not only from Latin but also, of course, from French. In this connection a translation attributed to Chaucer of the *Roman de la Rose* is of particular interest:

> Tho myghtist thou karoles sen,
> And folk daunce and mery ben,
> And made many a fair tournyng
> Upon the grene gras springyng.[11]

---

[8] LBL, Cotton Vespasian, A. III (s.xiv$^{1/4}$), fol. 42^{v}. This is the reading in *Cursor Mundi (The Cursor of the World): A Northumbarian Poem of the XIVth Century in Four Versions*, ed. Rev. Richard Morris, The Early English Text Society, Original Series, No 101 (London, 1893), ll. 7599–604. For dates of the manuscripts of this poem, see John J. Thompson, *The* Cursor Mundi: *Poem, Texts and Contexts*, Medium Aevum Monographs, New Series, No 19 (Oxford, 1998), pp. 30–46.

[9] Ranulph Higden, *Polychronicon Ranulphi Higden Monachi Cestrensis*, with a translation by John Trevisa, ed. Churchill Babington and Joseph Rawson Lumby (London, 1879), VII, 122 .

[10] *Polychronicon*, VII, 123.

[11] Geoffrey Chaucer, *The Romaunt of the Rose*, ll. 759–62. The authorship of this translation is still a matter of debate, but as it is not central to my argument he is assumed

(There mightest thou see *caroles*, and people dancing and being happy, and they made many a graceful turn stepping in a lively manner on the green grass.)

Carole for Chaucer often has the same meaning as the general English term, *dance* and, in fact, at two later points in the passage cited he actually translates the French *carole* as *daunce*.[12] Consequently, when the term makes a rare appearance in one of his original works, it is doubtful whether it has any more precise choreographic significance. The text in question is a line in 'The Knight's Tale' of *The Canterbury Tales*, where he is describing the walls in the temple of Diana where could be seen 'Festes, instrumentz, caroles, daunces'.[13]

Compared to the Italian sources, and especially compared to the French, English ones are very sparse. Still, enough evidence has been gathered here to show that the *carole* still existed as a dance term in English in the fourteenth century, and it would appear that it referred to a circular dance, just as in French. One critical difference, however, separated the two. Whereas in French the word *carole* designated the choreography alone, in English the term could mean either the dance, or the song that accompanied it, or both together, or, as we shall see, eventually neither. In the lines from *Handlyng Synne* quoted above it refers unambiguously to the choreography alone, but then these lines follow:

Þys is þe karol þat þey sunge,
As telleþ þe latyne tunge:
Equitabat Beuo [etc.][14]

(This is the carol that they sang as the Latin language tells: *Bevo rode* [etc.].)

'Karol' here refers to the song sung. Precisely the same usage is found in Chaucer, in his version of the *Roman de la Rose* where, after the lines already quoted demonstrating that 'karoles' means dances exclusively, comes the passage:

This folk, of which I telle you soo,
Upon a karole wenten thoo.
A lady karolede hem that hyghte
Gladnesse, [the] blissful and the lighte.[15]

(These people, about whom I am telling you, performed a *carole* there, a lady called Gladness, cheerful and happy, sang a carol for them.)

---

to be the author here. Except where noted, citations from Chaucer are from *The Riverside Chaucer*, gen. ed, Larry D. Benson (1987, 3rd ed. Oxford, 1989).

12 *The Romaunt of the Rose*, ll. 802, 808.

13 'The Knight's Tale', l. 1931.

14 *Handlyng Synne*, ll. 9049–51.

15 *The Romaunt of the Rose*, ll. 743–6.

Karole here first means the dance, and then the verb *karolede* refers to the song that accompanies it. Did some special kind or kinds of song accompany it? In fact Chaucer, in his *Legend of Good Women*, writes of ladies dancing around a daisy 'And songyn as it were in carolewyse / This balade whiche that I schal ȝow deuyse' (and sang in the manner of a carole this ballade, which I shall set out for you.)[16] He then quotes a lyric in the form of a ballade. The ballade was not a lyric that accompanied dancing, so that it is difficult to discern what 'carolewyse' might mean here. It may indicate that a different lady sang each of its three stanzas just as in French texts a different person sings different short songs for *caroles*.

Dance lyrics are all but non-existent in Middle English, that is to say lyrics that can actually be shown to have been intended for dancing. Music is completely lacking. There is, however, one lyric that, by a circuitous route, may possibly be linked to the *carole*. This is 'Maiden in the Mor Lay' found with other lyrics (which may or may not be dance lyrics) on a loose leaf attached to a volume in the Bodleian Library in Oxford (see Appendix C).[17] The scribe has failed to copy out several of the lines that are required to be repeated, and there are a few scribal errors. This was evidently one of a number secular songs popular with the clergy of the diocese of Ossory in Ireland. Richard of Leatherhead, Bishop of Ossory between 1317 and 1369, thoroughly disapproved of such songs, however, and sought to remedy the situation by substituting sacred Latin words for the profane English ones. One of these *contrafacta* is 'Peperit Virgo', which bears an all but illegible marginal note identifying its original. Greene, however, has deciphered this note as '[M]ayde y[n] the moore [l]ay'.[18] Yet in neither the English source, nor in the Latin one, is the lyric called a *carol*. But Wenzel has drawn attention to a manuscript of the Latin text of a sermon preserved in Worcester Cathedral Library, in which the author dwells on the drink of mankind in the Golden Age: 'Et quis potus? Responditur in quodam cantico, viz. karole "þe mayde be wode lay"' (And what was their drink? The answer is to be found in a certain song, namely a carol called 'the maid lay by a wood').[19] Although the sermon refers to a wood rather than to a moor, a marginal note in English specifies 'þe cold water of þe well spryng', and thus identifies the lyric as that of the Moor Maiden.

While no positive evidence exists that the lyric is that of a song to accompany a *carole*, it seems at least plausible that this was so. The Latin *contrafactum* confirms

---

[16] Geoffrey Chaucer, *The Legend of Good Women*, ed. Janet Cowen and George Kane, Medieval Texts and Studies, No 16 (East Lansing, MI, 1995), ll. 199–202.

[17] OBL, MS Rawlinson, D. 913 (s. xiv), fol. 1v. The lyric has been published several times, not necessarily in the layout found here.

[18] See Richard Leighton Greene, '"The Maid of the Moor" in the Red Book of Ossory', *Speculum*, 27 (1952), 504–6, for his discovery of the *contrafactum* and for the Latin text; see also *The Lyrics of the Red Book of Ossory*, ed. Richard Leighton Greene, Medium Aevum Monographs, New Series, No 5 (Oxford, 1974), pp. ix-xiii.

[19] For text and comment, see Siegfried Wenzel, 'The Moor Maiden – A Contemporary View', *Speculum*, 49 (1974), 69–74 (especially pp. 71–2).

that every stanza of the original English consisted of nine lines. This means that every line has two stresses, which fit perfectly with the steps of the *carole*. Yet it is unlike any other dance song in English or in French. A tenuous connection exists between it and the rondeau in that both involve a substantial amount of repetition, but it is not a rondeau in spite of Greene's statement that 'it is in rondel verse-form, which is not found elsewhere in Middle English, nor does it occur, to my knowledge, in any other medieval Latin verse'.[20] It is only unique because no other candidates for English *carole* songs have so far been discovered. Certainly others must have existed, but are now lost, because they were not considered worth preserving, or they may exist but simply have not yet been identified as songs for *caroles*.

The French term, *carole*, was adopted into English as the name of a kind of dance and a kind of song that accompanied that dance. By the end of the fourteenth century, however, it was apparently becoming a lyric form unrelated to dancing. The poet Gower, in his *Confessio Amantis*, places the carol in the context of the French poetic *formes fixes*: 'And ek he can carolles make, / Rondeal, balade and virelai' (and he can also compose carols, rondeaux, ballades and virelais).[21] The carol, then, for Gower and others had a predetermined form. What that form was does not become evident until the first half of the fifteenth century. In a collection of verse in the British Library called the 'Thornton Miscellany', which could date from any time between 1414 and 1469, there is a piece entitled 'A Carolle ffor Crystynmesse … the Rose of Ryse'.[22] It is unfinished, but as it stands it begins with a refrain that is repeated after each of its three extant stanzas. Thus from the point of view of the placing of the refrain it broadly resembles the virelai. Moreover, a manuscript of the poems of John Audelay in the Bodleian Library dating from the second quarter of the fifteenth century contains 25 pieces in the same form prefaced by the injunction 'I pray ȝow syrus, boothe more and las, syng þese caroles in Cristemas' (I pray you sirs, both high and low, sing these carols at Christmas) and there are references such as 'þis carol' throughout the group.[23]

---

[20] *Red Book*, p. x.

[21] John Gower, *Confessio Amantis*, Liber Primus, ll. 2708–9 in *The English Works of John Gower*, ed. G. C. Macaulay, Early English Text Society, Extra Series, No 81 (1900; rpt, London, 1979), I; see also Liber Primus, ll. 2708–9, where the sense of *song* is quite explicit. Interestingly in this connection the French poet Charles d'Orléans, who was held prisoner in England from 1415 to 1440, composed four virelais, three in French and one in Latin, which he called 'caroles'; see *Charles d'Orléans: poésies*, ed. Pierre Champion (Paris, 1923) I, 287–90.

[22] LBL, Additional MS 31042 (s. xv^{1}), fol. 110^{v}. The poem and the dating of the manuscript are discussed in Karen Stern, 'The London "Thornton Miscellany": A New Description of British Museum Additional Manuscript 31042', *Scriptorium*, 30 (1976), 26–37 and 201–18.

[23] OBL, MS Douce 302 (s. xv$^{2/4}$), fols 27^{v}–32^{r}, printed in John Audelay, *The Poems of John Audelay*, ed. Ella Keats Whiting, The Early English Text Society, Original Series,

Some of the pieces have many stanzas. Lyrics such as these were manifestly not intended for dancing, and had, in fact, quite a different origin.

This lyric form, sometimes called the burden-and-stanza form, has been traced back by Robbins to a processional hymn in the liturgy for Palm Sunday in the Sarum Missal, of which the earliest manuscript dates from about 1264.[24] Seven boys begin the hymn with 'Gloria, laus et honor tibi sit, rex Christe redemptor / Cui puerile decus prompsit Hosanna pium' (Glory, praise and honour be to thee Christ, King and Redeemer, to whom virtuous boys proclaim a pious hosanna). The choir responds. The two earliest vernacular examples, however, are unambiguously secular love lyrics. One of these, 'Blow, Northerne Wynd', belongs to the second half of the thirteenth century or to the first decades of the fourteenth century, and consists of 10 stanzas with a burden.[25] The other, 'Nou Sprinkes the Sprai', has been dated on the manuscript evidence of the folio on which it is written to before 1303, and comprises a more modest three stanzas with a burden.[26] At least seven more fourteenth-century lyrics in this form, some incomplete, have been cited in anthologies, and are all religious. Notable among these is Friar Herebert's English version of 'Gloria, Laus et Honor', 'Wele Heriȝyng, and Worshype'.[27] An important source of four of the remaining six pieces is John Grimestone's commonplace book of 1372.[28] None of the English pieces, however, is called a

---

No 184 (London, 1931), pp. 181–214, where (p. vii) the manuscript is dated to the 'second quarter of the 15th Century'.

24 Rossell Hope Robbins, 'Friar Herebert and the Carol', *Anglia*, 75 (1957), 194–8. Robbins (pp. 195–6) cites the *Processionale ad Usum Insignis ac Praeclarae Ecclesiae Sarum*, ed. W. G. Henderson (1882; rpt Leeds, 1969), p. 52 for the Sarum text This edition, however, is itself a reprint of the processional printed by Morin of Rouen in 1508. I have preferred to use *The Sarum Missal Edited from Three Early Manuscripts*, ed. J. Wickham Legg (Oxford, 1916), p. 96, using a base manuscript dating from c. 1264 now in the John Rylands Library, Manchester. There are differences between the two texts, and the earlier one is obviously more relevant.

25 LBL, Harley MS 2253 (s. xiv^1), fols 72^v–73^v (*Index*, No 1395). This lyric has been edited several times, most notably in *The Harley Lyrics: The Middle English Lyrics of MS. Harley 2253*, ed. G. L. Brook (1948; 3rd ed. Manchester, 1964), No 14, where (p. 3) a date of c. 1314–25 is suggested for the manuscript. N. Ker, however, in his introduction to *Facsimile of British Museum Harley 2253*, Early English Text Society, No 255 (Oxford, 1965), p. xxi, states that the manuscript was copied in the 1340s.

26 London, Lincoln's Inn, MS Hale, 135 (before 1303), fol 137^v (*Index*, No 360). This is another popular anthology piece. It can be found, for example, in *English Lyrics of the XIIIth Century*, ed. Carleton Brown (Oxford, 1932), No 62. A note on p. 214 of this edition explains the dating.

27 LBL, Additional MS 46919 (formerly Phillipps 8336) (s. xiv), fol. 205^v. The lyric is edited in *Religious Lyrics of the XIVth Century*, ed. Carleton Brown (1924; 2nd ed. rev. G. V. Smithers, Oxford 1952), No 14.

28 *Religious Lyrics*, Nos, 352, 2024, 162 and 3961.

carol in their sources, notwithstanding the fact that they clearly have the form to which that appellation was later to be explicitly attached in the sources.

One awkward fact remains: no obvious relationship is discernible between the dance and its song on one hand and the burden-and-stanza form on the other, although the term *carol* came to be applied to both. The only similarity between a possible dance lyric, 'Maiden in the Mor Lay', and the non-dance form is that both involve much repetition. In one, different lines are repeated in each stanza; in the other the same lines are repeated for every stanza. It may be, then, that the term *carol* came to be applied to any lyric with this feature, whether it had a refrain or not.[29] Certainly the *formes fixes*, with their characteristic refrains, are extremely rare in English in the period under review.[30]

The two earliest lyrics in burden-and stanza form are secular, and carols in this sense on a variety of topics were common in the fifteenth century so that the subject matter in no way defines the form, as Greene is at pains to point out.[31] Nevertheless, apart from the two examples cited ('Blow Northern Wynd' and 'Nou Sprinkes the Sprai') the theme of remaining extant pieces is frequently the Nativity, and the connection with Christmas persists into the fifteenth century as exemplified in the 'Thornton Miscellany' and John Audelay's collection. And, of course, the word *carol*, if not the form, is still associated in English with Christmas to this day.

[29] Much later Shakespeare evidently understood 'carol' to mean a secular lyric of several stanzas each ending with a refrain, see *As You Like It*, V, 3, 'It was a lover and his lass'.

[30] Obvious exceptions are the rondeau at the conclusion of Chaucer's *Parliament of Fowls*, ed. Larry D. Benson, ll. 680–92, and the ballade in the interpolated lines of his *Legend of Good Women* cited above.

[31] See *The Early English Carols*, ed. Richard Leighton Greene, (1935; 2nd ed. Oxford, 1977), where Greene defines carol lyrics composed before 1550 as 'a song on any subject, composed of uniform stanzas and provided with a burden' (pp. xxxii–xxxiii). He stresses the variety of subject matter throughout his introduction.

Appendix A
Music Examples

Example 1 Jacquemart Gielée, *Renart le Nouvel*

(a) 'Vous n'ales mie' (ll. 2544ff)
'Rois Nobles' (male)

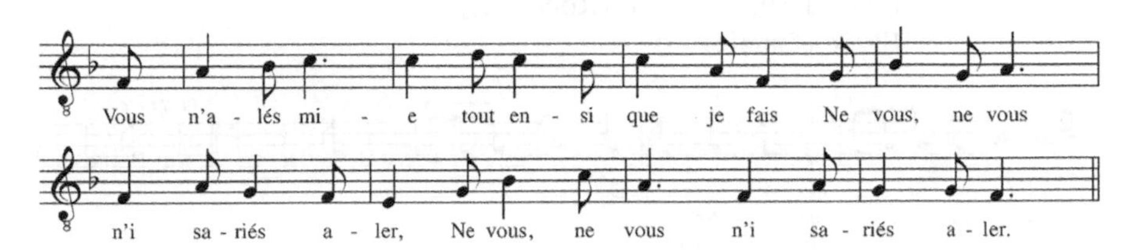

You do not go the way I do, nor would you go that way.

(b) 'Ja ne serai sans amour' (ll. 2548ff)
'La roine' (female)

I shall certainly never be without love all my life.

(c) 'Tres douche dame jolie' (ll. 2552ff)
'Renars' (male)

My very sweet lively lady, listen to my heart beseeching you.

(d) 'Hé Dieus' (ll. 2556ff)
'Hersens' (female)

Hé, Dieus, che - le m'a___ tra - ì___ Qui m'a to - lu mon___ a - mi.

Oh heavens, she has betrayed me by taking away my friend.

Example 2 Jean Brisebarre, *Li Restor du Paon*
'Ensi va' (ll. 1170–73) (Rondeau))
'Elyot' (female)

Last time
1 *En - si va___ qui A - mours* 2 *De - mai - ne - a son com - mant.*
3 A qui que___ soit do - lours,
4 *En - si va___ qui A - mours.*
5 As mau - vais___ est lan - gours 6 Nos biens, mais___ non por - quant,
7 *En - si va___ qui A - mours* 8 *De - mai - ne a son com - ment.*

Ensi va qui Amours	*Thus he goes whom Love*
Demaine a son commant.	*leads at his command.*
A qui que soit dolours,	Suffer who may,
Ensi va qui Amours.	*thus he goes whom Love.*
As mauvais est langours	To the bad our good
Nos biens mais nonporquant,	is ill, but nonetheless,
Ensi va qui Amours	*thus he goes whom Love*
Demaine a son commant.	*leads at his command.*

Appendix B
Manuscripts Cited in Chapter 9

Chrétien de Troyes, *Le Conte du Graal (Perceval)*

1. Montpellier, Bibliothèque de la Faculté de Médecine, MS 249 (s. xiii^{ex}), fol. no. not known; reproduction held in London, Courtauld Institute of Art, Conway Library, Box 28

Ysopet de Lyon

2. Lyon, Bibliothèque de l'Académie des Sciences, Belles-Lettres et Arts, MS 57 (s. xiii^{ex} / s. xiv^{int}), fol. 9^{v}

Jean Brisebarre, *Li Restor du Paon*

3. OBL, MS Bodley 264 (text finished 18 December 1338, but illustrations not completed until 18 April 1334), fol. 181^{v}

La Châtelaine de Vergy

4. London, British Museum, Ivories 367, ivory casket (s. xiv $^{2/4}$), left panel

Prose Lancelot

5. PBN, fonds fr. 110 (s. xiii^{ex}), fol. 358^{v}
6. LBL, Additional MS 10293 (c. 1316), fol. 292^{v}
7. LBL, MS Royal 20 D IV (1310-20), fol. 237^{v}
8. OBL, MS Douce 199 (1325-30), fol. 99^{v}
9. PBN, fonds fr. 333 (s. xiv^{int}), fol. 51^{v}
10. New Haven, Yale University, MS 229 (s. xiv^{int}), fol. 66^{v}

Guillaume de Lorris, *Le Roman de la Rose* (first part)

11. OBL, MS Additional A. 22 (c. 1300), fol.15^{r}
12. LBL, MS Stowe 947 (s. xiv^{int}), fol. 7^{r}
13. Lyon, Bibliothèque Municipale, MS 23 (s. xiv^{int}), fol. 7^{v}
14. New York, Pierpont Morgan Library, MS M 372 (s. xiv^{int}), fol. 6^{v}
15. Princeton, Princeton University, Medieval and Renaissance MSS Garnett 126 (s. xiv^{int}), fol. 7^{r}
16. PBN, fonds fr. 1569 (s. xiv^{int}), fol. 6^{v}
17. PBN, fonds fr. 24388 (s. xiv^{int}), fol. 8^{r}
18. PBN, fonds fr. 9345 (s. xiv^{int}), fol. 4^{v}
19. PBN, fonds fr. 1560 (s. xiv^{int}), fol. 6^{v}
20. PBN, fonds fr. 1565 (s. xiv^{int}), [fol. 6^{v}]
21. OBL, MS Selden supra 57 (s. xiv^{int}), fol. 6^{v}

22. PBN, fonds fr. 1558 (s. xiv$^{1/3}$), fol. 7^{v}
23. LBL, MS Royal 20 A XVII (s. xiv$^{1/4}$), fol. 9^{r}
24. Tournai, Bibliothèque de la Ville, MS C1 (dated 1330), p. 30
25. New York, Pierpont Morgan Library, MS M 503 (c. 1340), fol. 6^{v}
26. Paris, Bibliothèque de l'Arsenal, MS 5209 (c.1340), fol. no. not known
27. LBL, MS Royal 19 B XIII (s. xiv^{1}), fol. 10^{v}
28. PBN, fonds fr. 1567 (s. xiv^{1}), fol. 7^{r}
29. PBN, fonds fr. 19156 (s. xiv^{1}), fol. 6^{r}
30. PBN, fonds fr. 1564 (s. xiv^{1}), fol. 4^{r}
31. PBN, fonds fr. 12588 (s. xiv^{1}), fol. 6^{r}
32. Germany, Private Collection (MS formerly on loan to OBL, where it had the pressmark MS Astor A 12), (c. 1350), fol. 9^{v}
33. (Same MS), fol. 11^{v}
34. (Same MS), fol. 12^{r}
35. Chantilly, Musée Condé, MS 1480 (c. 1350), fol. 13^{r}
36. PBN, fonds fr. 12593 (s. xiv^{med}), p. xiii
37. PBN, fonds fr. 25526 (s.xiv^{med}), fol.7^{r}
38. Brussels, Bibliothèque Royale de Belgique, MS 11187 (c. 1360), fol. 1^{r}
39. LBL, MS Yates Thompson 21 (c.1360), fol. 8^{v}
40. PBN, fonds fr. 24390 (s. xiv$^{2/3}$), 'fol. 7^{v}' [*recte* fol. 6^{v}]
41. PBN, fonds fr. 24389 (s. xiv$^{2/3}$), fol. 6^{v}
42. LBL, MS Additional 31840 (s. xiv$^{2/3}$), fol.11^{r+v}
43. Vienna, Hofbibliothek, Codex 2592 (s. xiv^{2}), fol. 6^{v}
44. OBL, MS e Museo 65 (c.1380), fol. 3^{v}
45. PBN, fonds fr. 1665 (s. xiv^{ex}), fol.7^{r}
46. PBN, fonds fr. 1570 (s. xiv^{ex}), fol. 8^{r}
47. Amsterdam, MS (s. xiv^{ex}) sold on 3 April 1906, fol. no. not known; reproduction in London, Courtauld Institute of Art, Conway Library, Box 37
48. LBL, MS Additional 12042 (c. 1400), fol. 7^{r}
49. PBN, fonds fr. 380 (c. 1400), [fol. 7^{v}]
50. PBN, fonds fr. 1563 (c. 1400), fol. 7^{r}

Appendix C
'Maiden in the Mor Lay'

Maiden in the mor lay –		A maiden lay in the moor,
In the mor lay		lay in the moor,
Sevenyght[es][1] fulle –		full seven nights,
Sevenight[es][2] fulle.		full seven nights.
Maiden in the mor lay –	5	A maiden lay in the moor,
In the mor lay		lay in the moor,
Sevenightes[3] fulle –		full seven nights,
[Sevenightes fulle]		full seven nights,
Ant a day.		and a day.
Welle[4] was hire mete.	10	Her food was good.
Wat was hire mete?		What was her food?
Þe primerole ant the –		The primrose and the—
Þe primerole ant the –		the primrose and the—
Welle was hire mete		Her food was good.
Wat was hire mete?	15	What was her food?
The primerole and the –		The primrose and the—
[The primerole ant the]		the primrose and the
Vïolet.		violet.
Welle [was hire dryng.]		Her drink was good
Wat was hire dryng?	20	What was her drink?
Þe chelde water of þe –		The cold water of the –
[Þe chelde water of þe –		the cold water of the –
Welle was hire dryng.		Her drink was good.
Wat was hire dryng?		What was her drink?
Þe chelde water of þe –	25	The cold water of the –
Þe chelde water of þe]		the cold water of the –
Welle-spring.[5]		wellspring.

[1] 3. MS: seuenyst
[2] 4. MS: seuenist
[3] 7. MS: seuenistes
[4] 10. MS: wat
[5] 27. MS: springe*s*

Welle was hire bour		Her chamber was good.
Wat was hire bour?		What was her chamber?
Þe rede rose ant the –[6]	30	The red rose and the –
[Þe rede rose ant the –		the red rose and the –
Welle was hire bour.		Her chamber was good.
Wat was hire bour?		What was her chamber?
Þe rede rose ant the –		The red rose and the –
Þe rede rose ant the]	35	the rede rose and the
Lilie flour.		lily flower.

[6] 30. MS: ante

Bibliography

Manuscripts

London, The British Library

Additional, 10293 (c. 1316). 'The Prose Lancelot'
Additional, 11880 (s. ix^{int}). Venantius Fortunatus, 'Vita Sanctae Radegundae'
Additional, 31042 (s. xv^{1}). The Thornton Miscellany Additional, 46919 (formerly Phillipps 8336) (s. xiv). Friar Herebert, 'Wele Heriȝying and Worshype'
Cotton Caligula, A XI (1320–30). 'The Metrical Chronicle of Robert of Gloucester'
Cotton Vespasian, A III (s. xiv$^{1/4}$). 'Cursor Mundi'
Harley, 1605 (s. xii^{med}). Stonehenge in the Harley Fragment
Harley, 2253 (s. xiv^{1}). 'Blow, Northerne Wynd'

London, Lincoln's Inn

Hale, 135 (before 1303). 'Nou Sprinkes the Sprai'

Oxford, The Bodleian Library

Douce, 302 (s. xv$^{2/4}$). The Poems of John Audelay
Douce, 320 (s. xii^{1}). The Oxford Psalter
Rawlinson, D. 913 (s. xiv). 'Maiden in the Mor Lay'

Paris, Bibliothèque Nationale de France

Fonds fr. 12615 (1270s–80s). The Chansonnier de Noailles
Fonds fr. 25566 (1291–97). The La Vallière Manuscript. Jacquemart Gielée, *Renart le Nouvel* and the works of Adam de la Halle
Fonds fr. 9113 (xiii^{ex}). Jean d'Antioche, 'Le Livre de grant delict'
Fonds fr. MS Rothschild 3085.IV. I. 5 (c. 1330). Jean de Vignay, 'Le Livre des oisivetez des emperieres'
Fonds lat. 17509 (s. xiii). Jacques de Vitry, 'Sermones Vulgares'

Printed Works

(Writers living before c. 1500 will be found under their *first* name or, in the case of Classical Greek and Latin authors, under the common English form of their names e.g. Pliny the Elder, Virgil)

Abert, Herman, 'Die Musikästhetik der Echecs Amoureux'. *Sammelbände der Internationalen Musikgesellschaft*. 6 (1904–05), 346–55

Adam de la Bassée, *Ludus super Anticlaudianum*. Ed. Abbé Paul Bayart. Tourcoing, 1930

Adam de la Halle, *Le Jeu de Robin et de Marion*. Ed. Kenneth Varty. London, 1960

— *The Lyric Works of Adam de la Halle*. Ed. Nigel Wilkins. Corpus Mensurabilis Musicae, No 44. n.p., 1967

Adenet le Roi, *Les Oeuvres d'Adenet le Roi*. Ed. Albert Henry. Université Libre de Bruxelles, Travaux de la Faculté de Philosophie et Lettres, Nos 45 and 46. Brussels, 1963–71

Aeppli, Fritz, 'Die wichtigsten Ausdrücke für das Tanzen in den romanischen Sprachen'. *Beihefte zur Zeitschrift für romanische Philologie*. 75 (1925), 33–6, 90–95

Alain Chartier, *The Poetical Works of Alain Chartier*. Ed. J. C. Laidlaw. London, 1974

Alexander Neckam, 'De Laudibus Divinae Sapientiae Distinctiones Decem' in *De Naturis Rerum*. Ed. Thomas Wright. London, 1863, pp. 355–503

Alford, Violet, 'The Farandole'. *Journal of the English Folk Dance and Song Society*. 1 (1932), 18–33

Anglo-Norman Dictionary. Ed. William Rothwell *et al*. London, 1992

Antonio da Tempo, *Summa Artis Rithimici Vulgaris Dictaminis*. Ed. Richard Andrews. Collezione di opere inedite o rare pubblicata dalla Commissione per i Testi di Lingua, No 136. Bologna, 1977

Apuleius, *Apulée: opuscules philosophiques*. Ed. and trans. Jean Beaujeu. Paris, 1973

Arbeau, Thoinot [pseud. Jean Tabourot], *Orchesographie par Thoinot Arbeau: réimpression précédée d'une notice sur les danses du XVIe siècle par Laure Fonta*. Facsimile of the edition of 1589. Biblioteca Musica Bononiensis, II, No 102. Bologna, 1981

Armannino Giudice, 'La Fiorita' in *Testi inediti di storia trojana* [etc.]. Ed. Egidio Gorra. Biblioteca di testi inediti e rari, No 1. Turin, 1887, pp. 532–61

L'Art d'amours: *traduction et commentaire de l'*Ars Amatoria *d'Ovide*. Ed. Bruno Roy. 3 vols. Leiden, 1974

Aubry, Pierre, 'La Danse au Moyen Age'. *La Revue Musicale* [originally *La Revue d'Histoire et de Critique Musicales*]. 9 (1909), 109–15

Aucassin et Nicolette: *édition critique*. Ed. and trans. Jean Dufournet. Paris, 1973

Avril, François, *L'Enluminure à la Cour de France*. Paris, 1978

— *Manuscript Painting at the Court of France: The Fourteenth Century (1310–1380)*. Trans. Ursule Molinaro and Bruce Benderson. London, 1978 (translation of the preceding work)

Baldwin, John, W., 'Once there was an emperor ...: A Political Reading of the Romances of Jean Renart' in *Jean Renart and the Art of Romance: Essays on* Guillaume de Dole. Ed. Nancy Vine Durling. Gainsville, FL, 1997, pp. 45–82

Bartholomaeis, Vincenzo de, *Le origini della poesia drammatica italiana*. Bologna, 1924

Bataillon, M., rev. of *Etude sur la carole médiévale*, by Margit Sahlin. *Bulletin Hispanique*. 42 (1940), 328–31

Battaglia, Salvatore, *et al.* (eds), *Grande dizionario della lingua italiana*. 21 vols. Turin, 1961–2002

Baudouin de Condé, *Dits et contes de Baudouin de Condé et de son fils Jean de Condé*. Ed. Auguste Scheler. 3 vols. Brussels, 1866–67

Baudouin de Sebourc. Ed. Larry S. Crist. 2 vols. Abbeville, 2002

Baumel, Jean, *Les Danses populaires, les farandoles, les rondes, les jeux chorégraphiques et les ballets du Languedoc méditerranéan*. Paris, 1958

Bec, Pierre, *La Lyrique française au Moyen Age (XIIe–XIIIe siècles): contribution à une typologie des genres poétiques médiévaux*. Publications d'Etudes Supérieures de l'Université de Poitiers, No 6. 2 vols. Paris, 1977–78

Bédier, Joseph, 'Les Plus Anciennes Danses françaises'. *Revue des Deux Mondes*. 31 (jan–fév. 1906), 398–424

Bédier, Joseph and Paul Hazard, *Histoire de la littérature française illustrée*. 2 vols. Paris, 1923–24

Benoît de Sainte-Maure, *Le Roman de Troie*. Ed. Léopold Constans. 6 vols. Paris, 1904–12

Berman, Peggy, R., 'French Names for the Dance to 1588: A Dissertation in Romance Languages'. PhD Diss. University of Pennsylvania, 1968

Bernabei, Bruno, 'Riddare'. *Enciclopedia dantesca*. 2nd ed. Rome, 1984

Bernard of Clairvaux, *Saint, Li Sermon Saint Bernart: älteste franzsösische Übersetzung der lateinischen Predigten Bernhards von Clairvaux* [etc.]. Ed. Wendelin Foerster. Erlangen, 1885

— *Sancti Bernardi Primi Abbatis Claravallensis Sermones de Tempore, de Sanctis, de Diversis, ad Tertiam Editionem Mabilloniam cum Codicibus Austriacis Bohemicis Styriacis Collatam*. 2 vols. Vienna, 1891

Bertoni, Giulio, *L'elemento germanico nella lingua italiana*. Genoa, 1914

Besseler, Heinrich, *Die Musik des Mittelalters und Renaissance*. Potsdam, 1931

The Bible. Old Testament: I Book of Samuel, The Psalms, The Proverbs. New Testament: The Gospel According to Matthew

Blancandin et l'Orgueilleuse d'Amour: roman d'aventure du XIIIe siècle. Ed. Franklin P. Sweetser. Geneva, 1964

Boogaard, Nico H. J. van den, 'Jacquemart Gielée et la lyrique de son temps' in *Alain de Lille, Gautier de Châtillon, Jakmart Giélée et leur temps*. Actes du

Colloque de Lille, Octobre 1978. Ed. H. Roussel and F. Suard. Lille, 1980, 333–53

Borck, Karl-Heinz, 'Der Tanz zu Kölbigk'. *Beiträge zur Geschichte der deutschen Sprache und Literatur*. 76 (1954), 243–320

Borel, Pierre (ed.) *Trésor de recherches et antiquitez gauloises et françoises, reduites en order alphabétique*. Paris, 1655

Borinski, Karl, 'La Chastelaine de Vergy in der Kunst des Mittelalters'. *Monatshefte fuer Kunstwissenschaft*. 2 (1909), 58–63

Bowles, Edmund A., 'Instrumente des 15. Jahrhunderts und Ikonographie'. *Basler Jahrbuch für historische Musikpraxis* [vol. for 1984], 8 (1985), 11–50

Brainard, Ingrid, 'Dance, Art. 3 (1)' *New Grove 2*

— 'Medieval Dance'. *International Encyclopedia of Dance: A Project of Dance Perspectives Foundation*. Ed. Selma Jeanne Cohen *et al*. New York, 1998

Brown, Carleton, 'Text and the Man: Presidential Address Given in London, June 30, 1928'. *M.H.R.A.:Bulletin of the Modern Humanities Research Association*. 2 (1928), 97–111

Brüll, Hugo (ed.), *Untergegangene und veraltete Worte des französischen im heutigen Englisch*. Halle, 1913

Brunet, Jacques-Charles, *Manuel du libraire et de l'amateur de livres*. 5th ed. Paris, 1860–65

The Brut or The Chronicles of England. Ed. Friedrich W. D. Brie. The Early English Text Society, Original Series, No 131. London, 1906

Caldwell, James R., 'The Autograph Manuscript of Gervase of Tilbury (Vatican, Vat. Lat. 933)'. *Scriptorium*. 11 (1957), 87–98

— 'The Interrelationship of the Manuscripts of Gervase of Tilbury's *Otia Imperialia*'. *Scriptorium*. 16 (1962), 246–74

— 'Manuscripts of Gervase of Tilbury's *Otia Imperialia*'. *Scriptorium*. 16 (1962), 28–45

The Canterbury Psalter. Facsimile with an introduction by M. R. James. London, 1935

Cavallo, Marco A., 'Carola'. *Enciclopedia dantesca*. 2nd ed. Rome, 1984

The Chansons of the Troubadours and Trouvères. Ed. Hendrik van der Werf. Utrecht, 1972

Charles d'Orléans, *Charles d'Orléans: poésies*. Ed. Pierre Champion. 2 vols. Paris, 1923–27

La Châtelaine de Vergy. Ed. and Fr. trans. Jean Dufournet and Liliane Dulac. Paris, 1994

Le Chevalier du Papegau. Ed. Ferdinand Heuckenkamp. Halle, 1896

Chrétien de Troyes, *Le Chevalier de la Charrette*. Les Romans de Chrétien de Troyes, III. Ed. Mario Roques. Paris, 1958

— *Le Conte du Graal* (*Perceval*). Les Romans de Chrétien de Troyes, V. Ed. Félix Lecoy. 2 vols. Paris, 1972–75

— *Eric et Enide*. Les Romans de Chrétien de Troyes, I. Ed. Mario Roques. Paris, 1952

— (attrib.), *Guillaume d'Angleterre*. Ed. A. J. Holden. Geneva, 1988

Christine de Pizan, *Oeuvres poétiques de Christine de Pisan*. Ed. Maurice Roy. 3 vols. Paris, 1886–96

Chronique du religieux de Saint Denys, contenant le règne de Charles VI, de 1380 à 1422. Ed. L. Bellaguet. 6 vols. Paris, 1839–52

La Court de Paradis: poème anonyme du XIIIe *siècle*. Ed. Eva Vilamo-Pentti. Suomalaisen Tiedeakatemian Toimituksia, Series B, No 79/1. Helsinki, 1953

Cursor Mundi (The Cursor of the World: A Northumbrian Poem of the XIVth Century in Four Versions). Ed. Rev. Richard Morris. 3 vols. The Early English Text Society, Original Series, Nos 57, 59, 62, 68, 99 and 101. London, 1874–93

Czerwinski, Albert, *Geschichte der Tanzkunst bei den cultiven Völkern von den ersten Anfängen bis auf die gegenwärtige Zeit*. Leipzig, 1862

Dahms, Sibylle, 'Tanz. 1. Mittelalter'. *MGG 2*

Dante Alighieri, *The Divine Comedy of Dante Alighieri*. Ed. and trans. John D. Sinclair. 3 vols. Rpt, New York, 1961

— *Rime: rime dubbie*. Vol. VII. Ed. Domenico de Robertis. 3 Testi. Società Dantesca Italiana. Florence, 2002

Dauzat, Albert (ed.), *Dictionnaire étymologique de la langue française*. Paris, 1938

Delany, Joseph F., 'Baptismal Vows'. *The Catholic Encyclopedia*. Ed. Charles G. Herbermann *et al*. New York, 1907–12

Delbouille, Maurice, 'Sur les traces de "Bele Aëlis"'. *Mélanges de philologie romane dédiés à la mémoire de Jean Boutière (1899–1967)*. Vol. I. Ed. Irénée Cluzel and François Pirot. Liège, 1971, 199–218

Dictionnaire de la musique. Ed. Marc Honegger. 4 vols. Paris, 1970–76

Diefenbach, Laurentius (ed.), *Glossarium Latino–Germanicum Mediae et Infimae Aetatis*. Frankfurt-am-Main, 1857

Diez, Friedrich (ed.), *Etymologisches Wörterbuch der romanischen Sprachen*. 1st ed., Bonn, 1853

— *Etymologisches Wörterbuch der romansichen Sprachen*, 2nd ed., 2 vols. Bonn, 1861–62

— *Etymologisches Wörterbuch der romanischen Sprachen*. 5th ed., Bonn, 1887

Dino Compagni, *Cronica*. Ed. Gino Luzzato. NUE, nuova serie, No 46. Rpt, Turin, 1978

Dizionario enciclopedico universale della musica e dei musicisti. Ed. Alberto Basso. 13 vols. Turin, 1983–90

Doss-Quinby, Eglal, *Les Refrains chez les trouvères du XII*[e] *siècle au début du XIV*[e] *siècle*. American University Studies, Series II, No 17. New York, 1984

Dronke, Peter, *The Medieval Lyric*. 3rd ed., Cambridge, 1996

Du Fresne, Charles, seigneur du Cange (ed.), *Glossarium Mediae et Infimae Latinitatis* [1678], rev. Léopold Favre. 10 vols. Niort, 1883–87

The Eadwine Psalter: Text, Image, and Monastic Culture in Twelfth-Century Canterbury. Ed. Margaret Gibson, T. A. Heslop and Richard Pfaff. Publications of the Modern Humanities Research Association, No 14. London, 1992

The Early English Carols. Ed. Richard Leighton Greene. 2nd ed., Oxford, 1977

Early Middle English Verse and Prose. Ed. J. A. W. Bennett and G. V. Smithers. Rpt, Oxford, 1974

Earp, Lawrence, 'Lyrics for Reading and Lyrics for Singing in Late Medieval France: The Development of the Dance Lyric from Adam de la Halle to Guillaume de Machaut' in *The Union of Words and Music in Medieval Poetry*. Ed. Rebecca A. Baltzer, Thomas Cable and James I. Wimsatt. Austin, TX, 1991, 101–31

Eggebrecht, Heinrich, *Handwörterbuch der musikalischen Terminologie*. 4 vols. Stuttgart, 1972–94

Enciclopedia della musica. Ed. Claudio Sartori. 4 vols. Milan, 1963–64

Encyclopédie de la musique. Ed. François Michel. 3 vols. Paris, 1958–61

English Lyrics of the XIIIth Century. Ed. Carleton Brown. Oxford, 1932

Epigrammatum Anthologia Palatina. Ed. Friedrich Dübner. 3 vols. Paris, 1864–90

L'Ere baroque en France: répertoire chronologique des éditions de textes littéraires. Ed. Roméo Arbour. Geneva, 1977–

Etienne de Bourbon, *Anecdotes historiques, légendes et apologues tirés du recueil inédit d'Etienne de Bourbon*. Ed. Richard Albert Lecoy de la Marche. Paris, 1877

Eustache Deschamps, *Oeuvres complètes de Eustache Deschamps*. Ed. Auguste Henri Edouard, marquis de Queux de Saint-Hilaire and Gaston Raynaud. 11 vols. Paris, 1878–1903

Ewert, Alfred, *The French Language*. Rpt, London, 1969

Fabyan Robert, *The New Chronicles of England and France, in Two Parts, by Robert Fabyan* [1516]. Ed. Henry Ellis. London, 1811

Falk, Paul, rev. of *Etude sur la carole médiévale*, by Margit Sahlin. *Studia Neophilologica*. 13 (1940–41), 134–9

Faral, Edmond, *La Vie quotidienne au temps de Saint Louis*. Rpt, Paris, 1956

Fazio degi Uberti, *Il dittamondo e le rime*. Ed. Giuseppe Corsi. 2 vols. Scrittori d'Italia, Nos 206 and 207. Bari, 1952

Federico Frezzi, *Il quadriregio*. Ed. Enrico Filippini. Bari, 1914

Fleming, John V., *The* Roman de la Rose*: A Study in Allegory and Iconography*. Princeton, NJ, 1969

Fleuriot, Léon (ed.), *A Dictionary of Old Breton: Dictionnaire du vieux Breton*. 2 vols. Rpt, Toronto, 1985

Floriant et Florete. Ed. Harry F. Williams. University of Michigan Publications, Language and Literature, No 23. Ann Arbor, MI, 1947

Flutre, Louis-Ferdinand. 'Etudes sur le Roman de *Perceforêt*: premier article'. *Romania*. 70 (1948), 474–522

Foerster, W., 'II Etymologisches'. *Zeitschrift für romanische Philologie*. 6 (1882), 108–16

Folgore da San Gimignano [i.e. Jacobo di Michele], *Le rime di Folgore da San Gemignano e di Cene da la Chitarra d'Arezzo*. Ed. Giulio Navone. Bologna, 1880

Förster, Max, 'Can Old French *caroler* be of Celtic Origin?' *Language*. 4 (1928), 200–01

Fortescue, Adrian, 'Durandus, William the Younger'. *The Catholic Encylopedia*. Ed. Charles G. Herbermann *et al*. NewYork, 1907–12

Fouché, Pierre, *Phonétique historique du français*. 3 vols. Paris, 1966–69

Fourez, Lucien, 'Le *Roman de la Rose* de la Bibliothèque de la Ville de Tournai'. *Scriptorium: Revue Internationale des Etudes Relatives aux Manuscrits / International Review of Manuscript Studies*. 1 (1946–47), 213–39

Fowler, Maria Vedder, 'Musical Interpolations in Thirteenth- and Fourteenth-Century French Narratives'. 2 vols. PhD Diss., Yale University, 1979

Francesco da Barberino, *Reggimento e costume di donna*. Ed. Giuseppe E. Sansone. Collezione di 'Filogia Romanza', No 2. Turin, 1957

Francesco di Bartolo da Buti, *Commento di Francesco da Buti sopra la Divina Comedia di Dante Allighieri*. Ed. Crescentino Giannini. 3 vols. Pisa, 1858–62

Franco Sacchetti, *Opere*. Ed. Alberto Chiari. 2 vols. Bari, 1936–38

Französisches etymologisches Wörterbuch. Ed. Walther von Wartburg. Bonn, 1928–

Gaimar (Geffrei), *L'Estoire des Engleis*. Ed. Alexander Bell. Anglo-Norman Texts, Nos 14–15. Oxford, 1960

Gaydon: *chanson de geste*. Ed. F. Guessard and S. Luce. Paris, 1862

Geoffrey Chaucer, *The Legend of Good Women*. Ed. Janet Cowen and George Kane. Medieval Texts and Studies, No 16. East Lansing, MI, 1995

— *The Riverside Chaucer*. Gen. ed. Larry D. Benson. 3rd ed., Oxford, 1989

Geoffrey of Monmouth, *The* Historia Regum Britannie *of Geoffrey of Monmouth*. Ed. Neil Wright and Julia C. Crick. 5 vols. Cambridge, 1985–91

Georges Chastellain (attrib.), 'Le Livre des faits du bon chevalier messire Jacques de Lalaing' in *Oeuvres de Georges Chastellain*. Ed. Baron Joseph Kervyn de Lettenhove. Vol. VIII. Brussels, 1866, 1–259

Gérard d'Amiens, *Der Roman von Escanor von Gerard von Amiens*. Ed. H. Michelant. Tübingen, 1886

Gerbert de Montreuil, *Le Roman de la Violette, ou de Gérart de Nevers par Gerbert de Montreuil*. Ed. Douglas Labaree Buffum. Paris, 1928

Gérold, Théodore, *Histoire de la musique des origines à la fin du XIVe siècle*. Paris, 1936

— *La Musique au Moyen Age*. Paris, 1932

Gervase of Tilbury, *Gervasii Tilberiensis Otia Imperialia ad Ottonem IV Imperatorem* [c. 1209–c. 1214] in *Scriptores Rerum Brunsvicensium Illustrationi Inservientes*. Ed. Godfried Wilhelm Leibnitz. Hannover, 1707, pp. 881–1004

Gilles Le Muisit, *Poésies de Gilles Li Muisis*. Ed. Baron Joseph Kervyn de Lettenhove. 2 vols. Louvain, 1882

Giovanni Boccaccio, *Decameron*. Ed. Vittore Branca. 6th ed., Turin, 1992

— *Esposizioni sopra la comedia di Dante*. Ed. Giorgio Padoan. Tutte le opere di Giovanni Boccaccio. Ed. Vittore Branca. Vol VI. Milan, 1965

Giraldus Cambrensis, 'Gemma Ecclesiastica' in *Giraldi Cambrensis Opera*. Vol II. Ed. J. S. Brewer. London, 1862

Godefroy, Frédéric (ed.), *Dictionnaire de l'ancienne langue française et de tous ses dialectes du IXe siècle au XVe siècle*. 10 vols. Paris, 1880–1902

Goetz, Georg *et al.* (eds), *De Glossariorum Latinorum Origine et Fatis*. 7 vols. Rpt, Amsterdam, 1965

Grandgent, Charles Hill, *An Introduction to Vulgar Latin*. Rpt, New York, 1962

Greene, Richard Leighton, '"The Maid of the Moor" in the Red Book of Ossory'. *Speculum*. 27 (1952), 504–6

Greimas, Algirdas Julien and Teresa Mary Kane (eds), *Dictionnaire du moyen français*: *la Renaissance*. Paris, 1992

Gröber, G., 'Vulgärlateinische Substrate romanischer Wörter' in *Archiv für lateinische Lexikographie und Grammatik*. 1 (1884) , p. 552, 'Corolla'

Gross, Laila, '"La Chastelaine de Vergi" Carved in Ivory'. *Viator: Medieval and Renaissance Studies*. 10 (1979), 311–21

Grosskreuz, Peter, 'Tanzquellen des Mittelalters und der Renaissance'. *Gutenberg Jahrbuch*. 66 (1991) 324–39

Grundriss der romanischen Literaturen des Mittelalters. Ed. Jürgen Beyer and Franz Koppe. Vol VI. Heidelberg, 1968–70

Guglielmus Durandus, *Rationale Divinorum Officiorum* [etc.]. Ed. V. D'Avino. Naples, 1859

Guibert de Nogent, *Autobiographie*. Ed. and Fr. trans. Edmond-René Labande. Les Classiques de l'Histoire de France au Moyen Age, No 34. Paris, 1981

— *Guibert de Nogent*: *histoire de sa vie (1053–1124)*. Ed. Georges Bourgin. Paris. 1907

Guido Faba, 'Gemma purpurea' in *La Prosa del Duecento*. Ed. Cesare Segre and Mario Marti. La letteratura italiana: storia e testi, No 3. Milan, 1959

Guillaume de Lorris and Jean de Meun, *Le Roman de la Rose*. Ed. Félix Lecoy. 3 vols. Paris, 1965–70

Guillaume de Machaut, *Le Jugement du roy de Behaigne* and *Remède de Fortune*. Ed. James I. Wimsatt and William W. Kibler; mus. ed. Rebecca A. Baltzer. Athens, GA, 1988

— *La Prise d'Alixandrie (The Taking of Alexandria)*. Ed. and trans. R. Barton Palmer. New York, 2002

— *Oeuvres de Guillaume de Machaut*. Ed. Ernest Hoepffner. 3 vols. Paris, 1908–21

Guillaume de Nangis, *Gesta Philippi Regis Franciae Filii Sanctae Memoriae Regis Ludovici*. Ed. [P.] Daunou and [J.] Naudet. Recueil des Historiens des Gaules et de la France. Vol. XX. Paris, 1840

Guiter, Henri, rev. of *Etude sur la carole médievale*, by Margit Sahlin. *Revue des Langues Romanes*. 69 (1945), 345–6

Guy, Henri, *Essai sur la vie et les oeuvres littéraires du trouvère Adan de la Hale*. Paris, 1898

Haberl, Rudolf, 'Neue Beiträge zur romanischen Linguistik'. *Zeitschrift für romanische Philologie*. 36 (1912), 303–11

Harding, Ann, *An Investigation into the Use and Meaning of Medieval German Dancing Terms*. Göppinger Arbeiten zur Germanistik, No 93. Göppingen, 1973

The Harley Lyrics. *Facsimile of British Museum, MS. Harley 2253*. Introduction by N. Ker. The Early English Text Society, No 255. Oxford, 1965

— *The Harley Lyrics*: *The Middle English Lyrics of MS. Harley 2253*. Ed. G. L. Brook. 3rd ed., Manchester, 1964

Hauréau, Jean Barthélemy, *Notices et extraits de quelques manuscrits latins de la Bibliothèque Nationale*. 6 vols. Paris, 1890–93

Hemon, Roparz (ed.), *Geriadur istorel ar brezhoneg* [etc.]: *Dictionnaire historique du Breton*. 2nd ed., Quimper, 1979–

Henri d'Andeli, *Le Lai d'Aristote*. Ed. Maurice Delbouille. Bibliothèque de la Faculté de Philosophie et Lettres de l'Université de Liège, No 123. Paris, 1951

Herbert, *Le Roman de Dolopathos*. Ed. Jean-Luc Leclanche. 3 vols. Paris, 1997

Hindley, Alan, Frederick W. Langley and Brian J. Levy (eds.), *Old French–English Dictionary*. Cambridge, 2000

History of William Marshal. Ed. A. J. Holden; trans. S., Gregory [historical notes by D. Crouch]. Anglo-Norman Text Society. Occasional Publications Series, No 4. London, 2002–

Hofman, (…) (ed.), 'Das zweitälteste unedirte altfranzösische Glossar'. *Sitzungberichte der Königlichen Bayerischen Akademie der Wissenschaften zu München*. 1 (1868), 121–34

Holmes, Urban T., 'Old French *Carole*'. *Language*. 4 (1928), 28–30

Honoré of Autun, *Honorii Augustodunensis Operum Pars Tertia Liturgica*: *Gemma Animae* [etc.]. Ed. J.-P. Migne. Patrologiae [Latinae] Cursus Completus. Vol. CLXXII. Paris, 1854, cols 542–738

Huguet, Edmond (ed.), *Dictionnaire de la langue française du seizième siècle*. 7 vols. Paris, 1925–67

Ibos-Augé, Anne, 'Les Insertions lyriques dans le roman de Renard le Nouvel: éléments de recherche musicale'. *Romania*. 118 (2000), 375–93

Imbs, Paul (ed.), *Trésor de la langue française*: *dictionnaire de la langue du XIX*[e] *et du XX*[e] *siècle (1789–1960)*. Paris, 1971–94

The Index of Middle English Verse. Ed. Carleton Brown and Rossell Hope Robbins. New York, 1943

Jacobus de Voragine, *Jacobi a Voragine Legenda Aurea Vulgo Historia Lombardica Dicta*. Ed. Theodor Graesse. Dresden, 1846

Jacopone da Todi [i.e. Jacopone de' Benedetti], 'Secreto spirituale' in *Le poesie spirituali del B. Jacopone da Todi, frate minore*. Ed. Francesco Tresatti. Venice, 1617, pp.1024–7

Jacquemart Gielée, *Renart le Nouvel*. Ed. Henri Roussel. Paris, 1961

Jacques Bretel, *Le Tournoi de Chauvency*. Ed. Maurice Delbouille. Bibliothèque de la Faculté de Philosophie et Lettres de l'Université de Liège, No 49. Liège, 1932

Jakemes, *Le Roman du Castelain de Couci et de la Dame de Fayel*. Ed. from notes by John E. Matzke by Maurice Delbouille. Paris, 1936

Jammers, Ewald, 'Studien zur Tanzmusik des Mittelalters'. *Archiv für Musikwissenschaft*. 30 (1973), 81–95
Jean Brisebarre, *Jean Brisebarre*: *Li Restor du Paon*. Ed. Enid Donkin. London, 1980
— *Le Restor du Paon*. Ed. Richard J. Carey. Geneva, 1966
Jean de Lescurel, *The Works of Jehan de Lescurel*. Ed. Nigel Wilkins. Corpus Mensurabilis Musicae, No 30. n.p., 1966
Jean de Wavrin, *Recueil des croniques et anchiennes istories de la Grant Bretaigne a present nomme Engleterre*. Ed. Sir William Hardy and Edward L. C. P. Hardy. 5 vols. London, 1864–91
Jean Froissart, *Chroniques de J. Froissart*. Ed. Siméon Luce *et al*. 15 vols. Paris, 1869–1975
— *The Lyric Poems of Jean Froissart*: *A Critical Edition*. Ed. Rob Roy McGregor, Jnr. North Carolina Studies in the Romance Languages and Literatures, No 143. Chapel Hill, NC, 1975
— *Méliador par Jean Froissart*. Ed. Auguste Longnon. 3 vols. Paris, 1895–99
— *Oeuvres de Froissart*. ed. Baron Joseph Kervyn de Lettenhove. 28 vols. Brussels, 1867–77
— *Oeuvres de Froissart: poésies*. Ed. Auguste Scheler. 3 vols. Brussels, 1870–72
— *La Prison amoureuse*. Ed. Anthime Fourrier. Bibliothèque Française et Romane, Série B, No 13. Paris, 1974
Jean Le Bel, *Chronique de Jean Le Bel*. Ed. Jules Viard and Eugène Déprez. 2 vols. Paris, 1904–05
Jean Le Fèvre, *Les Lamentations de Matheolus et le Livre de Leesce de Jehan Le Fevre de Resson*. Ed. Anton-Gérard van Hamel. 2 vols. Paris, 1892–1905
Jean Maillart, *Le Roman du comte d'Anjou*. Ed. Mario Roques. Paris, 1931
Jean Renart, *L'Escoufle*: *roman d'aventure*. Ed. Franklin Sweetser. Geneva, 1974
— *Le Roman de la Rose ou de Guillaume de Dole*. Ed. G. Servois. Paris, 1893
— *Le Roman de la Rose ou de Guillaume de Dole*. Ed. Rita Lejeune. Paris, 1936
— *Le Roman de la Rose ou de Guillaume de Dole*. Ed. Félix Lecoy. Rpt, Paris, 1979
— *The Romance of the Rose or of Guillaume de Dole* (*Roman de la Rose ou de Guillaume de Dole*). Ed. and trans. Regina Psaki. Garland Library of Medieval Literature, No 92A. New York, 1995
Jeanroy, Alfred, *Les Origines de la poésie lyrique en France au Moyen Age*. 3rd ed. Paris, 1925
'Jehan', *Le Mervelles de Rigomer von Jehan*: *altfranzösischer Artusroman des XIII. Jahrhunderts nach der einzigen Aumale-Handschrift in Chantilly*. Ed. Wendelin Foerster. Dresden, 1908
Johannes de Garlandia, 'The *Dictionarius* of John de Garlande'. *A Library of National Antiquities*. Vol. 1: *A Volume of Vocabularies*. Ed. Thomas Wright. n.p., 1857, pp. 120–38
— 'Les Gloses en langue vulgaire dans les MSS de *l'Unum Omnium* de Jean de Garlande'. Ed. Tony Hunt. *Revue de Linguistique Romane*. 43 (1979), 162–78

— *Lexicographie latine du XII*[e] *et du XIII*[e] *siècle: trois traités de Jean de Garlande, Alexandre Neckam et Adam du Petit-Pont*. Ed. Auguste Scheler. Leipzig, 1867

Johannes de Grocheo, *Die Quellenhandschriften zum Musiktraktat des Johannes de Grocheio im Faksimile herausgegeben nebst Übertragung des Textes und Übersetzung ins Deutsch, dazu Bericht, Literaturschau, Tabellen und Indices*. Ed. and Ger. trans. Ernst Rohloff. Leipzig, 1972

John Audelay, *The Poems of John Audelay*. Ed. Ella Keats Whiting. The Early English Text Society, Original Series, No 184. London, 1931

John Gower, *The English Works of John Gower*. Ed. G. C. Macaulay. 2 vols. The Early English Text Society, Extra Series, Nos 81 and 82. Rpt, Oxford, 1979

Jordan, Leo, 'Der Reigentanz Carole und seine Lieder'. *Zeitschrift für romanische Philologie*. 51 (1931), 335–53

— 'Wortgeschichtliches' in *Festschrift zum XII. allgemeinen deutschen Neuphilologentage in München*, Pfingsten, 1906. Ed. E. Stollreither. Erlangen, 1906, 61–80

Jud, J., rev. of *Etude sur la carole médiévale*, by Margit Sahlin. *Vox Romanica*. 5 (1940), 302–4

Jung, Marc-René, 'Gui de Mori et Guillaume de Lorris'. *Vox Romanica*. 27 (1968), 106–37

Juvenal, *Satires*

Knapp, Janet, 'Conductus'. *New Grove 2*

Komma, Karl Michael, *Musikgeschichte in Bildern*. Stuttgart, 1961

Körting, Gustav (ed.), *Lateinisch–romanisches Wörterbuch* (*Etymologisches Wörterbuch der romanischen Hauptsprachen*). 3rd ed., Paderborn, 1907

Kuhn, Alfred, *Die Illustration des Rosenromans*. Jahrbuch der kunsthistorischen Sammlungen des allerhöchsten Kaiserhauses, No 31/1. Vienna, 1912

Kyng Alisaunder. Ed. G. V. Smithers. 2 vols. The Early English Text Society, Original Series, Nos 227 and 237. London, 1952–57

Lacroix-Novaro, Yves, 'La Carole: ses origines'. *Revue de Musicologie*. 19 (1935), 1–26

La Curne de Sainte-Palaye, Jean-Baptiste (ed.), *Dictionnaire historique de l'ancien langage françois ou glossaire de la langue françoise depuis son origine jusqu'au siècle de Louis XIV* [1762]. 10 vols. Ed. L. Favre and M. Pajot. Niort, 1875–82

La Porte, Maurice de, *Les Epithetes de M. de la Porte, Parisien*. Paris, 1571

Lambarde, William (ed.), *Dictionarium Angliae Topographicum et Historicum* [1576]. London, 1730

Lancelot: roman en prose du XIIIe *siècle*. Ed. Alexandre Micha. 9 vols. Paris, 1978–83

Lapesa, Rafael, rev. of *Etude sur la carole médiévale*, by Margit Sahlin. *Revista de Filología Española*. 25 (1941), 122–4

Latham, R. E. (ed.), *Dictionary of Medieval Latin from British Sources*. London, 1975–

Le Gentil, Pierre, 'A propos du *Guillaume de Dole*'. *Mélanges de linguistique romane et de philologie médiévale offerts à M. Maurice Delbouille*. Vol. II. Ed. Madeleine Tyssens. Gembloux, 1964, pp. 381–97

Lefevre, Sylvie, 'Le Fragment Bekker et les anciennes versions françaises de l'*Historia Regum Britanniae*'. *Romania*. 109 (1988), 225–46

Legge, M. Dominica, *Anglo-Norman Literature and its Background*. Oxford, 1963

Lejeune, Rita, 'Le *Roman de Guillaume de Dole* et la Principauté de Liège'. *Cahiers de Civilisation Médiévale: X*[e] *–XII*[e] *Siècles*. Vol. XVII. Poitiers, 1974, 1–24

Lerch, Eugen, rev. of *Etude sur la carole médiévale*, by Margit Sahlin. *Cultura Neolatina*. 1 (1941), 236–44

Levy, Emil *et al.* (eds), *Provenzalisches Supplement-Wörterbuch*: *Berichtigungen und Ergänzungen zu Raynouards Lexique roman*. 8 vols. Leipzig, 1894–1924

Lexikon des Mittelalters. Ed. Liselotte Lutz *et al.* Munich, 1979–

Liber Eliensis. Ed. E. O. Blake. Camden Third Series, No 92. London, 1962

Libri Psalmorum Versio Antiqua Gallica e Cod. MS. in Bibl. Bodleiana Asservato una cum Versione Metrica aliisque Monumentis Pervetustis. Ed. Francisque Michel. Oxford, 1860

Liddell, Henry George and Robert Scott (eds), *A Greek–English Lexicon*, rev. Sir Henry Stuart Jones *et al.* 9th ed., Oxford, 1940

Liebermann, F, 'Zu Liedrefrain und Tanz im englischen Mittelalter'. *Archiv für das Studium der neueren Sprachen und Literaturen*. 140 (1920), 261–2

Liliencron, R. von, 'Über Neidharts höfische Dorfpoesie'. *Zeitschrift für deutsches Alterthum*. 6 (1848), 69–117

Le Livre d'Artus. The Vulgate Version of the Arthurian Romances. Vol. VII. Ed. Oskar Sommer. Carnegie Institution of Washington, Publication No 74. Washington, 1909–16

Le Livre de Lancelot del Lac. Ed. H. Oskar Sommer. The Vulgate Version of the Arthurian Romances. Vols III–V. Carnegie Institution of Washington, Publication No 74. Washington, 1909–16

Le Livre des psaumes: *ancienne traduction française publiée pour la première fois d'après les manuscrits de Cambridge et de Paris*. Ed. Francisque Michel. Paris, 1876

Louis, Maurice A.-L., *Le Folklore et la danse*. Paris, 1963

The Lyrics of the Red Book of Ossory. Ed. Richard Leighton Greene. Medium Aevum Monographs, New Series, No 5. Oxford, 1974

Le Magnus Liber Organi de Notre-Dame de Paris. Vol. I. Ed. Edward H. Roesner. Monaco, 1993

McGee, Timothy, 'Medieval Dances: Matching the Repertory with Grocheio's Descriptions'. *The Journal of Musicology*. 7 (1989), 498–517

Maillard, Jean, 'Les Refrains de caroles dans *Renart le Nouvel*'. *Alain de Lille, Gautier de Châtillon, Jakemart Gielée et leur temps*. Actes du Colloque de Lille, octobre, 1978. Ed. H. Roussel and F. Suard. Lille, 1980, 277–93

Marle, Raimond van, *Iconographie de l'art profane au Moyen-Age et à la Renaissance et la décoration des demeures*: *la vie quotidienne*. The Hague, 1931

Martial, *Epigrams*

Matériaux pour l'édition de Guillaume de Jumièges. Ed. Jules Lair with a preface and notes by Léopold Delisle. n.p. 1910

Matthew Paris, *Matthaei Parisiensis, Monachi Sancti Albani Historia Anglorum*. Ed. Sir Frederic Madden. 3 vols. London, 1866–69

Matthieu le Poirier, *Le Court d'Amours de Mahieu le Poirier et la Suite anonyme de la* Court d'Amours. Ed. Terence Scully. Waterloo, Ontario, 1976

Medieval English Songs. Ed. E. J. Dobson and F. Ll. Harrison. London, 1979

Metzner, Ernst Erich, *Zur frühesten Geschichte der europäischen Balladendichtung: der Tanz in Kölbigk* [etc.]. Frankfurter Beiträge zur Germanistik, No 14. Frankfurt-am-Main, 1972

Meyer-Lübke, W. *Romanisches etymologisches Wörterbuch*. Sammlung romanischer Elementar-und Handbücher, 3rd Series No 3. 3rd ed. Heidelberg, 1935

Middle English Dictionary. Ed. Hans Kurath, Sherman Kuhn *et al*. 14 vols. Ann Arbor, MI, 1956–99

Middle English Humorous Tales in Verse. Ed. George H. McKnight. Boston, MA, 1913

Le Mireour du monde: manuscrit du XIVme siècle découvert dans les Archives de la Commune de la Sarra. Ed. Félix Chavannes. Mémoires et documents publiés par la Société d'Histoire de la Suisse Romande, No 4. Lausanne, 1845

The Montpellier Codex. *Polyphonies du XIIIe siècle: le manuscrit H. 196 de la Faculté de Médecine de Montpellier*. Ed. Yvonne Rokseth. 4 vols. Paris 1935–39

— *The Montpellier Codex*. Ed. Hans Tischler. Recent Researches in the Music of the Middle Ages and Early Renaissance. 4 vols. Madison, WI, 1978–85

Moreau, Sébastien, *La Prinse et délivrance du roy* [etc.]. Ed. L. Cimber and F. Danjou. *Archives curieuses de l'histoire de France depuis Louis XI jusqu'à Louis XVIII*. 1re Série, No 2. Paris, 1835

La Mort Aymeri de Narbonne: chanson de geste. Ed. J. Couraye du Parc. Paris, 1884

Mullally, Robert, 'The Ballade before Machaut'. *Zeitschrift für französische Sprache und Literatur*. 104 (1994), 252–68

— 'Cançon de Carole'. *Acta Musicologica*. 58 (1986), 224–31

— 'Carole'. *New Grove 2*

— 'Dance Terminology in the Works of Machaut and Froissart. *Medium Aevum*. 59 (1990), 248–59

— 'Houes Danses'. *Neophilologus*. 76 (1992), 29–34

— 'Johannes de Grocheo's "Musica Vulgaris"'. *Music & Letters*. 79 (1998), 1–26

— 'Vireli, Virelai'. *Neuphilologische Mittelungen*. 101 (2000), 451–63

Die Musik in Geschichte und Gegenwart. Ed. Ludwig Finscher. 9 vols. 2nd ed., Kassel, 1994–98

The New Grove Dictionary of Music and Musicians. Ed. Stanley Sadie. 20 vols. 1st ed., London, 1980

— Ed. Stanley Sadie and John Tyrell. 2nd ed. 29 vols. London, 2001

Nicole Oresme, *Le Livre du ciel et du monde*. Ed. Albert D. Menut and Alexander J. Denomy CSB; trans. Albert D. Menut. Madison, WI, 1968

Nicot, Jean *et al.* (eds), *Le Grand Dictionaire françois–latin augumenté*. Paris, 1573

Nigra, C., 'Notes étymologiques et lexicales'. *Romania*. 31 (1902), 499–526

Nixon, Terry, 'Romance Collections and the Manuscripts of Chrétien de Troyes' in *Les Manuscripts de Chrétien de Troyes: The Manuscripts of Chrétien de Troyes*. Ed. Keith Busby *et al*. Etudes de la langue et littérature françaises, No 72. Amsterdam, 1993

Nominale sive Verbale. Ed. Walter W. Skeat. Transactions of the Philological Society, 1903–06. London, 1906

Notre Dame and Related Conductus: *Opera Omnia*. Collected Works, X, Part 8, The Latin Rondeau Repertoire. Ed. Gordon A. Anderson. Henryville, UT, 1979

Ouen, *Saint*, *S. Eligii Episcopi Noviomensis Vita a Sancto Audoeno Rothomagensi Episcopo Scripta*. Ed. J.-P. Migne. Patrologiae [Latinae] Cursus Completus, Vol. LXXXVII. Paris, 1851, cols 478–594

The Oxford English Dictionary. 2nd ed., rev. A. Simpson and E. S. C. Weiner. 20 vols. Oxford, 1989

Oxford Latin Dictionary. 2 vols. Oxford, 1968–82

Page, Christopher, *The Owl and the Nightingale*: *Musical Life and Ideas in France, 1100–1300*. London, 1989

— *Voices and Instruments of the Middle Ages*: *Instrumental Practice and Songs in France, 1100–1300*. London, 1987

Paris, Gaston, rev. of 'Carole' by W. Foerster. *Romania*. 11 (1882), 444–7

— 'Bele Aaliz' in *Mélanges de littérature française du Moyen Age*. Ed. Mario Roques. Rpt Paris, 1912, 616–24

— rev. of *Les Origines de la poésie en France au Moyen Age*, by Alfred Jeanroy in *Mélanges de literature française du Moyen Age*. Ed. Mario Roques. Rpt Paris, 1912, 539–615

Pastourelles. Ed. Jean-Claude Rivière. 3 vols. Paris, 1974–76

Paulys Real-Encyclopädie der classischen Alterumswissenschaft. Ed. August Friedrich von Pauly, rev. Georg Wissowa *et al*. 83 vols. Stuttgart, 1893–1978

Perceforest: *quatrième partie*. Ed. Gilles Roussineau. 2 vols. Paris, 1987

Petronius, *Satyricon*

Philippe de Remi, *Le Roman de la Manekine*. Ed. and trans. Barbara Sargent-Baur with contributions by Alison Stones and Roger Middleton. Etudes de la langue et littérature françaises, No 159. Amsterdam, 1999

Pierre d'Abernon of Fetcham, *La Vie de Seint Richard, evesque de Cycestre*. Ed. D. W. Russell. Anglo-Norman Text Society, No 51. London, 1995

Pliny the Elder, *Pline l'Ancien*: *histoire naturelle*. Gen. ed. and Fr. trans. Alfred Ernout (Book XXVII, trans. E. de Saint Denis). Paris, 1972

Plutarch, *Lives*

Le Poème moral: *Traité de vie chrétienne écrit dans la région wallonne vers l'an 1200*. Ed. Alphonse Bayot. Brussels, 1929

Poesie musicali del Trecento. Ed. Giuseppe Corsi. Collezione di opere inedite o rare. No 131. Bologna, 1970

Poésies populaires latines du Moyen Age. Ed. Edélestand du Méril. Paris, 1847

Pope, M. K., *From Latin to Modern French with Especial Consideration of Anglo-Norman*. Publications of the University of Manchester, No 229. Rpt, Manchester, 1966

Pound, Louise, 'King Cnut's Song and Ballad Origins'. *Modern Language Notes*. 34 (1919), 162–5

A Primer of Medieval Latin: An Anthology of Prose and Poetry. Ed. Charles H. Beeson. Rpt Folkestone, 1973

Probus, *Probi, Donati, Servii Qui Feruntur de Arte Grammatica Libri*. Ed. Heinrich Keil. Grammatici Latini. Vol. IV. Hildesheim, 1961

Processionale ad Usum Insignis ac Praeclarae Ecclesiae Sarum. Ed. W. G. Henderson. Rpt, Leeds, 1969

Li Quatre Livre des reis: die Bücher Samuelis und der Könige in einer französischen Bearbeitung des 12. Jahrhunderts nach der ältesten Handschrift unter Benutzung der neu aufgefundenen Handschriften. Ed. Ernst Robert Curtius. Gesellschaft für romanische Literatur, No 26. Dresden, 1911

Ranconnet, Aimar (ed.), *Thrésor de la langue francoise, tant ancienne que moderne*, rev. Jean Nicot. 1621, facsimile, Paris, 1960

Ranulph Higden, *Polychronicon Ranulphi Higden Monachi Cestrensis*, with a translation by John Trevisa. Ed. Churchill Babington and Joseph Rawson Lumby. 9 vols. London, 1865–86

Raoul de Houdenc, *Raoul von Houdenc: sämtliche Werke nach allen bekannten Handschriften*. Ed. Mathias Friedwagner. 2 vols. Halle, 1897–1909

Re Giovanni [i.e. Jean de Brienne], 'Donna audite como' in *Le rime della scuola siciliana*. Ed. Bruno Panvini. Biblioteca dell 'Archivum Romanicum'. Serie 1, No 65. Florence, 1962, pp. 85–8

Recueil de motets français des XIIe et XIIIe siècles. Ed. Gaston Raynaud. 2 vols. Paris, 1881–83

Recueil de poésies françoises des XVe et XVIe siècles – morales, facétieuses, historiques. Ed. Anatole de Montaiglon. 6 vols. Paris, 1855–57

Recueil général et complet des fabliaux des XIIIe et XIVe siècles imprimés ou inédits. Ed. Anatole de Montaiglon and Gaston Raynaud. 6 vols. Paris. 1872–90

Religious Lyrics of the XIVth Century. Ed. Carleton Brown. 2nd ed. rev. G. V. Smithers. Oxford, 1952

Renouard, François (ed.), *Lexique roman ou dictionnaire de la langue des troubadours* [etc.]. 6 vols. Paris, 1838–44

Rheinfelder, Hans, rev. of *Etude sur la carole médiévale*, by Margit Sahlin. *Volkstum und Kultur der Romanen*. 15 (1942–43), 186–8

Richard Rolle, *English Writings of Richard Rolle, Hermit of Hampole*. Ed. Hope Emily Allen. Oxford, 1931

— *The Incendium Amoris of Richard Rolle of Hampole*. Ed. Margaret Deanesly. Publications of the University of Manchester, Historical Series, No 26. Manchester, 1915

Richelet, Pierre (ed.), *Nouveau Dictionnaire françois*. 2 vols. Amsterdam, 1732

Rimmer, Joan, 'Dance Elements in Trouvère Repertory'. *Dance Research*. 3/2 (1985), 23–34

— 'Medieval Instrumental Dance Music', *Music & Letters*, 72 (1991), 61–8

Rinaldo d'Aquino, 'In amoroso pensare' in *Le rime della scuola siciliana*. Serie 1, No 65. Ed. Bruno Panvini. Florence, 1962, pp. 114–15

Robbins, Rossell Hope, 'The Earliest Carols and the Franciscans'. *Modern Language Notes*. 53 (1938), 239–45

— 'Friar Herebert and the Carol'. *Anglia*. 75 (1957), 194–8

— 'Middle English Carols as Processional Hymns'. *Studies in Philology*. 56 (1959), 559–82

Robert Mannyng, *Handlyng Synne*. Ed. Idelle Sullens. Medieval and Renaissance Texts and Studies, No 14. New York, 1983

Robert of Gloucester, *The Metrical Chronicle of Robert of Gloucester*. Ed. William Alois Wright. 2 vols. London, 1887

Robert, Paul (ed.), *Le Grand Robert de la langue française*. 2nd ed., rev. Alain Rey. Paris, 1985

Robertus de Handlo, *Regule / The Rules* and Johannes de Hanboys, *Summa / The Summa*. Ed. and trans. Peter M. Lefferts. Lincoln, NE, 1991

Le Roman de Laurin, fils de Marques le Sénéchal. Ed. Lewis Thorpe. University of Nottingham Research Publication, No 2. Cambridge, 1960

Le Roman de Perceforest: première partie. Ed. Jane H. M. Taylor. Geneva. 1979

Le Roman de Renart. Ed. Ernest Martin [i.e. Ernst Martin]. 4 vols. Strasbourg, 1882–87

Le Roman de Renart le Contrefait. Ed. Gaston Raynaud and Henri Le Maître. 2 vols. Paris, 1914

Le Roman de Thèbes. Ed. Guy Raynaud de Lage. 2 vols. Paris, 1966–68

Le Roman des Sept Sages. Ed. Jean Misrahi. Paris, 1933

The Romance of Alexander: A Collotype Facsimile of MS Bodley 264. Introduction by M. R. James. Oxford, 1933

Romances et pastourelles françaises des XIIe et XIIIe siècles: altfranzösische Romanzen und Pastorellen. Ed. Karl Bartsch. Leipzig, 1870

Li Romans de Bauduin de Sebourc, IIIe roy de Jhérusalem: poème du XIVe siècle. [Ed. Louis-Napoléon Boca]. 2 vols. Valenciennes, 1841

Le Romans de la Dame a la Lycorne et du biau Chevalier au Lyon: ein Abenteuerroman aus dem ersten Drittel des XIV. Jahrhunderts. Ed. Friedrich Gennrich. Gesellschaft für romanische Litteratur, No 18. Dresden, 1908

*Rondeaux et refrains du XIIe siècle au début du XIVe*. Ed. Nico H. J. van den Boogaard. Bibliothèque française et romane, Série D. No 3. Paris, 1969

Rondeaux, Virelais und Balladen. Ed. Friedrich Gennrich. Gesellschaft für romanische Literatur, Nos 43 and 47. Dresden, 1921 and Göttingen, 1927

Roques, Mario, rev. of *Etude sur la carole médiévale*, by Margit Sahlin. *Romania*. 67 (1942–43), 419–20

Rowley, George, *Ambrogio Lorenzetti*. Princeton Monograph in Art and Archaeology, No 32. 2 vols. Princeton, NJ, 1958

Rutebeuf, *Oeuvres complètes*. Ed. and Fr. trans. Michel Zink. Paris, 1989

Sachs, Curt, *Eine Weltgeschichte des Tanzes*. Berlin, 1933

— *World History of the Dance*, trans. Bessie Schönberg. London, 1938 (translation of the preceding work)

Sahlin, Margit, *Etude sur la carole médiévale: l'origine du mot et ses rapports avec l'église*. Uppsala, 1940

Salmen, Walter, 'Ikonographie des Reigens im Mittelalter'. *Acta Musicologica*. 52 (1980), 14–26

— *Tanz und Tanzen vom Mittelalter bis zur Renaissance*. Hildesheim, 1999

The Sarum Missal Edited from Three Early Manuscripts. Ed. J. Wickham Legg. Oxford, 1916

Schmitz, Guilelmus (ed.), *Comentarii Notarum Tironianarum cum Prolegomenis Adnotationibus Criticis et Exegeticis Notarumque Indice Alphabetico*. Leipzig, 1893

Schmolke-Hasselmann, Beate, '*La Chastelaine de Vergi* auf Pariser Elfenbein-Kästchen des 14. Jarhunderts: zum Problem der Interpretation literarischer Texte anhand von Bildzeugnissen'. *Romanistisches Jahrbuch*. 27 (1976), 52–76

Schneider, Otto, *Tanz Lexikon*. Frankfurt-am-Main, 1985

Schultz, Alwin, *Das höfische Leben zur Zeit der Minnesinger*. 2 vols. 2nd ed., Leipzig, 1889

Schultz, Oscar, rev. of *Untersuchungen über die Rondeaux und Virelais speciell des 14. und 15. Jahrhunderts*, by Heinrich Pfuhl. *Literaturblatt für germanische und romanische Philologie*. 8 (1887), 444–7

Secular Lyrics of the XIVth and XVth Centuries. Ed. Rossell Hope Robbins. 2nd ed., Oxford, 1955

Servius, *Servii Grammatici Qui Feruntur in Vergilii Carmina Commentarii*. Ed. Georg Thilo and Hermann Hagen. 3 vols. Leipzig, 1923–27

Seymour, M. C., 'Chaucer's *Legend of Good Women*: Two Fallacies'. *The Review of English Studies*. New Series, No 37 (1986), 528–34

Shakespeare, William, *As You Like It*

Short, Ian, 'Patrons and Polyglots: French Literature in Twelfth-Century England'. *Anglo-Norman Studies*. 14 (1991), 229–49

Skeat, Walter W. (ed.), *An Etymological Dictionary of the English Language*. Oxford, 1882

Sneddon, Dorothy A., 'The Anglo-Norman Psalters: I, A Note on the Relationship between the Oxford and Arundel Psalters'. *Romania*. 99 (1978), 395–400

Sone de Nansay. Sone von Nausay. Ed. Moritz Goldschmidt. Bibliothek des Litterarischen Vereins in Stuttgart, No 216. Tübingen, 1899

Spanke, Hans, rev. of *Etude sur la carole médiévale*, by Margit Sahlin. *Literaturblatt für germanische und romanische Philologie*. 64 (1943), 106–07

— 'Tanzmusik in der Kirche des Mittelalters'. *Neuphilologische Mitteilungen*. 31 (1930), 143–70

— 'Volkstümliches in der altfranzösischen Lyrik'. *Zeitschrift für romanische Philologie*. 53 (1933), 258–86

— 'Zum Thema "Mittelalterliche Tanzlieder"'. *Neuphilologische Mitteilungen*. 33 (1932), 1–22

Spitzer, Leo, rev. of *Etude sur la carole médiévale*, by Margit Sahlin. *Modern Language Notes*. 56 (1941), 222–5

Stainer, J. and W. A. Barrett (eds), *A Dictionary of Musical Terms*. London, [1876]

A Stanzaic Life of Christ Compiled from Higden's Polychronicon *and the* Legenda Aurea. Ed. Francis A. Foster. The Early English Text Society, Original Series, No 166. London, 1926

Stern, Karen, 'The London "Thornton Miscellany": A New Description of British Museum Additional Manuscript 31042'. *Scriptorium*. 30 (1976), 26–37, 201–18

Stevens, John, 'Carole'. *New Grove 1*

— *Words and Music in the Middle Ages*: *Song, Narrative, Dance and Drama, 1050–1350*. Cambridge, 1986

Stones, Alison, 'The Illustrations of BN fr. 95 and Yale 229: Prolegomena to a Comparative Analysis' in *Word and Image in Arthurian Literature*. Ed. Keith Busby. New York, 1996, pp. 203–83

Strabo, *Geography*

Suchier, Walther, rev. of *Etude sur la carole médiévale*, by Margit Sahlin. *Deutsche Literaturzeitung*. 62 (1941), cols 1214–16

Suetonius, *Lives of the Caesars*

Taylor, Jane H. M., 'The Fourteenth Century: Context, Text and Intertext' in *The Legacy of Chrétien de Troyes*. Ed. Norris J. Lacy, Douglas Kelly and Keith Busby. Vol I, Faux Titre, 31. Amsterdam, 1987, pp. 267–332

Thesaurus Linguae Latinae. Leipzig, 1900–

Thomas de Cantimpré, *Liber Qui Dicitur Bonum Universale de Proprietatibus Apum* [13th cent.] [Cologne, 1480?]

Thompson, John J., *The* Cursor Mundi: *Poem, Texts and Contexts*. Medium Aevum Monographs, New Series, No 19. Oxford, 1998

Tobler, Adolf and Erhard Lommatzsch (eds), *Altfranzösisches Wörterbuch*. 11 vols. Berlin, 1925–2002

Uc Faidit, *The* Donatz Proensals *of Uc Faidit*. Ed. J. H. Marshall. London, 1969

Variétés historiques et littéraires: *recueil de pièces volantes rares et curieuses en prose et en vers*. Ed. Edouard Fournier. 10 vols. Paris, 1855–68

Venantius Fortunatus, *Venance Fortunat*: *poèmes*. Ed. and Fr. trans. Marc Reydellet. 2 vols. Paris, 1994–98

— *Venanti Honori Clementiani Fortunati Presbyteri Italici Opera Pedestria*. Ed. Bruno Krusch. Monumenta Germaniae Historica, Auctorum Antiquissimorum Tomi IV Pars Posterior. Berlin, 1885, pp. 38–49. 'Vita Sanctae Radegundae'

Verrier, Paul, 'La Plus Vieille Citation de carole'. *Romania*, 58 (1932), 380–421 and 61 (1935), 95–7

— *Le Vers français: formes primitives, développement, diffusion*. 3 vols. Paris, 1931–32

Virgil, *Deux Livres de l'Eneide de Virgile, a scavoir le quatrieme, et sixieme, traduicts en vers francois par J. Du Bellay, Angevin*. Paris, 1560

— *Eclogues*

Vising, Per Johan, *Anglo-Norman Language and Literature*. London, 1923

Wace, *Le Roman de Brut de Wace*. Ed. Ivor Arnold. 2 vols. Paris, 1938–40

Walter de Bibbesworth, *Le Trétiz*. Ed. William Rothwell. Anglo-Norman Text Society, Plain Texts Series, No 6. London 1990

Watriquet de Couvin, *Dits de Watriquet de Couvin*. Ed. Auguste Scheler. Brussels, 1868

Wenzel, Siegfried, 'The Moor Maiden – A Contemporary View'. *Speculum*. 49 (1974), 69–74

Werf, Hendrik van der, 'Jean Renart and Medieval Song' in *Jean Renart and the Art of Romance: Essays on* Guillaume de Dole. Ed. Nancy Vine Durling. Gainsville, FL, 1997, 157–87

William Rishanger, 'Willelmi Rishanger Gesta Edwardi Primi, Regis Angliae' in *Chronica Monasterii S. Albani*. Ed. Henry Thomas Riley. London, 1865, pp. 409–33

Woledge, Brian and H. D. Clive (eds), *Répertoire des plus anciens textes en prose française depuis 842 jusqu'aux premières années du XIIIe siècle*. Publications romanes et françaises, No 79. Geneva, 1964

Wolf, Johannes, 'Die Tänze des Mittelalters: eine Untersuchung des Wesens der ältesten Instrumentalmusik'. *Archiv für Musikwissenschaft*. 1 (1918–19), 10–42

Ysopet de Lyon. *Bibliothèque de la Ville de Lyon: documents paléographiques, typographiques, iconographiques*. Ed. R. Cantinelli. Vol. II /1. Lyon, 1923

— *Lyoner Yzopet: altfranzösische Übersetzung des XIII. Jahrhunderts in der Mundart der Franche-Comté*. Ed.Wendelin Foerster. Altfranzösische Bibliothek, No 5. Heilbronn, 1882

Zink, Michel, 'Suspension and Fall: The Fragmentation and Linkage of Lyric Insertions in *Le Roman de la Rose* (*Guillaume de Dole*) and *Le Roman de la Violette*' in *Jean Renart and the Art of Romance: Essays on* Guillaume de Dole. Ed. Nancy Vine Durling. Gainsville, FL, 1997, pp. 105–21

Zumthor, Paul, rev. of *Etude sur la carole médiévale*, by Margit Sahlin. *Zeitschrift für romanische Philologie*. 64 (1944), 182–4

Index